ADJUSTING TO DEMOCRACY
THE ROLE OF THE MINISTRY OF
LABOUR IN BRITISH POLITICS,
1916-1939

Adjusting to Democracy

*The Role of the Ministry of Labour
in British Politics, 1916–1939*

RODNEY LOWE

CLARENDON PRESS · OXFORD
1986

Oxford University Press, Walton Street, Oxford OX2 6DP

Oxford New York Toronto
Delhi Bombay Calcutta Madras Karachi
Kuala Lumpur Singapore Hong Kong Tokyo
Nairobi Dar es Salaam Cape Town
Melbourne Auckland

and associated companies in
Beirut Berlin Ibadan Nicosia

Oxford is a trade mark of Oxford University Press

Published in the United States
by Oxford University Press, New York

British Library Cataloguing in Publication Data
Lowe, Rodney
Adjusting to democracy: the role of
the ministry of labour in British politics,
1916-1939.
1. Labor policy——Great Britain——History
——20th century
I. Title
331.12'5'0941 HD8391
ISBN 0-19-820094-3

Library of Congress Cataloging in Publication Data
Lowe, Rodney.
Adjusting to democracy.
Bibliography: p.
Includes index.
1. Great Britain. Ministry of Labour. 2. Labor
policy——Great Britain——History——20th century. 3. Great
Britain——Economic policy——1918-1945. 4. Great Britain——
Politics and government——20th century. I. Title.
HD8390.L68 1986 354.410083 86-733
ISBN 0-19-820094-3

Printed and bound in Great Britain
by Butler & Tanner Ltd,
Frome and London

PREFACE

THIS book, as many 'friends' have fallen over themselves to point out, has been a long time in the writing. It is the product of 14 years' research in which over 30 collections of private papers have been consulted as well as the records of nine government departments. It has trespassed into many academic disciplines other than economic and social history: politics, public administration, industrial relations, and social administration. The overwhelming impression from these labours, nevertheless, is one of incompleteness. Consequently, the book is not a definitive history of the Ministry of Labour but a discussion of some of the broader issues arising from the research which will, I hope, stimulate and inform further debate on a predominant feature of twentieth-century British history—the expansion of central government.

One major reason for the book's necessary incompleteness is the nature of the research material. The records of the inter-war Ministry of Labour alone comprise 25 classes, the most important of which for this study (Lab 2, a comprehensive class of records between 1916 and 1933) contains 2,191 boxes of, on average, over 10 files each. This class is not among the best-indexed at the Public Record Office (PRO). From the bulk of this material, I have tried to select the most relevant documents but (as I have discovered with mounting terror when talking to fellow academics) I have not always been successful and (as I soon learnt as a postgraduate student working on the period from 1916 to 1924) the major policy documents do not always contain the most revealing information. Since one of my objects has been to analyse policy-formation at all levels within the Ministry, much relevant work has also, inevitably, been left undone. However, the reconstruction papers of the Second World War (which might not immediately appear relevant) have been consulted because they contain comprehensive reviews of inter-war policy and often make explicit the opinions of leading inter-war politicians and civil servants.

Many records have also, wittingly or unwittingly, been destroyed. The papers of the Publicity Department of the Ministry, for example, which might have shed light on the government's propaganda offensive against 'revolutionary' Labour between 1917 and 1921, have not survived. Nor has any detailed record of the collusion of the Ministry with the Scottish Office against the Treasury over unemployment policy in the 1930s. Papers relating to the first Labour Government are also sparse, reinforcing (no doubt unfairly) the impression of many officials that Tom Shaw, as minister, had little if anything to contribute to policy. Private records can sometimes compensate for official lacunae. The historian of the Ministry is particularly well served by the papers of Sir Arthur Steel-Maitland, the minister during the 1924-9 Conservative Government, and of Tom Jones and Violet Markham, two members of the Unemployment Assistance Board (UAB). The Steel-Maitland papers provide evidence of considerable political bargaining between the Baldwin Government and bankers and industrialists, at which official records only hint. The latter collections achieve the seemingly impossible feat of making the Treasury's attitude towards social policy in the 1930s appear almost prodigal.

Finally, it would be naïve to expect the written record to reveal everything. Cabinet records are notoriously bland and the reasons for many key political decisions, such as the suspension of the UAB scales in 1935, were deliberately not recorded. The records of the civil service are similarly incomplete. Many 'real' decisions were taken in unrecorded 'little private and informal conferences, committees and interviews', correspondence was often started only after decisions had been taken, and the most senior officials tended to talk and listen rather than write.[1] The increasing use of the telephone, moreover, provided a technical reason who many official transactions went unrecorded: the Trades Union Congress (TUC) (somewhat surprisingly in view of its cart-horse image) would seem to have been one of the few inter-war institutions systematically to record telephone conversations. Certain areas of administrative activity were also particularly secretive. No mere collection of files, for instance, could ever do full justice to the rise of Sir Horace Wilson from the lower reaches of the pre-war Board of Trade through the permanent secretaryship of the Ministry of Labour to

[1] H. E. Dale, *The Higher Civil Service of Great Britain* (1941), pp. 116, 163. There is also, of course, the much-vexed question of official preservation policy. One of the few good things the Finance Department of the inter-war Ministry of Labour did was to preserve vital policy-making records.

the headship of the civil service. The whole policy area of industrial relations is also unconducive to the written record. The hard bargaining between parties was often best left obscure and many leading participants depended for their success on personalities which no office routine could contain. Between the wars, for example, one chief industrial conciliator was well recognized as the ideal person to whom to send a troublesome memorandum because he would never rest content until it had been flung on top of, or preferably behind, the furthest filing cabinet. Oral history can provide an indication, but no more, of such omissions from official archives.

A second reason for the necessary incompleteness of the book is the question of interpretation. Any research connected with 'the state' and bureaucracy is immediately confronted by both rival ideological concepts and the competing theoretical approaches of different academic disciplines. Little sleep need be lost over identifying within this book an 'incrementalist' approach, whereby policy is deemed largely to be a pragmatic and often erratic response by government to the immediate problems with which it is faced— 'organized chaos rather than carefully-planned conspiracy'.[2] The book's evidence, it is hoped, is deployed in a manner which will be of value to those who do not share this basic assumption, but assumptions inevitably dictate structure and hence the selection of evidence. This may have resulted in omissions that others think unjustified.

A further problem of interpretation is one that all former civil servants try to impress on historians at an early age, that the criteria by which academics tend to judge public policy and memoranda are not always the most appropriate. The civil servant is essentially a practical man of action not a thinker and therefore he should be judged, in ordinary circumstances, not by a nice turn of phrase in a memorandum or an acute perception of a wide range of academic possibilities, but by an ability to identify the needs of specific client groups and, within a given range of political practicalities, to fashion the most appropriate response. Such considerations mean that the history of any department and of any government has to be judged carefully against an assessment of what was at any given time feasible. Judgment is necessarily fine, as the fate of successive inquiries into the civil service illustrates. The 1918

[2] J. Higgins, *The Poverty Business* (Oxford, 1978), p. 20.

Haldane Committee and 1968 Fulton Committee provided academically sound, but essentially impractical, recommendations for the reform of the civil service; the intervening Tomlin Royal Commission (1931) concluded, despite much evidence to the contrary, that all that could be done was being done. A historian has, if possible, to steer his way between these two extremes.

In the course of my research I have accumulated many debts. Foremost are those to my past and present colleagues at Heriot-Watt University (in particular Dr N. K. Buxton) and Bristol University (above all to Professor B. W. E. Alford and Professor W. Ashworth, whose teaching reinforced my interest in twentieth-century British history and whose idea it was originally that I should study the Ministry). My research has run parallel to that of many fellow academics, all of whom have produced or are about to produce major contributions to modern British history: Dr Alan Booth, Dr Roger Davidson, Dr Alan Deacon, Tony Lynes, Richard Roberts, Dr Terry Rodgers, and Dr Noel Whiteside. I have benefited enormously from the help of 12 former Ministry officials, all of whom have striven to alert me to the realities of inter-war administration and whose generosity has made it all the harder to criticize the Ministry. In particular I should like to thank Sir James Dunnett, Sir Harold Emmerson, C. H. Sisson, Sir John Walley, and above all P. H. St. J. Wilson. I have received generous financial assistance from the Carnegie and Nuffield Trusts, the Economic and Social Research Council, and Bristol University. I should also like to acknowledge the assistance of holders of copyright material for access to relevant material, librarians and archivists for their expert help, and the compilers of various historical aids. Foremost among the latter is Dr Brenda Swann, to whom all inter-war social scientists owe a considerable debt.

Finally, I should like to thank for their forbearance those who have helped in the final preparation of the typescript, in particular Rosemary Graham and Anne Griffiths. I have also been reminded by my wife that I should acknowledge her help and that of both my parents and the rest of my family. This I gladly do. Virginia, Alexander, Heriot, and Watt have each, over the years, made their own peculiar contributions to the manuscript.

ACKNOWLEDGEMENTS

I SHOULD like to thank for access to and permission to quote from copyright material: Viscount Bridgeman (Bridgeman papers), Sir William Lithgow (Lithgow papers), Mrs Longhurst Murphy (Rey papers), Mrs R. M. Stafford (Steel-Maitland papers), Miss P. Tallents (Markham papers), the late Dr C. R. Tribe (Tribe papers), Mr A. J. P. Taylor and the Beaverbrook Foundation (Lloyd George and Bonar Law papers). I should similarly like to thank the following libraries and institutions: Birmingham University, the British Library of Political and Economic Science, the Syndics of Cambridge University Library, Churchill College, the CBI, the House of Lords Record Office, the National Library of Wales, the TUC and the Trustees of the Mass Observation Archive, University of Sussex. Finally, I should like to thank the Controller of HM Stationery Office for permission to quote from papers at the Public Record Office and the Scottish Record Office, and the Social Science Research Council (NY) for permission to use extracts from E. M. Burns, *British Unemployment Programs, 1920-38*.

CONTENTS

Contents

ABBREVIATIONS

EEF	Engineering Employers' Federation
FBI	Federation of British Industries
ICI	Imperial Chemical Industries
ILO	International Labour Organisation (or Office)
ILP	Independent Labour Party
NIC	National Industrial Conference
NCEO	National Confederation of Employers' Organisations
PAC	Public Assistance Committee
PEP	Political and Economic Planning
PJC	Provisional Joint Committee (of the NIC)
PRO	Public Record Office
SRO	Scottish Record Office
TUC	Trades Union Congress
UAB	Unemployment Assistance Board
UGC	Unemployment Grants Committee
UISC	Unemployment Insurance Statutory Committee
YMCA	Young Men's Christian Association

CHAPTER I

THE ADVENT OF DEMOCRACY

Two predominant themes in recent British politics have been the reform of industrial relations and the power of the civil service. Concern over the former was officially acknowledged by the appointment of the Donovan Royal Commission on Trade Unions and Employers' Associations in 1965 and has increased with each subsequent attempt to reform industrial relations law; concern over the latter was acknowledged by the appointment of the Fulton Committee on the Civil Service in 1966 and escalated after the publication of the Crossman *Diaries* in 1975. The resolution of both issues is still widely held to be essential to national recovery. Concurrently, there has also been a less publicized but no less important debate over the means by which increasingly complex legislation can be efficiently administered. Attention here, before the preoccupation with 'privatization' in the mid-1980s, had been concentrated on the devolution of power to semi-autonomous corporate bodies (quangos) and in particular on the 'hiving-off' of the Department of Employment's responsibilities for industrial relations and unemployment to the Advisory, Conciliation and Arbitration Service and the Manpower Services Commission.

The contemporary debate on these issues is nothing if not old. It is concerned with the fundamental issue of the location and exercise of power within democracy and it was thus initiated, in its present form, over 60 years ago following the rapid democratization of Britain during the First World War. The purpose of this book is to put the debate in historical perspective by examining, first, the political response to the advent of democracy and, secondly, the administrative repercussions. The medium for analysis is the Ministry of Labour, the forerunner of the presently beleaguered Department of Employment and itself a creation of the First World War.

The terms 'democratization' and 'the advent of democracy' can, of course, be defined in many different ways. Both refer here to the political not the economic system and 'the advent of democracy' signifies the completion of a long-drawn-out process of 'democratization'—the time at which the political system became effectively responsive to the wishes of the whole adult population. 'The advent of democracy' does not mean that the mass electorate had an increasingly active share in government but only an increased influence over it. As Max Weber has defined democracy:

The *demos* itself, in the sense of a shapeless mass, never 'governs' larger associations, but rather is governed. What changes is only the way in which the executive leaders are selected and the measure of influence which the *demos*, or better, which social circles from its midst are able to exert upon the content and the direction of administrative activities by means of 'public opinion'.[1]

It was Weber also who observed that mass democracy was inevitably accompanied by bureaucracy (in the sense of an increased number of officials) and this is an observation with which the majority of political commentators, albeit for very different reasons, would concur.

By these definitions, it might be claimed that Britain was effectively a democracy before 1914. As Donald Read, for instance, has written of late Victorian England: 'many contemporaries rightly believed that the political system had become sufficiently responsive to the wishes of the many to make it "democratic" in practice.'[2] Successive reform bills together with increasing economic prosperity (which enabled a growing number of men to meet the property qualification) had greatly extended the franchise and thereby encouraged political and administrative adjustment. Politically, party leaders claimed to consider more seriously the wishes of the 'people', industrial relations law was changed to meet the increasingly influential demands of organized Labour, and parliamentary procedure was made more professional with such innovations as afternoon sittings. Administratively, there was a slow erosion of power from local to central government with an expansion of the social services and the bureaucracy needed to administer them. The climax to these adjustments came with the Liberal Government of 1906-15 which not only reached an accommodation with the new

[1] G. Roth and C. Willich, *Max Weber: Economy and Society* (New York, 1968), vol. 3, pp. 983-5. For the various definitions of bureaucracy, see M. Albrow, *Bureaucracy* (1970), ch. 5.

[2] D. Read, *England 1868-1914* (1979), p. x.

Labour Party and passed the 1906 Trade Disputes Act but also initiated welfare services (such as employment exchanges, old age pensions, and social insurance) which greatly enlarged the civil service. In the volume of his history of the English people entitled *The Rule of Democracy*, the French historian Halévy noted of Edwardian England: 'A very serious change was taking place and for the first time attracting notice. England was becoming bureaucratic.'[3]

On the eve of the First World War, however, Britain was far from being a political democracy. Over 4.7m. adult men, and all adult women, were without the vote and the complex franchise qualifications were deliberately designed to exclude half the potential working-class electorate.[4] As late as 1910, only 40 per cent of adult males in working-class cities such as Liverpool and Glasgow were enfranchised (in comparison with an average figure for English and Welsh boroughs of 60 per cent) and the distribution of seats was similarly biased so that only 89 pre-war constituencies were predominantly working class. Such restrictions inevitably hampered the evolution of an effective working-class political party, although the main impediment to such a development was the low cultural aspirations of manual workers in general. The vote was granted in Victorian England not so much as a right but as a trust—a trust that the newly enfranchised would defer to the existing political establishment—and it was a trust which the pre-war electorate seemed unwilling to betray. Thus, although various adjustments did take place before 1914, there was no fundamental political or administrative change. Pre-war parties remained illequipped either to appeal to or organize mass electorates and the civil service remained remarkably small (80,000 in 1914, if the General Post Office is excluded)[5] and too ill-organized to administer an interventionist domestic policy. Expenditure on pre-war social services never rose above 4.2 per cent of GNP. Before 1914, in other words, democracy was more a threat than a reality.

[3] E. Halévy, *The Rule of Democracy* (1961 edn.), p. 262. Halévy also observed the appointment of 400 trade-unionists to the civil service to administer the new welfare services.

[4] Much of this paragraph is based on H. G. C. Matthew, R. I. McKibbin and J. A. Kay, 'The franchise factor in the rise of the Labour Party', *English Historical Review*, 91 (1976), 723-52. In Northern towns, low property prices and traditional labour mobility (if only over short distances) conspired with complex registration procedures to disenfranchise the majority of manual workers.

[5] W. H. Beveridge, *The Public Service in War and Peace* (1920).

It was the First World War that was the occasion, if not necessarily the cause, of the effective democratization of Britain. The 1918 Reform Act trebled the electorate at both national and local levels and revolutionized the assumptions on which British politics were based. Middle-class voters were reduced to an estimated 20 per cent (instead of 40 per cent) of the electorate and many of the new voters, enfranchised on an age rather than a property qualification, were not seen—like their nineteenth-century predecessors—overtly to have earned such a trust. Consequently electoral priorities were permanently transformed and an air of increased uncertainty injected into party politics. 'The 1918 Act', it has been argued, 'did more than just treble the electorate: it transformed its character by significantly lowering its political awareness. Not only was the new electorate divided by class ... it was less likely to respond to policies that demanded a comparatively high level of political intelligence.'[6] This electoral revolution, moreover, was underpinned by a significant advance in working-class organization and aspirations. As a result of full employment and increased wartime responsibilities, the trade union movement almost doubled its membership between 1914 and 1919 from 4.1m. to 7.9m. (23 to 43 per cent of the work-force) and, assisted by the new franchise, the Labour Party quickly established itself as an alternative party of government.[7] Working-class culture became more assertive. One observer of working-class life characterized the war as the 'great release' in which traditional deference died and a 'new dignity' emerged:

1917! The year when the twentieth century really began. New ideas ran abroad in the world.... At home people remarked continually on the change among the undermass: regular wages and the absence of class pressure from above had wrought in many a peculiar quality which looked uncommonly like self-respect.... Life had broadened in scope; a certain parochialism had gone for ever.[8]

This assertiveness, even if it did not always display as mature a 'political awareness' as some commentators might wish, presented

---

[6] Matthew *et al.*, 'The franchise factor', 749.

[7] The degree of working-class organization is contentious, in the absence of any exact knowledge of the size and composition of the work-force. These figures are taken from A. H. Halsey, *Trends in British Society* (1972), table 4.12. See Appendix 2(A).

[8] R. Roberts, *The Classic Slum* (1973 edn.), pp. 210–15.

a fundamental challenge in both industry and parliament to pre-war capitalist certainties already rocked by the war itself. A final shock to the traditional assumptions on which the pre-war political system had been based was that, under the new electoral pressures, government was slowly propelled by the structural weaknesses of the economy into new areas of responsibility such as intervention in industry. Here, confronted by the TUC and the new employers' organizations that working-class assertiveness had provoked (the Federation of British Industry (FBI) and the National Confederation of Employers' Organisations (NCEO)), both politicians and civil servants were brought face to face with the realities of pluralist politics.[9]

The response of inter-war politicians to the advent of democracy was, it has been generally agreed, far from heroic. The one government seriously to attempt to harness the power of democracy and to direct it to 'positive ends' was the first, the Lloyd George Coalition of 1918–22.[10] Thereafter, inter-war politics were largely a reaction against its perceived political and personal amorality. It was Baldwin who, over the next 15 years, was to exercise an unrivalled 'moral authority' over the whole electorate and significantly it had been he who had sealed the Coalition's fate with the remark to a critical meeting of the Conservative Party that 'a dynamic force is a very terrible thing'.[11] Rather than being excited by the challenge of democracy, Baldwin was concerned mainly for its fragility, believing as he did that the 'rapid political evolution brought about by the war' had produced an electorate whose 'political status' was too far in advance of its cultural status. As he asked, for example, in 1927: 'How often has mankind travelled on the circumference of a wheel, working its way to a point you could call democracy? Go but a little further and democracy becomes licence, licence becomes anarchy, then the wheel goes full circle and anarchy

[9] Pluralism, like democracy, can be defined in a variety of ways. The implicit model here is one of bounded pluralism as defined in P. Hall, H. Land, R. Parker and A. Webb, *Change, Choice and Conflict in Social Policy* (1975), ch. 8. Policy-making is pluralistic in that the interest of the 'élite' may be challenged at any time but, owing to a variety of factors such as the inequality of access to policy-making experienced by different pressure groups, the range of decisions that can actually be made is limited or 'bounded'.

[10] K. O. Morgan, *Consensus and Disunity* (Oxford, 1979), p. 375.

[11] E. Percy, *Some Memories* (1958), p. 128; K. Middlemas and J. Barnes, *Baldwin* (1969), p. 123.

comes back to tyranny.'[12] The rise of totalitarianism in Fascist and Communist Europe gave added substance to his fears.

Like the two other politicians who dominated inter-war politics (MacDonald and Neville Chamberlain), Baldwin constantly reminded himself of the responsibility of democratic leadership: the need to 'do one's duty', 'to face up to and not to run away from responsibility', and, above all, to seek national rather than sectional interest. The test of their joint leadership came with the formation of the National Government with its massive majorities of 493 and 248 after the elections of 1931 and 1935. The test was largely failed for, whatever its achievement in maintaining social order, the Cabinet was able to provide neither the positive moral example to 'educate' the new mass electorate nor the executive leadership to establish beyond doubt the effectiveness of parliamentary democracy as a system of government. On the one hand, election pledges (such as the promise to support the Gold Standard in 1931 and the League of Nations over Abyssinia in 1935) were immediately broken, and there was a resort, even under Chamberlain's supposedly austere chancellorship, to 'electoral bribery' by means of extensive propaganda, unsound finance, and economic 'stunts'.[13] On the other hand, the two major challenges of mass unemployment and the maintenance of European peace were failed, whilst the men of action in each party (Lloyd George, Churchill, and Mosley) were berated for seeking to corrupt or take advantage of an immature electorate. In Churchill's incomparable phrase, Cabinet policy seemed solely to be 'decided to be undecided, resolved to be irresolute, adamant for drift, solid for fluidity, all powerful to be impotent'.[14]

The perceived impotence of the National Government spawned a general disillusion with democracy. It is possible perhaps to exaggerate the extent of popular disillusion, as opposed to apathy, as Mass Observation—to its evident chagrin—discovered from its

[12] Quoted in Middlemas and Barnes, *Baldwin*, pp. 530, 503. Lloyd George at one time significantly did call himself a 'nationalist-socialist': *Lord Riddell's War Diary* (1933), p. 324.

[13] Use of contemporary records is the more rewarding for their revelation of widely held obsessions. 'Stunts' was the frequent term of abuse for any public works scheme (preferably from the Lloyd George stable) designed to counteract unemployment; 'sentimental' was likewise the vogue word used by employers to denounce the readiness of democratic politicians to concede social reforms.

[14] Quoted in F. Williams, *A Pattern of Rulers* (1965), p. 50.

surveys in the early 1940s.[15] Amongst informed insiders, however, disillusion was endemic. As one liberal group of public figures noted in 1933:

The prevailing view ... was that 'democracy' has never recovered its faith after the knock-out blows of the General Strike and its disillusionment with two Labour Governments. It has lost its faith in any sudden change or complete panacea, does not believe Government can do much anyway, is not actively discontented with such food and shelter and amusement as it now has.[16]

As new initiatives, such as Mosley's New Party, and Political and Economic Planning (PEP), collapsed or failed to make an impact, so disillusion deepened. Aneurin Bevan provided a perceptive explanation of the *malaise*. It was, he wrote,

a dangerous period in the lifetime of a nation when the convictions, beliefs and values of one epoch are seen to be losing their vitality and those of the new have not yet won universal acceptance. Many believe they are witnessing the decline of human society, when all that is happening is a change from one type of society to another.[17]

Inter-war politicians of both left and right certainly appeared incapable of effecting the political changes demanded by the advent of democracy. For this failure they were subjected during the early years of the Second World War to a vitriolic press campaign, spearheaded by Cato's *Guilty Men*.

The advent of democracy also posed considerable political and administrative problems for the civil service which, amidst political vacillation and public disillusion, had at the very least to carry on the King's government. In the first place, the establishment as the alternative party of government of the Labour Party, with its socialist constitution of 1918, challenged the basic principle of civil service neutrality. The civil service had long stood for the concept of the impartial state, holding the ring between competing interests, but this presumed a capitalist consensus: how could it now serve with equal impartiality capitalist and socialist ministers assured that, in its necessary restriction of the flow of information and

---

[15] See, for example, 'Popular attitudes towards wartime politics, 20 November 1940' (Mass Observation archives, FR 496).
[16] The Romney Street Group, Tom Jones diary, 17 Jan. 1933 (Tom Jones papers).
[17] A. Bevan, *In Place of Fear* (1961), p. 122.

policy options to ministers, personal or class bias would not intrude? In the second place, the increasingly interventionist role of government posed the twin problems of how to develop effective long-term policies, which would satisfy two parties with rival ideologies, and of how to act under a patently weak or incompetent minister. Should the tradition of Chadwick, Kay-Shuttleworth, and Morant be honoured and the decline of democracy into bureaucracy risked? Or should the constitutionally correct response of submission to minister and parliament be adopted, risking further public disillusion and the decline of departmental morale into cynical negativism? Growing interventionism, moreover, raised doubts as to the specialist expertise, competence, and flexibility of the service. By the 1930s, for instance, central government was paying out annually £115m. in over two hundred million separate weekly transactions and officials were being drawn, not only into new areas of policy advice, but also into a totally new relationship with the public.

The conventional wisdom of both contemporaries and historians is that the administrative response to the advent of democracy was as unheroic as the political.[18] The civil service, it is argued, remained an elite caste which used its increasing power to discourage much-needed reform. Despite the social and educational revolution of the First World War and the changing role of administration, for instance, the class and educational bias of the higher civil service hardly altered. Indeed, certain reforms tended to intensify existing bias, so that 80 per cent of inter-war recruits to the higher civil service were children of parents in classes I and II of the Registrar General's 1911 social classification (whereas only 18 per cent of the population fell into these categories) and the percentage of recruits from Oxbridge actually rose to 89 per cent from the 1909-14 figure of 80 per cent. With the rise of the Labour Party, it had become easier for the child of a manual worker to become a Cabinet minister than a top civil servant. The ease with which many senior administrators such as Sir John Anderson, Sir James Grigg, and

---

[18] For a fuller examination of the conventional wisdom, see R. Davidson and R. Lowe, 'Bureaucracy and innovation in British welfare policy, 1870-1945', in W. J. Mommsen (ed.), *The Emergence of the Welfare State in Britain and Germany* (1981), pp. 263-95. For the statistical evidence, see R. K. Kelsall, *Higher Civil Servants in Britain* (1955). Kelsall defined the higher civil service both as the whole administrative class, which numbered 1,500, and the senior 500 officials who were in regular contact with ministers.

Sir Maurice Hankey slipped into the role of Cabinet ministers during the Second World War also suggests that, like many of their nineteenth-century predecessors, they had long been acting as 'statesmen in disguise'; and, as both a frustrated reformer and an ex-Treasury civil servant, Keynes for one had no doubt that they had used their power negatively. In 1939, for instance, he wrote:

> The civil service is ruled today by the Treasury school, trained by tradition and experience and native skill to every form of intelligent obstruction.... We have experienced in the twenty years since the war two occasions of terrific retrenchment and axing of constructive schemes [1922 and 1931]. This has not only been a crushing discouragement for all who are capable of constructive projects, but it has inevitably led to the survival of those to whom negative measures are natural and sympathetic.[19]

Keynes was undoubtedly right to detect in the inter-war period a major, and not wholly beneficent, increase in the formal power and influence of the Treasury. Treasury control had been formally extended immediately after the war to unify the civil service in anticipation of more interventionist government, but ironically it concentrated power in a department whose officials had little contact with the public and such predetermined views on the restriction of public expenditure (and hence the role of government) that they were widely known as 'abominable no-men'. Consequently, at the very time that administrative initiative was needed, it was centrally discouraged.

A formidable case against the bias and negative influence of the inter-war civil service can be, and indeed has been, made; but, when the service is judged as part of, rather than apart from, contemporary society, particular criticisms lose much of their apparent validity. The educational and social bias of higher civil servants, for instance, is somewhat irrelevant because such prejudice as officials did display was largely the product of influences after appointment which no new recruitment procedure could have counteracted: the shared experience of work, fortified by life in the south-east of England in general and in London clubs in particular. In any case, between the wars, senior positions were filled by men recruited under pre-war regulations. Sir Horace Wilson, for instance, the head of the civil service between 1939 and 1942, had enjoyed none of the supposed privileges of the Treasury mandarin,

---

[19] *New Statesman*, 28 Jan. 1939.

being the son of a Bournemouth furniture dealer, educated part time at the London School of Economics and having worked his way up from the pre-war equivalent of the executive class via one of the less glamorous departments, the Ministry of Labour. It is also doubtful how much real power the civil service could have accreted at a time when politicians had become noticeably more professional (in their attendance if not their attainment at work) and politics had become more pluralist. Any increase in power was more apparent than real, explicable in terms of numerical expansion (approximately 200 per cent between 1914 and 1939 if the General Post Office is excluded) and increased public prominence owing to the growth of the social services.

The alleged negativism of the civil service should also be placed in its proper cultural and political context. There was at no time in the inter-war period any widespread acceptance of the assumption, which underpinned criticism of the civil service by reformist groups such as PEP, that civil servants should adopt a more aggressive role in the determination of economic and social priorities and the planning of policy. The British public as a whole was opposed to the expansion of central government and (as the results of the 1931 and 1935 elections showed) for every reformer urging increased expenditure there were a thousand taxpayers urging less. Parliamentary government by its nature also constrained the service because, as the Fabian Society belatedly acknowledged in 1947, 'the civil service could only achieve a speed comparable to efficient private business by the sacrifice both of democratic control (questions in Parliament etc.) and of the principle of uniform treatment for all citizens'.[20] This was a price presumably few reformers were willing to pay. Even charges of bureaucratic incompetence and incivility lose force when closer examination is made of an area under-researched by historians, the implementation (as opposed to the formulation) of policy. Indeed, much of the criticism levelled against the inter-war civil service would seem to have been formed without due appreciation of the real economic, political, and parliamentary constraints within which it worked.

The time is, therefore, ripe for a reassessment of the administrative, if not necessarily the political, response of government to the advent of democracy. Such a reassessment is dependent on two preconditions: first, the separation, so far as is practical, of political

[20] Fabian Society, *The Reform of the Higher Civil Service* (1947), p. 6.

and administrative influences on the formulation of policy and, secondly, a recognition of the fundamental dynamism of public administration. A balanced analysis of policy must, above all, scrutinize the phrase 'official policy', conventionally used so loosely by historians and political commentators alike, to establish whether it refers to the decisions of Cabinet, a specific departmental minister, or the civil service; and, if the latter, whether it refers to the Treasury view, the consensus of departmental officials (before or after discussion with their minister), or the opinion of a predominant official who may be at variance with his colleagues. Just as political decisions are often taken in opposition to administrative advice, so the civil service (despite the frequent assumption of the Treasury) is not a monolithic organization propagating a single orthodox view. Nor are individual ministries inorganic entities devoid of internal tensions. As Max Beloff has remarked, the anonymity of the service may perhaps be a valuable constitutional convention, but it is certainly not a valuable convention for the historian.[21]

To strip anonymity from the whole inter-war civil service, however, is clearly a task beyond the scope of a single book, and, therefore, one department has to be singled out for particular attention. The Ministry of Labour provides a most apposite case-study. Not only was it the second largest inter-war department and often the most expensive, but also it had an exceptional range of responsibility—industrial relations, social policy (unemployment relief), and economic policy (in particular regional policy)—which involved it directly in the government's response to democracy.[22] Founded in 1916 by Lloyd George as a concession to the Labour movement, it was from its inception the foremost token of the government's adjustment to pluralism. Its responsibility for industrial relations made it the prime channel of industrial and popular opinion to the Cabinet, whilst its responsibility for unemployment policy involved it deeply in the bargaining between government and vested interest. This latter responsibility also established it as a

---

[21] M. Beloff, 'The Whitehall factor: the role of the higher civil service', in G. Peele and C. Cook (eds.), *The Politics of Reappraisal* (1975), p. 227.

[22] Owing in particular to its responsibility for employment exchanges and unemployment pay, the Ministry was second in size only to the General Post Office and had a peak expenditure, in 1932, of £78.62m.—just under one-fifth of net public expenditure. See Appendix 1, C and D. In 1939, rival domestic departments such as the Ministry of Health and the Board of Trade had establishments of under 7,000 and 5,000 respectively in contrast to the Ministry's total of 30,000.

pioneer in many of the administrative adjustments to democracy (such as the extension of delegated legislation and administrative discretion) and made it highly influential in the development of a wide range of economic and social policy. It was, after all, as Asa Briggs has remarked, unemployment 'more than any other social contingency which ... determined the shape and timing of modern "welfare" legislation'.[23]

The Ministry also provides a perfect illustration of the contrast between the political and administrative response of government to the advent of democracy. It was permanently denied strong political leadership, for a low salary (£2,000 p.a. as compared to the £5,000 of an established secretary of state) and the constant threat of parliamentary embarrassment did little to attract ambitious ministers. Administratively, however, it was rapidly transformed from the 'cinderella of government offices', as diagnosed by MacDonald in 1924, to a 'bloody soviet', as feared by a Treasury official in 1936.[24] The Ministry's extensive local and regional organization— in particular the employment exchanges—gave its officials the practical administrative experience and the direct contact with the public that other departments (such as the Ministry of Health, working largely through local authorities, or the Treasury, dependent on other government departments and the Bank of England) lacked. As a result they were able to develop an independent source of information and an appreciation of public needs which gave their advice in Whitehall distinction and authority. They were consequently chosen in the 1930s to plan and staff the new quangos (such as the UAB and the Special Areas Commissions) which were the most significant administrative adjustment to democracy; and some, like Sir Horace Wilson, were eventually appointed to senior positions within the Treasury itself. By the late 1930s, indeed, officials trained or serving in the Ministry had developed both the confidence and the competence which made their services so highly prized during the Second World War and enabled the Ministry to become one of the most important wartime departments.

The Ministry of Labour, therefore, is an excellent medium through which to examine the political and administrative response

[23] A. Briggs, 'The welfare state in historical perspective', *European Journal of Sociology*, 2 (1961), 229.
[24] Beatrice Webb diary, 18 Jan. 1924 (Passfield papers); V. Markham to T. Jones, 27 Mar. 1936 (Tom Jones diary).

of government to the advent of democracy. Its history can also assist in a reappraisal of inter-war economic and social policy, clarifying the role that civil servants played in the quiet pragmatic experiments which, under a blighted political surface, gradually revolutionized political and administrative practice. Bureaucrats have, of course, been assigned many distinct roles by theorists: the conscious or unconscious agents of class rule; an independent social and political force with a propensity for either enervation or self-aggrandisement; and a professional body essential to the rational development of resources and social relationships in an increasingly complex world. Reality is more complex for, as a heterogeneous body of men and women, civil servants discharge a variety of roles. Weber himself acknowledged this. He urged that *a priori* the indispensability of expert officials need not guarantee them power in a democracy any more than the economic indispensability of manual workers had guaranteed the working class power. Nevertheless, the danger of bureaucracy (in the sense of 'rule by officials') did exist and so 'one must in every historical case analyse in which ... special direction bureaucratization has ... developed'.[25] The following chapters are just such a case-study.

[25] Roth and Willich, *Max Weber*, pp. 983, 991.

CHAPTER 2

THE POLITICAL CHALLENGE

THE creation of the Ministry in December 1916, as one of the three principal concessions made by Lloyd George to secure the Labour Party's support for his premiership, was hailed at the time as a major political development. Lloyd George opined:

the Department would certainly be one of the most important Departments in the Government because, however important a Labour Ministry would be in time of peace—and it would essentially be a Department whose decisions would very materially affect the lives of millions of people in this country—in times of war it is almost doubly important.[1]

Not for the only time, however, the rhetoric of the new prime minister and wartime expectations were to prove deceptive. Despite retaining its Cabinet status throughout the inter-war period (a feat unmatched by any other department created in the First World War), the Ministry remained politically 'one of the least important home departments'.[2] When the first Labour Government assumed office in 1924, it was considered insufficiently prestigious to receive either the prime responsibility for unemployment or the Party's leading theorist (Sidney Webb). The leading inter-war trade unionist (Ernest Bevin) found no place for it in his 1931 plans for a reformed Whitehall—despite having been one of its earliest proponents—and, on his own assumption of office in 1940, dismissed as a 'waste of time' its peacetime role as a 'glorified conciliation board with the register for national service, unemployment and public assistance'.[3] Conservative politicians reacted similarly. Churchill, the political author of much of the pre-war legislation

---

[1] Transcript of Lloyd George's meeting with a deputation from the Labour Party, 7 Dec. 1916 (Lloyd George papers, G 245). The other concessions were a place in the War Cabinet for Henderson and the establishment of a ministry of pensions.

[2] A. Bullock, *The Life and Times of Ernest Bevin*, vol. 2 (1967), p. 119. The Ministry was briefly out of the Cabinet during the emergency National Government of Aug.-Nov. 1931.

[3] Beatrice Webb diary, 18 Jan. 1924. Bullock, *Ernest Bevin*, vol. 1 (1960), pp. 501, 652.

for which the Ministry became responsible, proclaimed soon after the war: 'I do not myself hold with such a Ministry. Arbitration and Conciliation are the functions of an impartial department like the Board of Trade. *Factories* etc. are well managed by the Home Office. Labour *policy* belongs to the Government.'[4] Baldwin and Chamberlain also, despite various encouraging noises, had little positive regard for the Ministry. With its low salary and status, it was shunned by the politically ambitious.

The Ministry's lack of political importance, however, is significant, for it epitomized a fundamental contradiction in British inter-war politics. Under electoral pressure, economic and more particularly social policy became the essence of party politics and yet the new interventionist ministries enjoyed little political prestige. They were dismissed as 'a transitional step to higher office or a graveyard where a dying career could be quietly buried'; and not until the 1940s did their fortunes so revive that they became (as they had been briefly before the First World War, when Lloyd George and Churchill were presidents of the Board of Trade) the 'surest way' for an ambitious politician to 'get on'.[5] The disappointment of the high expectations initially held for the Ministry symbolized the unresponsiveness of the formal political system to the challenge of democracy.

Political Expectation

The creation of the Ministry had a certain air of inevitability.[6] Not only had many other industrial countries established ministries of labour before the First World War but in Britain, too, there had been mounting debate. After 1892, 15 parliamentary bills and two amendments to the Address (in 1904 and 1908) had sought the Ministry's establishment; and two Royal Commissions, those on Labour (1892-4) and the Civil Service (1912-14) had specifically examined the issue. Meanwhile the administrative and political momentum had been inexorable. A Labour Department was established within the Board of Trade in 1886, given greater autonomy in 1892, placed under its own comptroller-general in 1909, and

---

[4] Lloyd George papers, F 8/2/49.
[5] B. B. Gilbert, *British Social Policy, 1914-1939* (1970), p. 307; N. Fisher, *Iain Macleod* (1973), p. 75.
[6] The pre-war demands for the Ministry are fully examined in R. Lowe, 'The Ministry of Labour, 1916-1924: a graveyard of social reform?', *Public Administration*, 52 (1974), 415-38.

finally under a second secretary in 1912. Simultaneously the increasing power of Labour was given political recognition. In 1886 Henry Broadhurst (the general secretary of the TUC) became the first minister of working-class origin and in 1905 and 1915 respectively John Burns and Arthur Henderson were appointed to Cabinet posts. That they were appointed to advise generally on labour matters and not just to discharge departmental duties was made explicit in August 1916 by Henderson's translation from the Board of Education to the newly created Office of Labour Adviser.

Administrative momentum played a vital part in the Ministry's eventual creation and will be examined more fully in the next chapter. Political momentum was sustained by two main concerns—the realization that the power of Labour, in particular organized Labour, had to be formally acknowledged and the desire of reformers to draw attention to supposedly neglected areas of policy. The former was the more straightforward. As early as 1892, Haldane urged on Gladstone this 'useful and popular' reform to demonstrate the Liberal Party's sympathy for social reform and thereby to assist the frustration of an independent labour party.[7] Two years later, the minority report of the Royal Commission on Labour recommended the Ministry's establishment on account of 'the increasing prominence of industrial problems and the growing participation in politics of the wage-earning class'.[8] Thereafter, Ben Tillett, of the Dockers' Union, became its most consistent advocate, demanding a minister 'who for the first time in history would be able to speak in the name of the workers, as the President of the Board of Trade does of trade, as the President of the Board of Agriculture does of agricultural interests'. This demand was still being reiterated during the First World War when the Parliamentary Committee of the TUC, for instance, asked:

What more fitting recognition could be given to labour's cooperation during the war than by the establishment of a Ministry of Labour, which would enable the workers to realize that at last they were taking a direct, active and real part in the administrative affairs of their country? It behoves the Trade Union movement to see to it that the recent consultations

---

[7] Maj.-Gen. Sir F. West, *Haldane*, vol. 1 (1937), p. 59.

[8] C. 7421, PP (1894), xxxv, 9, para. 308. The succeeding quotations are from Dockers' Union, *Minutes of the Triennial Delégate Meeting*, 1911, General Secretary's Report, p. 27 and TUC *Annual Report*, 1916, p. 185.

with its representatives were something more than a mere passing phase of the direct association of Labour with the government of the State.

For many, however, mere consultation was not enough; the Ministry was conceived as a remedy for particular grievances. First, it was championed, as by Keir Hardie in his amendment to the Address in 1904 and by the minority report of the Royal Commission on the Poor Laws in 1909, as a remedy for unemployment.[9] Thus the minority report envisaged a Ministry as the 'national authority for unemployment' which would have, apart from one department administering the factory acts, five further divisions: a statistics department (to predict and then assist in the regulation of cyclical unemployment), a national labour exchange and a migration division (to organise the labour market), a trade insurance division (to assist the temporarily unemployed), and a maintenance and training division (to mop up the residuum). Secondly, during the war, when attention had become focused on the weaknesses of industry rather than of the labour market, the TUC sought a ministry of labour and industry to nationalize the commanding heights of the economy as well as to safeguard the industrial and environmental health of the worker; and the 'Athenaeum' group of liberal reformers (who were to play a central role in the actual establishment of the Ministry) championed a similarly titled ministry to stimulate productive efficiency.[10] The first proposal was to be broadly endorsed by the 1918 Haldane Committee on the Machinery of Government in its blueprint for a ministry of employment. The latter was reminiscent of the very first demand for the Ministry, by the Association of the Chambers of Commerce in 1892, which had sought to divest the Board of Trade of its labour responsibilities so that it could assume the role of a 'ministry of industry'.

Before 1916, these demands for the Ministry were officially rejected for a variety of general reasons. The creation of any new department, it was argued, would increase public expenditure, decrease political independence (as more back-benchers accepted office), and make the Cabinet unwieldy. Moreover, government had grown too complex for a 'scientific allocation' of departmental

---

[9] *Parl. Deb.*, 1904, 130, col. 474; Cd. 4499, PP (1909), xxxvii, 1208–14.
[10] TUC, *Annual Report*, 1916, p. 250; *The Athenaeum*, no. 4613, 1917. These reforms anticipated the transformation of the Ministry into a Department of Employment and Productivity in 1968.

responsibility and, were such a reallocation to be attempted, any benefit accruing would be disproportionate to the disruption caused.[11] Two more specific objections were raised: first, that all government departments should be impartial and, secondly, that a division in the responsibility for industrial and labour policy would impair good government. As Llewellyn Smith, the head of the Board of Trade's Labour Department, argued in a powerful memorandum provoked by Keir Hardie's amendment to the Address in 1904:

> Undoubtedly the intention is that the Minister of Labour should be a man specially 'sympathetic' with labour interests. But the decision and administration of all ... [employment] matters requires equal weight to be given to the interests and representations of labourers and the employers of labour. It would be most undesirable to have a Minister of Labour supposed to stand for the 'labour' side of each economic question and a Minister of Commerce taking the other side. But beyond this experience shows that the best guarantee for wise dealing with matters relating either to labour or commerce is to deal with each in the light of the other: i.e. to keep questions of the 'condition of the people' in mind in dealing with a commercial question, and to remember the effects on commerce and foreign competition when dealing with such matters as the regulation of labour.[12]

These official objections were matched by opposition from within the Labour movement. At the 1909 TUC conference, for example, Tillett argued for the appointment of a minister of labour on the grounds that: 'If the Government could organize a military and naval force it could do the same thing for its labour force. Such a minister should have all the means of ammunition for organizing the labour market, as had a Minister of War or an Admiralty Lord.'[13] Syndicalists rejected such reasoning, as did many other trade unionists who did not share the collectivist assumption that the working class should seek the assistance of the state. They preferred to keep their own hands on the ammunition, so that they could themselves direct the firing.

Before 1916, therefore, there was a lengthy debate over the need for and the potential role of the Ministry but, wide-ranging though this debate was, it lacked penetrative depth. Foremost amongst the

---

[11] See, for instance, Asquith in *Parl. Deb.*, 1909, 3, col. 1499.
[12] Lab 2/213/L 156/1904.   [13] TUC, *Annual Report*, 1909, pp. 140-1.

critical issues left unresolved was the question of 'impartiality'. As has been seen, the rise of the Labour Party as the alternative party of government presented a real challenge for the whole civil service; but a Ministry of Labour would be faced with the particular dilemma of whether or not it should be (even under a Labour cabinet) a permanent pressure group within government for the Labour movement. Official plans all reaffirmed the principle of departmental disinterest, but there was a significant disagreement over the means of its attainment. On the one hand, the Board of Trade (as Llewellyn Smith's memorandum made plain) advocated a comprehensive 'ministry of commerce and labour' so that any clash of sectional interests might be contained within one department. On the other hand, the 1918 Haldane Committee was convinced that a single minister would be prevented from 'exercising effective control' by the superior 'technical knowledge' of 'corporate bodies representing either employers or workmen'. Moreover, with uncharacteristic insight into the imperfections of the real world, the Committee argued:

If the same Minister and the same Department were responsible for determining the conditions of employment and for encouraging private enterprise in the production of wealth it is inevitable that there should be, if not undue subordination of the one purpose to the other, at least a general suspicion, on the one side or the other, of such a sacrifice of interests.[14]

Consequently its solution was to establish two separate ministries (the ministries of industry and employment) so that any sectional dispute might be resolved in Cabinet. Such official niceties, however, were peremptorily swept aside by the TUC, which, before 1916, had indeed been suspicious of the Board of Trade's bias. It demanded an openly partisan Ministry of Labour to champion its own interests.

Even had such partisanship been embraced, it is unclear how the Ministry could have succeeded, for the TUC's pre-war campaign never satisfactorily explained how one minister could represent so volatile an interest as 'Labour'. Fundamental disagreement within the Labour movement was illustrated by the pre-war clash between collectivists and syndicalists over the need for a Ministry, by continuing disputes over the nature of the Ministry's potential powers (for example, the degree of compulsion to be exercised in

[14] Cd. 9230, PP (1918), xii, 1, pp. 41–3.

industrial relations or in the treatment of the residuum) and by trade union hostility to welfare services, such as the employment exchanges, which were to be the kernel of the Ministry's responsibilities.[15] Such disagreements raised fundamental questions about the role the Labour movement really wanted the state and thus the Ministry to play. What social services, for example, could the Ministry provide without threatening to some the imposition of a 'servile state'? How could welfare services be efficiently administered without some degree of standardization and coercion? How could government discharge (presumably with the use of taxpayers' money) its obligation to the majority of working people, who were unorganized, wihout unduly benefiting them in relation to the trade unionist who, to safeguard his independence, rejected collectivism?

Constant changes to the small print of the pre-war bills promoting the Ministry were also indicative of an inability satisfactorily to resolve the major administrative and constitutional obstacles which beset the discharge of the Ministry's projected responsibilities. Nowhere was this more apparent than in unemployment policy where the Webbs (in the minority report of the Royal Commission on the Poor Laws) and the Labour Party (in its Right to Work Bills) had initially advocated very different concepts of the Ministry as a 'national authority for unemployment'. Later they tried to co-ordinate their plans in the 1913 Prevention of Unemployment Bill, which projected the Ministry as a 'national authority' with the power to execute anti-cyclical programmes of public works (and not just to advise the Treasury, as suggested by the Webbs) whilst the unemployment committees of local authorities (to which the Labour Party had wished to devolve power) became merely the 'local agencies' of the national authority.[16] This compromise, however, begged more questions than it answered. Were local authorities, with their long tradition of independence and their experience of administering public relief, prepared to act as the 'local agencies' of central government? Would, or indeed could, the Treasury cede such control over public expenditure to another government

[15] Tillett and the Webbs were amongst those to demand greater compulsory powers for the state; Tillett's lieutenant, Ernest Bevin, in his maiden speech to Congress in 1916, articulated union fears that state welfare would undermine their economic, social, and hence political role.

[16] PP (1913), v, 399.

department? Inter-war experience was to show and Beatrice Webb, by signing the Haldane Report, was to admit that neither was a practical possibility. All that pre-war planning had, therefore, managed to produce was the spectre of a 'national authority' devoid of both financial independence and executive powers.

With such lacunae at the heart of pre-war demands for the Ministry as a welfare department, how many more bedevilled the brief wartime campaign for a 'ministry of industry and labour', which raised a whole gamut of problems from nationalization to increased productivity. The strategy favoured by wartime reformers for the solution of these problems was the devolution of responsibility to each individual industry—'home rule for industry'. But how practical was such a policy given the mutual antipathy of both sides of industry? Could government, with its responsibilities to the new mass electorate, devolve such power to vested interest? Could democratic freedom (in particular free collective bargaining) indeed be reconciled with the swift attainment of economic efficiency and social justice? Like other blueprints for the Ministry, the concept of a 'ministry for industry and labour' seemed to be a political slogan designed to draw attention to a particular grievance rather than a serious attempt to adapt the machinery of government to new responsibilities.

The actual creation of the Ministry of Labour in 1916, therefore, raised major political, constitutional, and administrative problems which its advocates had done little to resolve. The problems were far from insoluble. Indeed their solution went to the very heart of democratic politics and offered to those who successfully grappled with them a political prestige comparable to that enjoyed by Lloyd George and Churchill as social reformers before 1914. Their successful resolution, however, did depend on exceptional political leadership at both Cabinet and ministerial level and a measure of public consensus. All these the Ministry was denied.

Political Constraints

For its proper development the Ministry required from successive governments leadership that was positive and reasonably consistent, especially in relation to the role of the state in society. This was not forthcoming. Between 1916 and 1922 it was roughly buffeted and indeed almost sunk by the positive inconsistency of Lloyd George. Thereafter, it was abandoned to the irresolution

of Baldwin and MacDonald and the expediency of the National
Government.

Of all inter-war governments, the Lloyd George Coalition promised the most positive response to the challenge of democracy: but
in fact its legacy was to delay it. After the war, it is true, Lloyd
George enacted a programme of reform which, in retrospect, might
appear equal to that of the 1906-15 Liberal or the 1945-51 Labour
Governments. At the time, however, it was viewed very differently,
as an improvised series of opportunist concessions consistent only
in their betrayal of the high wartime expectations which the Prime
Minister's own rhetoric had done so much to excite. By 1922, the
necessary preconditions for political reform had been dissipated.
The germ of wartime unity had been transformed into 'a more
divided, more sectionalized society with classes at war with each
other and with the government'; intellectual ability was discredited
owing to its association with 'personal corruption and rackety private lives'; and bold state action had become identified with 'incipient caesarism'.[17]

The fault was by no means Lloyd George's alone. As prime
minister he was often poorly served by his political colleagues and
frustrated by vested interest groups, which circumscribed his freedom of action; but his ultimate isolation was largely of his own
making. First, even when preoccupied with wartime strategy and
the Versailles Peace Treaty, he had been reluctant to delegate
authority or to select ministers who might 'pave the way not only
to a democratic peace but a democratic reconstruction at home'.[18]
Secondly, in his public dealings he displayed an unprincipled flexibility typified by an instruction to his Minister of Labour in 1919 at
the start of some important negotiations: 'no one ever convinced
anyone by an argument.'[19] Thirdly, he was unable to reconcile his
intuitive radicalism, bred in rural Wales, with the needs of industrial society. As a consequence, he was ultimately unable to provide
either a consistently reasoned response to the immense challenge of
democracy or a firm focus for those who wished to give him assistance. For Keynes, amongst many, he had a 'final purposelessness'.

[17] Morgan, *Consensus and Disunity*, p. 299; R. Blake, *The Conservative Party
from Peel to Churchill* (1968), p. 216.
[18] T. Jones, *Whitehall Diary*, vol. 1 (1969), p. 44.
[19] A. J. P. Taylor (ed.), *Lloyd George: A Diary by Frances Stevenson* (1971),
p. 323.

'Lloyd George', argued Keynes, 'is rooted in nothing: he is a void and without context: he lives and feeds on his immediate surroundings.'[20] After the economic collapse of 1920 those surroundings, in the shape of a Cabinet dominated by the Conservative Party, increasingly required a return to 'pre-war normalcy', not a radical adaptation to democracy.

The Conservative Party, after a brief flirtation with die-hard government under Bonar Law in 1922–3, did not sink into pure reaction. Baldwin, despite an earlier career of the 'utmost insignificance', entertained so definite a view of his duty to secure national harmony that the Party's principal agent was reduced to describing him as 'semi-socialist'.[21] His greatness was to sense and represent the national mood, his weakness a failure to translate this mood into positive action. He never lived up to his speeches. In 1924, he had led a reunited Conservative Party to 'the greatest party victory that modern Britain has ever seen' and for the next five years presided over a government of considerable talent.[22] Initially he used his power to prepare the ground for moderate reforms, but he was broken both in health and resolve by the General Strike. As John Ramsden has argued:

He had suffered physically and emotionally from the events of 1926 and he was to need regular rests for recuperation for the rest of his career. Although he continued to preach conciliation, he had lost the certainty that it was the practical course to pursue and he was no longer optimistic.

Consequently he abandoned his positive commitment to social reform as quickly as, in 1924, he had jettisoned tariff reform (the economic policy which only a few months earlier he had been

---

[20] 'Mr. Lloyd George: a fragment', *The Collected Writings of John Maynard Keynes*, vol. 10 (1971), p. 24. Humbert Wolfe, Lloyd George's wartime private secretary and the most charismatic inter-war Ministry official, confirmed this judgement. Lloyd George was 'a hundred per cent wicked. The Welsh wizard had a mind and imagination that functioned from minute to minute, moving with an inspired power of extemporization as each necessity arose, either practical towards events or psychological towards men. But after that moment all was forgotten, promises and commitments obliterated from his memory, his conscience left treacherously virgin.' R. Church, *The Voyage Home* (1964), p. 81.

[21] J. Ramsden, *The Age of Balfour and Baldwin* (1979), p. 226.

[22] The Conservatives had more seats than either the Liberals in 1906 or Labour in 1945, and polled over 50 per cent of the vote if allowance is made for uncontested seats. See Ramsden, ibid., p. 206. Quotations in the remainder of the paragraph are from the same source, pp. 212, 285, 214.

proclaiming was essential to economic recovery). Thereafter, Conservative policy slid into a 'pragmatic realism' which required
neither periodic reappraisals of policy-objectives nor the provision
of inspirational leadership, but rather judged all proposals by the
simple test of what was 'practical political business'. Judgement
became increasingly pessimistic.

Baldwin's administration was sandwiched between two Labour
Governments. The first, in 1924, achieved little. 'What a joke—
what an unexpected and ludicrous adventure!' was the reaction of
Sidney Webb to the opportunity of putting into practice what he
had long been preaching in regard to unemployment policy.[23] The
second Labour Government (1929-31) started with more verve,
threatening, in the eyes of one observer, not 'socialism in our time'
but socialism before Christmas.[24] Even before the world economic
crisis, however, it had run up against the fundamental contradictions in party policy, above all the incompatibility of its economic
conservatism and social idealism. MacDonald, as prime minister,
quickly slid into a mood of 'despairing agnosticism', ever willing
to listen to new ideas but ever more pessimistic about what, in the
real world, the state could achieve.[25]

The election of the National Government in 1931, with its massive majority of 493, was hailed as a major turning-point in inter-
war politics—a signal triumph for democracy, demonstrating that
in a crisis a mass electorate would vote for national and not sectional interest. As has been seen, however, such optimism soon
evaporated and by 1934 even Baldwin was considering the inclusion
in the Cabinet of Bevin and, more seriously, Lloyd George to form
a truly national government. Little happened. With its ruthless
election machine and a lack of credible alternatives, the Government was under little real threat except from the YMCA group of
Conservative MPs who feared for their marginal Northern seats.[26]
Most could be squared by patronage, and so government remained
under the leadership of ageing, infirm men, all harbouring old
hatreds (especially Baldwin for Churchill, Chamberlain for Lloyd
George) and judging policy by past parallels not by future objectives.

---

[23] Beatrice Webb diary, 3 Jan. 1924.
[24] Tom Jones diary, 23 Dec. 1929.
[25] D. Marquand, *Ramsay MacDonald* (1977).
[26] See Tom Jones diary, in particular entries for 27 Feb. 1934 and Feb. 1935.

Such driving force as there was within the National Government was provided by Neville Chamberlain, first as chancellor of the exchequer and then as prime minister. His personality greatly influenced policy in the 1930s. He was a man whose personal charm and modesty were peculiarly at variance with his public persona: as he admitted in 1937, after watching a film of himself: 'If I had not previously seen the person who addressed us from the screen I should have called him pompous, insufferably slow in diction and unspeakably repellent in person.'[27] In the 1920s he had constantly protested his lack of ambition and qualification for the chancellorship and the premiership, and yet in the 1930s he found himself in both positions owing to the perceived absence of credible alternatives. His original instincts were duly confirmed. He was a man of formidable energy who, as leader, won the hearts of the Conservative Party after Baldwin's lassitude. However, as ministers of Labour were to discover after 1931, he lacked both imagination and tolerance. He tried to steamroller by executive drive reasoned objections to his predetermined course of action. He vigorously denied any lack of imagination, citing long lists of major reforms he had inspired; but in truth the intention behind many of these reforms was not progressive but rather an attempt to deny the consequences of democracy (the reform of local government after Labour successes at municipal elections and the removal from politics of the most political of issues, unemployment relief). Behind his abrasiveness, moreover, there was a lack of self-confidence, which led him to abandon principle—even financial rectitude—in times of crisis. This weakness was compounded by the need to retain the confidence of restless young back-benchers during his long vigil as Baldwin's heir apparent.

Thus under the leadership of MacDonald, Baldwin, and Chamberlain, the National Government lacked an essential sympathy with the novel remedies needed to solve the problems with which it was confronted. This can best be illustrated by the three leaders' reaction to Roosevelt's New Deal. MacDonald recognized that the Government must act with 'vision and energy' once 'the appetite of the world for spectacular effects' had been whetted, but

[27] Quoted by Peter Clarke, *The Times Literary Supplement*, 11 Feb. 1977, p. 158. Later impressions are culled from Chamberlain's papers, in particular NC 18/1/405, 656 and 867.

rejected any imitation of American policy and had no alternative suggestions.[28] Baldwin noted:

I have come to the conclusion the world is stark mad. I have no idea what is the matter with it but it's all wrong and at times I am sick to death of being an asylum attendant.... I always dreaded Roosevelt's experiments and I think there will be an appalling mess up in America in a few months.[29]

Chamberlain, characteristically with greater force and contempt, dismissed 'the Yanks as a barbarous tribe and Roosevelt as a medicine man whose superiority over other medicine men consisted in the astonishing agility with which when one kind of mumbo jumbo failed, he provided another'.[30] The Government accordingly sank beneath, rather than rose to, the challenge of democracy.

It was not only successive Cabinets but also industrial and public opinion that placed political constraints on the Ministry of Labour. Industrial attitudes will be examined fully in Chapter 4 but briefly it may be noted that (officially at least) employers implacably opposed, and the TUC remained curiously ambivalent towards, state intervention. As the NCEO, the most influential of the employers' national pressure groups, argued during the economic crisis of 1931:

We are convinced that the colossal expenditure on the social services is far greater than this country can afford: that the financial burdens which it imposes on industry are in no small measure accountable for our industrial depression and that this country by concentrating upon insuring its people against all the risks of life, has in large measure deprived them of the employment which is the greatest security of all.[31]

Between 1916 and 1926 the TUC was equally uncompromising, arguing in its official evidence to the National Industrial Conference (NIC) in 1919:

Unless and until the Government is prepared to realise the need for comprehensive reconstruction on a democratic basis, and to formulate a constructive policy leading towards economic democracy, there can be at most no more than a temporary diminution of industrial unrest to be followed inevitably by further waves of constantly growing magnitude.[32]

Only after the General Strike did this challenge to economic and

---

[28] Marquand, *Ramsay MacDonald*, pp. 733-4.
[29] Tom Jones diary, 14 Sept. 1933.
[30] Neville Chamberlain papers, NC 18/1/848.
[31] NCEO, *The Industrial Situation* (1931).
[32] Cmd. 501, PP. (1919), xxiv, 21, appendix 1, xi.

political orthodoxy start to fade and state intervention become accepted in principle as a means of extending social benefits to the unorganized and of forcing the pace of reform against recalcitrant employers.

Behind the vested interest of industry there lay the ultimate sanction of public opinion. Public opinion is, of course, notoriously difficult to define, but throughout the inter-war period it was widely interpreted as being hostile to any bureaucratic encroachment on individual freedom. Perhaps public opinion was confused—particularly by the civil service—with the sectional interests of middle-class taxpayers, the judiciary, or the popular press, but nevertheless it was this interpretation that dominated policy. Its pervasive influence is best illustrated by a note written in 1929 by the head of the civil service for the Cabinet, covering an official report on the Liberal Party's pamphlet *We Can Conquer Unemployment*. It read:

Even if a Mussolini regime could be proved to be desirable for the 'war' against unemployment, speaking as an ordinary British citizen I do not believe for one moment that the country would stand it. The full rigour of D.O.R.A. [Defence of the Realm Act] was tolerated during the war because 100% of the population felt themselves to be in urgent danger of something worse; today 90% of the population have more material happiness and amenity than in all our previous history; and sad though the plight of the other 10% is ... the 90% would never even on that account acquiesce in full peacetime in a bureaucracy of such wide and arbitrary powers.[33]

The inter-war civil service perceived and felt consequently constrained by an innate public hostility towards its own expansion.

Ministerial Leadership

To guide it successfully through the unresolved ambiguities in its role, whilst keeping within the political constraints imposed by government and public opinion alike, the Ministry needed exceptional leadership. Five qualities needed by a good minister of labour were identified first by *The Times* on 26 October 1924 and later by Sir Thomas Phillips, the permanent secretary from 1935 to 1944: sympathy with and foreknowledge of the problems to be tackled; vision to determine long-term objectives; courage to remain faithful to these objectives in the face of bitter opposition; conviction and persuasiveness to win support in parliament and in

[33] Cab 24/203/CP 104 (29).

industrial negotiations; and, finally, a capacity for self-efface-
ment.[34] Not until the appointment of Ernest Bevin in 1940 did any
minister display such an exceptional range of talent. None seriously
threatened, as pre-war syndicalists had feared, the regimentation of
Labour but all lacked either vision or political accomplishment.

The first two ministers were among the weakest. This was due in
part to Lloyd George's unwillingness to appoint front-rank Labour
politicians and in part to the political immaturity of the Labour
movement itself. J. H. Thomas, the general secretary of the National Union of Railwaymen, was first offered the Ministry. At the
time he undoubtedly had the practical realism, the industrial base,
and the verbal dexterity—not to mention the right Welsh connec-
tions—to achieve success. However, he declined, insisting, no doubt
correctly, that he 'could render more assistance to the nation and
also the best interests of Labour whose confidence I most value by
remaining outside the Ministry'.[35] In his place were appointed John
Hodge (December 1916–August 1917) and George Roberts (August
1917–January 1919). Neither had the ability to bridge the gap between Westminster and the shop-floor, especially when the latter
was controlled by the militant shop-stewards' movement. Both,
indeed, had Conservative leanings. Hodge was 'a rampaging and
most patriotic Tory working-man who would have delighted the
heart of Disraeli'.[36] At the time of his appointment, he was not
only acting chairman of the Labour Party but also president of the
British Workers' National League, the Party's antidote to the pa-
cifist Independent Labour Party (ILP), which was in negotiation
with the Conservative Party over a joint programme of 'national
efficiency' and protection. Roberts, on his appointment as minister,
was disowned by his local trades councils for opposing Henderson's
attendance at the Stockholm Peace Conference and actually joined
the Conservative Party in 1922.

Neither had sufficient political muscle or presence. Hodge's perceived strength was his profound distaste for unofficial strikes, for
his steel-smelters' union had had a strike-free record since the 1880s
and he had himself been a 'tower of strength' to the Ministry of
Munitions since 1915. At an earthy eighteen stone, he also 'looked

[34] T. W. Phillips in Bevin papers, 2/7.
[35] Lloyd George papers, F 94/1/10.
[36] A. Griffith-Boscawen, *Memories* (1925), p. 207. The undercover negotiations
are recorded in the Steel-Maitland papers, GD 193/99/2.

the part to perfection'.[37] He was notably deficient, however, in both breadth of vision and grasp of detail. Roberts, an altogether slighter figure, was a former organizer for the Typographical Association and Labour Party whip. As a founder of the Industrial League, he had a sincere commitment to reform but lacked the political presence to force reconstruction programmes through Cabinet and to win a popular following. He was treated by his audiences as 'a good music-hall turn rather than as the preacher of a new social gospel'.[38] Both ministers—no doubt as Lloyd George had intended—represented the simple loyalties of the pre-war trade union movement. In the rapidly changing world of Labour politics, their values became increasingly obsolete.

The first middle-class minister and the first to cut a truly public figure was a Scottish Conservative, Sir Robert Horne (January 1919–March 1920). He was one of the few new political personalities to emerge from the war and his ability was marked by an ascent even more meteoric than that of Lloyd George. The latter had risen from the back-benches to the chancellorship of the exchequer in three years; Horne was chancellor three years after entering parliament. This success was due to his knowledge of wartime Labour, gained whilst a civil lord at the Admiralty; a debating skill, worthy of a former lecturer in philosophy and barrister, which enabled him to take the fight to the enemy; and a gift for friendship (based on affability, mimicry, and a store of dirty jokes) which embraced such unlikely bedfellows as Lloyd George, Lord Northcliffe, and selected trade union leaders. His defect was a lack of vision. Whilst maintaining a rapport with the Labour movement, he had, according to a senior adviser, 'little affection for progressive social policies. His foot instinctively sought the brake rather than the accelerator.'[39] He was a staunch believer in capitalism and became increasingly irritated by revolutionary rhetoric and the trade unions' inability to respond speedily and constructively to consensus politics. After the Sankey Commission, he became the leading opponent in Cabinet to coal nationalization and had to be given by Lloyd George the strange reminder for a minister of labour

---

[37] A. Fitzroy, *Memories*, vol. 2 (1925), p. 642. For his activities on behalf of the Ministry of Munitions, see C. Addison, *Politics from Within*, vol. 1 (1924), pp. 274-5.

[38] H. B. Butler, *The Confident Morning* (1950), p. 124.

[39] Ibid., p. 141.

that, 'while proper consideration must be given to the capitalist, the two other great interests—the miners and the consumers— must not be overlooked'.[40] By March 1920, his private views were considerably at variance with his public image. He prophesied 'red revolution and blood and war at home and abroad' and outvied Sir Basil Thompson in his efforts to expose the Co-operative Society as a series of Communist cells fermenting revolution in the Yorkshire coalfields. In short, he typified the refusal of Lloyd George's Conservative allies—even before the economic crisis of 1920—to contemplate any fundamental adjustment to private enterprise and thus the narrowness of their conception of consensus politics.

Horne's recommendation as his successor was the Coalition Liberal, T. J. Macnamara, 'a tall, horse-faced man with a large mouthful of teeth and the booming voice of a bully'.[41] Just as Roberts's promotion in 1917 had been a reward for opposing Henderson, so Macnamara's elevation was recognition of his loyal defence of the Coalition Liberals at the Spen Valley by-election. He had earned a somewhat doubtful reputation with Lloyd George as an election expert and with Horne as a 'big-organizer'. He had a genuine sympathy for the ex-serviceman (as befitted the son of a Crimean War veteran born in a Montreal barracks) and a popular reputation as a social reformer (as befitted an ex-president of the National Union of Teachers). However, his political ability had been well recognized by his failure to gain promotion from the financial secretaryship of the Admiralty during the explosion of government offices between 1908 and 1920. He was a vacuous orator, whose performance on the Cabinet's unemployment committee reminded one observer of a 'dud observation balloon ... the safety valve having been opened wide, the contents poured forth. Waves of sound wrapped the Council Chamber.'[42] Faced with the advent of mass unemployment he 'had no use for facts' and reverted continually to the dangers of the Communist menace; confronted with mounting labour unrest, he admitted he was 'no diplomatist'. His 'deceptive naïvety' antagonized employers, trade unionists, Cabinet

---

[40] Cab 23/14/WC 614A. His sabre-rattling is recorded, *inter alia*, in Jones, *Whitehall Diary*, vol. 1, p. 97 and Lloyd George papers, F 27/6/27.

[41] Church, *Voyage Home*, p. 82. Horne's endorsement is recorded in Taylor, *Lloyd George*, p. 201.

[42] Rey papers, box 1/3. His further failings are recorded in T 162/74/E 7112/01; Lloyd George papers, F 36/1/42; Jones, *Whitehall Diary*, vol. 1, p. 197.

colleagues, and civil servants in turn. He was the personification of, not the necessary foil to, government weakness during the last years of Lloyd George's rule.

In the die-hard Conservative Government of 1922-4, he was succeeded by his parliamentary secretary, Sir Montague Barlow. In the circumstances, Barlow's was an inspired appointment. As the chairman who had established Sotheby's reputation, he could reassure the die-hards as a practical businessman; at the same time he had a firm reputation with the Labour movement as a reformer. As parliamentary secretary he had worked secretly with Beveridge to plan the breakup of the Poor Law and to establish the Ministry's responsibility for the able-bodied unemployed. As minister he anticipated the Beveridge Report by planning for a more comprehensive system of social security (all-in insurance) so that 'any working man [could] have a perfectly clear guarantee ... against his three devouring terrors—Disease, Unemployment and Old Age'.[43] He tried to counter the 'absurd ignorance' and public prejudice from which the Ministry suffered by repeatedly stressing that unemployment insurance was a measure of self-help, which cost the exchequer little, and that Britain had a range of social services of which she should be proud, not ashamed.[44] He was, however, fighting an uphill battle. He was a poor speaker 'with the most soporific voice' the President of the Industrial Court (no doubt an expert) had heard.[45] Moreover, despite being a tariff-reformer, he had no weight even in Baldwin's Cabinet, being suspected of sympathies with ex-Coalition Conservatives and of having inspired anti-government articles in the *Daily Express*. He was broken in health by his labours.

Tom Shaw, the minister during the first Labour Government, was also broken not so much by hard work as by the attempt to reconcile party policy with political reality. Under parliamentary taunts about 'the positive remedy for unemployment' of which the Labour Party manifesto had boasted, Shaw at an early date exclaimed: 'Does anyone think that we can produce schemes like rabbits out of our hat?'[46] Thereafter cries of 'rabbits!' pursued him

[43] Baldwin papers, vol. 7, fols. 257-60.
[44] Bonar Law papers, 111/4/17; *The Times*, 15 Nov. 1922, 3 Nov. 1923.
[45] Sir H. Morris, *Back View* (1960), p. 204. Rumours of his treachery are recorded in Baldwin papers, vol. 159, fol. 192.
[46] *Parl. Deb.*, 1924, 170, col. 2003.

around the chamber. He was not a trade-unionist of national standing, being the secretary of the Labour and Socialist International and the International Textile Workers, and his lack of political weight was illustrated by his late inclusion in the Cabinet, as replacement to Sidney Webb, because it was felt the Cabinet lacked union representation. He was unable either to establish a working relationship with the TUC, or, as a Lancashire man, to advocate any expansion of state intervention especially in economic policy. He was remembered by his officials mainly for the pride he took in the private ministerial lavatory, which inevitably became known as 'Uncle Tom's cabin'.

Despite Shaw's best efforts, 1924 was a potentially significant year for the Ministry because (as has been noted) Shaw was a late replacement for Sidney Webb and Baldwin's initial, unsuccessful intention on the fall of the Labour Government had been to replace him with Horne. Thus, eight years after Thomas's refusal of office in 1916, the Ministry lost in quick succession the services of two more well-known politicians. Could either have provided the Ministry with the leadership it so desperately needed? The evidence is inconclusive. Webb's correspondence with MacDonald after he had been offered the Ministry showed little appreciation of the problems involved and his foremost proposal was the establishment of a Cabinet committee on unemployment which (as president of the Board of Trade) he did in fact establish and chair. He admitted later that it had failed and that he, like Shaw, had been unable to provide the necessary leadership in formulating unemployment policy—an admission that was in keeping with the contemporary wisdom that 'Webb's mountainous brain always succeeded in producing an infinitesimal mouse'.[47] Horne's political acumen would undoubtedly have been a considerable asset to the Ministry but whether (as the president of the Board of Trade who ended the mining subsidy in 1921) he could have handled the General Strike better or whether (as a former chancellor of the exchequer) he could have assisted the Ministry in its quest for a progressive economic and social policy, is open to doubt. He was also detested by Baldwin, not least for a life-style which *The Times* tactfully de-

---

[47] Jones, *Whitehall Diary*, vol. 1, p. 274. The Webb–MacDonald correspondence is in the Passfield papers, II, box 4, g and h, fols. 206 and 1, and the MacDonald papers, PRO 30/69/5/35. Webb's post-mortem on the Labour Government is in the Passfield papers, IV, item 18.

scribed as the warming 'of both hands at the fire of life'.[48] His official career, significantly, was broken by his refusal of the Ministry in 1924 and he remained thereafter on the fringes of politics, the perpetual joker in the search for a new Conservative leader.

After Horne's refusal of the Ministry, Baldwin admitted that his courage failed him and the subsequent appointment of Sir Arthur Steel-Maitland (November 1924–June 1929) was duly received with universal disbelief.[49] Superficially, it was by no means an inappropriate appointment since Steel-Maitland had had a wide range of social, political, and industrial experience. After a brilliant sporting and academic career at Oxford, he had been an investigator for the Poor Law Commission and thus became the only Conservative minister to have slept in a public lodging-house. His credentials as a social reformer were thereby established. From 1910 to 1916 he had been chairman of the Conservative Party, successfully adapting the party organization to new electoral needs, and then, after the disappointments of junior office, he had become (under Lord Milner's patronage) managing director of Rio Tinto Zinc. He had even been an early conspirator against Lloyd George although, in seeking an alliance with the Liberals, he had characteristically backed the wrong horse. He was hard-working with a wide range of contacts in the business and financial world and an ever-open mind. He fought hard for departmental interests, not fearing to take on Churchill as chancellor, the Party's right wing over trade union reform and the NCEO. All these battles, however, he lost. His weaknesses were his poor health, which immobilized him during much of 1928 when circumstances most favoured a reappraisal of government policy; his halting and apologetic manner, which limited his effectiveness as a parliamentary speaker and an industrial negotiator; his preoccupation with detail, which often led him to lose the wood for the trees; and the breadth of his imagination, which encouraged him to explore innumerable courses of action

---

[48] *The Times*, 6 Dec. 1920. Baldwin's hatred developed from Horne's regular appearance in parliament, dressed ready for a night-club (whilst the chancellor overseeing the Geddes Axe), his sinecure on the board of Baldwins (the family steel firm), and his dereliction of public duty by rejecting the offer of the chancellorship in 1923 in favour of more lucrative business appointments. Horne was the only ex-Coalition minister absent from Baldwin's second Cabinet. In offering Horne the post Baldwin reputedly failed to remember his pledge to Austen Chamberlain that the Minister's salary would be raised to £5,000 (Baldwin papers, vol. 42, fols. 244–248).

[49] Jones, *Whitehall Diary*, vol. I, p. 304.

whilst discouraging him from choosing between them. 'Steel-Maitland has been a complete failure in office before,' Austen Chamberlain remarked on his appointment; 'Bonar Law said he always had
plans under way but they never came to anything.'[50] Nothing
changed with his promotion to the Cabinet. His lack of incisiveness
prevented him from becoming a dominant figure in Cabinet or
from succeeding with the Party where Baldwin had failed. He was
first the beneficiary and then the victim of Baldwin's irresolution.

Steel-Maitland was succeeded by the first woman Cabinet
minister, Margaret Bondfield. Despite a later resemblance to Old
Peggotty, she had been all her life a pioneer, rising from a shop
girl via the ILP and the National Federation of Women Workers to
be the first woman chairman of the TUC in 1923. A year later, after
only one parliamentary speech, she had become parliamentary
secretary to the Ministry. As minister she was admired by her officials for her decisiveness and by employers for her courage; the TUC
and the *Daily Herald*, on the other hand, attacked her with such
bitterness for her alleged failure to consult the General Council over
the appointment of the 1931 Royal Commission on Unemployment Insurance, that she felt obliged to tender her resignation.
She was not (as her critics alleged) the tool of her officials. Rather,
she had a 'white-hot integrity' which prevented her from glossing
over the chasm between manifesto commitments and administrative
reality.[51] She vigorously sought practical compromises which would
satisfy everyone's honour and, when necessary, was an effective opponent of the Treasury although (as a devoted admirer of MacDonald)
she could hardly be accused of economic radicalism. Her political
position, like that of Barlow and Shaw, was hopeless from the start.

Another successful opponent of the Treasury, no doubt much to
his own surprise, was Sir Henry Betterton, parliamentary secretary
to the Ministry in all Conservative governments after 1923 and
minister from 1931 to 1934. His great achievement was to defeat in
1933 the Treasury's initial plans for the UAB—the unification of
all unemployment relief under a statutory commission independent
of parliamentary control. Betterton's campaign against so undemocratic a measure was very much a personal initiative and wrung
from Chamberlain the rare admission that 'a very good case' had

[50] Neville Chamberlain papers, NC 2/21.
[51] M. Stocks, *My Common-Place Book* (1970), p. 167. For the assault on her, see
the *Daily Herald*, 6 Jan. 1931 and T 172/1769.

been made against him.[52] Such a burst of energy and enlighten-
ment, however, was wholly uncharacteristic. Betterton was a man
of great superficial charm who was on excellent terms with Labour's left wing; but, despite his long sojourn at the Ministry, he
failed either to master the complexities of policy or to provide a
positive lead. Chamberlain discounted him initially as chairman for
the UAB because of his lack of 'initiative and originality and drive'
and he was widely recognized as someone 'not to be trusted when
it was necessary to stand firm over something disagreeable'. Tom
Jones provided a telling appraisal:

How he managed to survive and succeed for so many years as Minister of
Labour is a puzzle. He has a good presence, a friendly gossiping disposition
and a habit of saying the same thing over and over again ... He has not
a trace of distinction in thought or language and I suppose this ordinari-
ness is his secret and his determination to agree with the enemy at the gate
and avoid trouble.[53]

On Betterton's translation, as Lord Rushcliffe, to the part-time
chairmanship of the UAB (at a salary equal to that of the prime
minister), the most original and the most disastrous inter-war
appointment was made. Oliver Stanley (June 1934–June 1935) had
impeccable Conservative credentials, being the second son of Lord
Derby and a product of Eton and Oxford. He had also a good,
original mind which had led him in 1927 to co-author, with Robert
Boothby and Harold Macmillan, *Industry and State—a Conservative View*, a book seeking to establish within the Conservative Party
a positive attitude towards state intervention. His independence of
mind allegedly discouraged Baldwin from promoting him earlier
and, as always, Baldwin's reservations had some justification.[54]
Stanley was appointed at a most promising time for the Ministry
when the creation of the UAB and the Special Areas Commissions
had relieved it of much routine administration and thus permitted
new policy-initiatives. However, he lacked Betterton's stamina and
worldliness. At the first sign of trouble over the UAB's relief scales
he panicked, promising immediate concessions in parliament and

[52] Neville Chamberlain papers, NC 18/1/810. The following description is based
on information supplied by Betterton's private secretary, Sir Harold Emmerson.
[53] Ibid., NC 2/22; Tom Jones diary, 9 July 1935 (letter from Markham to Jones)
and 10 June 1936.
[54] Percy, *Some Memories*, p. 130. I am again indebted to Sir Harold Emmerson
for the character-sketch.

accusing officials of maladministration. From this débâcle, his reputation as minister never recovered. His failure was, indeed, proof
of the very real constraints inhibiting ministers of labour throughout the inter-war period.

The final inter-war minister, the National Liberal Ernest Brown
(June 1935–October 1940) was a throw-back to the expediency of
Betterton and the blusterings of Hodge and Macnamara. A self-
taught Baptist lay preacher, he had enormous self-confidence and
an equally enormous voice.[55] He was reputed to be an expert on
electioneering and hence on the public acceptability of policy;
official papers certainly do not reveal him as having ever been
unduly troubled by principle. Informed opinion was divided on his
character. To the jaundiced Snowden he was a 'tub-thumping
bounder' and to Tom Jones he appeared in Whitehall negotiations
like a 'cheap-jack at a fair', pretending to give 'away everything for
nothing ... [and] bringing his fists down on the table with a bang
every few minutes to clinch matters'.[56] Others, however, were impressed by his honesty and shrewdness. He won many battles for
the Ministry (for instance over the location of munition industries
in the depressed areas) but rarely provided a positive lead (failing,
for example, to grasp the nettle of wartime labour controls). He
appeared to his parliamentary secretary to be 'simplicitas itself' and
it indeed seems likely that his allegedly open mind was in fact an
empty one.[57] Significantly he was Baldwin's protégé and, as the
longest-serving inter-war minister, he well illustrated the negative
qualities seemingly necessary for political survival in the 1930s.

The Political Account

The Ministry was at once a victim and a symbol of the unheroic
political response to the advent of democracy. Its political status
depended on a broad agreement between Conservative and Labour
Parties over the positive role the state should play in society, public
acceptance of that role, and firm ministerial leadership. It was
denied all three. As a result it remained politically 'one of the least
important home departments'.

[55] The voice was so stentorian that Baldwin, on hearing uproar in the lobby of
the House of Commons and being informed that Brown was addressing his Edinburgh constituents, enquired why he did not use the phone.

[56] Grigg papers, 2/19/3(a); Tom Jones diary, 9 Feb. 1936. His private secretaries
concurred with this view. To one he was an 'essentially silly person'.

[57] R. A. Butler, *The Art of the Possible* (1971), p. 61.

The very circumstances of the Ministry's establishment were far from propitious. As the British government advised the government of the USA in 1917, on the latter's entry into war, 'the one clear piece of machinery necessary for the effective control of labour during the war is a single, powerful and wide Labour Department'.[58] The Ministry, however, was established in the third year of the war and was never able to break the vested interests of longer-established departments, most notably the Ministry of Munitions. The appointment of a Labour representative to the War Cabinet deprived it of the political prestige it might have gained from representing Labour at the highest level and the Prime Minister's aversion to detail caused an administrative and political confusion in which the weakest went to the wall. Throughout the war, therefore, the Ministry remained a 'still, small voice'.[59] In 1919, as the department responsible for industrial relations and unemployment relief at a time of incipient revolution and mass unemployment, it was projected into political prominence. Through the NIC it started to win public support for the academic plans of the Ministry of Reconstruction and through its Committee on Increased Production it started to tackle the technological weaknesses of British industry. However, just as its minister, Sir Robert Horne, was destroyed by his association with Lloyd George, so the Ministry fell a victim of the Prime Minister's 'final purposelessness'. Between 1919 and 1922 it was subjected to a continuing series of public inquiries, culminating in the Geddes Committee on National Expenditure which recommended its abolition, and not until December 1923, seven years after its establishment, was it officially recognized as a permanent department of state. It was, in Lloyd George's phrase, political 'chaff'.[60]

The evolution of the Labour Party as the alternative party of government and of Baldwin as leader of the Conservative Party held high political promise for the Ministry. It was disappointed. MacDonald quickly accepted Whitehall's low opinion of the Ministry and during the first Labour Government it became 'an aunt sally to be shied at from all quarters', not least the TUC.[61] The temper of industrial relations, as exemplified by the General Strike,

---

[58] Mun 5/346/300/2.   [59] Butler, *Confident Morning*, p. 121.
[60] Taylor, *Lloyd George*, p. 134.
[61] *Parl. Deb.*, 1924, 174, col. 704. Four times the House of Commons debated a reduction of the minister's salary.

dissolved Baldwin's good intentions. Under Steel-Maitland's leadership, the Ministry was the first to recognize the long-term structural weakness of British industry and fought hard for industrial reconciliation and a sound financial basis for unemployment insurance but it lacked the political muscle to secure a fundamental reappraisal of policy. In the 1930s, the Ministry's political fortunes did improve with its recognition as the government's laboratory for economic and social experiment; but it remained largely under uninspired ministerial leadership and ever under the watchful eye of Neville Chamberlain, who only belatedly recognized that it held a key to an understanding of the home front.[62]

In the particular political conditions of inter-war Britain, could the Ministry have played a more constructive political role? Many contemporaries thought so. With his fellow radical Conservatives, Stanley in 1927 had argued that 'clearly there would be no place for a Ministry of Labour under a system of laissez-faire' but that in the changed post-war world such a ministry was needed to 'correlate economic facts and social aspirations' so as to ensure that 'the persons whose contributions to ... financial prosperity is their labour are employed under conditions corresponding to the standard set by the conscience of the community'.[63] Bevin, as minister, envisaged the peacetime Ministry as a guardian of the 'productive capacity of industry' and of a comprehensive industrial code of 'conduct, inspection, enforcement and welfare'. After the General Strike, the trade union movement as a whole was also more willing to accept the state as the guarantor of minimum industrial and social standards. Many obstacles, however, barred the way. Economic orthodoxy encouraged employers to oppose any extension of the social services, the Treasury and local authorities (as has been seen) had entrenched vested interests in unemployment policy, and the public, whilst expecting economic efficiency and greater social justice, appeared unwilling to accept the erosion of traditional individual freedom. Successive governments lacked the resolve to answer positively the challenge and the contradictions of inter-war democracy.

The political weakness of the Ministry was also self-inflicted. The

[62] Butler, *Art of the Possible*, p. 61.
[63] R. Boothby, H. Macmillan, J. de V. Loder and O. Stanley, *Industry and State — A Conservative View* (1927), pp. 237–8. Bevin papers, 4/7/10 and Lab 10/248.

continuing reluctance of ministers to challenge, rather than merely question, financial orthodoxy seriously impaired its role as a 'national authority for unemployment'. Equally debilitating was the eventual response to the dilemma of impartiality. As Peter Jenkins has written, 'the Ministry operated in the manner of an embassy to a foreign power—the working classes. As with embassies, it was never entirely clear whether its first loyalty lay with the power it represented or the power to which it was accredited.'[64] This divided loyalty politically emasculated the Ministry, for it discouraged ministers (in particular Conservatives) from taking the hard political decisions that the bold development of economic and social policy demanded. Sir Montague Barlow argued, for example, in 1923 that:

he would deprecate any pressure upon the Minister of Labour directed at confusing his political functions with his industrial functions. In his capacity as conciliator he must in the industrial world hold the balance with severe impartiality between capital and labour. As a member of the Government he had to face representatives of one of those two antagonists—labour—as a political opponent. The sound basis for general policy was that the state should require employers and workers to manage their own affairs.[65]

This was a virtual admission that a key policy of all inter-war ministers—home rule for industry—was the consequence not of political conviction but of political convenience. It evaded the questions of whether both sides of industry could work together and, more especially, whether the national interest would thereby be served. It also assumed, rather disingenuously, that the industrial and political functions of government could be clinically separated. Hard decisions were evaded rather than faced.

Throughout the inter-war period the Ministry remained close to the political challenge of democracy. A successful response to that challenge demanded exceptional leadership but this, despite the courage of Margaret Bondfield, the conviction of Barlow, the vision of Steel-Maitland, and the affability of Horne and Betterton, it never enjoyed. As a result, its political significance was limited. Its survival in the early 1920s was largely due to administrative

[64] P. Jenkins, *The Battle of Downing Street* (1970), p. 5.
[65] *The Times*, 7 Nov. 1923.

necessity; thereafter it retained Cabinet status largely through the reluctance of successive governments to offend a trade union movement which, in fact, had no particular use for it and yet did not want it destroyed. Lack of effective political leadership inevitably circumscribed administrative achievement.

CHAPTER 3

THE ADMINISTRATIVE RESPONSE

THE Ministry's most substantial response to the challenge of democracy was administrative. This had been foreshadowed before 1916
when the campaign for its creation had been sustained largely by
administrative rather than political momentum. Between 1900 and
1914, for instance, the staff and expenditure of the Board of Trade
had increased by 821 per cent and 595 per cent respectively, mainly
as a result of increased social administration, and, although the
1914 Royal Commission on the Civil Service had rejected the proposal, administrative devolution had been accepted as inevitable by
many of the Board's officials.[1] After the war, the Ministry rapidly
developed into one of the largest departments of state and its size
immediately convinced a new permanent secretary (Sir James
Masterton-Smith), appointed in 1920 specifically to consider its
closure, that abolition was impossible.[2] His report was greeted with
disbelief in the Treasury but either it or Masterton-Smith's more
personal testimony (a nervous breakdown after 16 months owing
to overwork), secured the Ministry's future. Accordingly, no serious consideration was given to the implementation of the Geddes
Committee recommendation in 1922 that the Ministry should be
disbanded; and in 1927, when the suggestion was revived, Sir Warren Fisher (as head of the civil service) advised Baldwin that no
other department could 'absorb so large a volume of necessary
work as is now dealt with by the Ministry of Labour'.[3]

If size guaranteed the Ministry's future, it did not automatically
guarantee its importance. Like most social service departments, the
Ministry was initially regarded as little more than a second-rate
department responsible solely for routine administration; but this

---

[1] Llewellyn Smith opposed devolution but others including (surprisingly) G. R.
Askwith did not, see BT 13/134. The Board's elephantiasis is quantified in J. A. M.
Caldwell, 'Social policy and public administration' (unpublished Ph.D. thesis,
Nottingham University, 1956), appendices pp. xxvii, xxxvii.

[2] Austen Chamberlain papers, AC 25/4/37.

[3] Baldwin papers, vol. 8, fol. 3–4. Fisher continued: 'for what it is worth I would
add that for political reasons also the suggestion seems to be impractical.'

attitude did not last long.[4] Responsibility for the national network of employment exchanges and offices (numbering some 1,618 by 1939) gave its officials both an unrivalled statistical expertise in the most crucial area of domestic policy (unemployment) and an established reputation as practical administrators. Responsibility for the conciliation service also made them an authority on the public acceptability of government policy. Within Whitehall, therefore, Ministry officials soon became highly influential in both the formulation and implementation of most important welfare measures. In the 1930s, they were the obvious choice to plan and staff the new semi-autonomous bodies (the UAB and the Special Areas Commissions) responsible for unemployment relief and regional policy. Several also won promotion to senior positions in the Treasury (so that by 1939, for instance, Sir Horace Wilson was permanent secretary and head of the civil service, Sir Alan Barlow third secretary, and F. N. Tribe principal assistant secretary in charge of social service expenditure). Despite the hiving-off of responsibilities and the promotion of senior officials, moreover, the Ministry itself continued to expand.[5]

The key to the development of the Ministry's administrative importance (as with its immediate predecessor, the labour departments of the pre-war Board of Trade) was statistical expertise and departmental morale. Statistical expertise made it the natural focus for experiments in domestic policy; and its officials were able to respond to the challenge because they were hand-picked and used to working in expanding, uncharted areas of government where precedent did not always predominate and access to policy-making was relatively open. There was, however, a significant difference in the use to which the Board and the Ministry put their influence; and this epitomized the radical difference between the Edwardian and inter-war civil service. The Board had used its position as the government's 'data bank' to initiate policy at an official level; its administration had also been characterized by an enlightened paternalism in which 'you govern labour, for the good of labour, on behalf of labour, but keep labour at a distance'.[6] The Ministry,

---

[4] For the Treasury's initial attitude, see T1/12610/24460/1920.

[5] See Appendix 1, C.

[6] The most authoritative studies of the pre-war Board are those by Roger Davidson. See 'Llewellyn Smith, the Labour Department and government growth', in G. Sutherland (ed.), *Studies in the Growth of Nineteenth-Century Government*

on the other hand, whilst often questioning economic orthodoxy, was hesitant to promote alternative policies, and its officials had little of the pre-war faith in bureaucracy. The Ministry's administrative weight, therefore, depended less on its imaginative initiation of policy than on its political realism and its ability, within pluralistic constraints, to sustain pragmatic experiment.

This difference in departmental attitudes was highly significant for two reasons. First, it demonstrated the extent to which the First World War had undermined the arrogance of Edwardian bureaucracy. As one contemporary commentator noted, most officials had seen 'too much of government to believe in the indefinite extension of its functions'.[7] Secondly, it reflected a conscious attempt by a reformed civil service to adjust itself to the perceived needs of democracy. The purpose of this chapter is to analyse the changing nature of inter-war bureaucracy, the criticisms which it attracted, and the light which the administrative history of the Ministry—as the department most exposed to public view—sheds on such criticisms.

The Reformed Civil Service and Its Critics

Between 1919 and 1924, the civil service underwent a major reorganization, the results of which were to dominate inter-war public administration. First, the economic authority of the Treasury was strengthened so that by 1924 it had the right to vet, before submission to Cabinet, all departmental memoranda proposing increased public expenditure. Secondly, the permanent secretary of the Treasury was appointed—or rather officially confirmed as—the head of the civil service and the staffing of all departments standardized under the auspices of the newly created National Whitley Council. The general purpose of this managerial reorganization was threefold: to eradicate waste, to forestall political corruption of the service by Lloyd George and his businessmen–ministers (on the lines of early nineteenth-century or contemporary American administration), and to increase efficiency by unifying the service and fostering within it a common purpose. In particular, the new head of the civil service (Sir Warren Fisher) sought to eradicate the

(1972), p. 261 and 'The Board of Trade and industrial relations, 1896–1914', *Historical Journal*, 21 (1978), 590.

[7] Dale, *Higher Civil Service*, p. 107.

traditional friction between the Treasury and the major spending departments by broadening the outlook of the Treasury and instilling a sense of 'responsibility' into the other departments. Treasury officials were no longer to be recruited direct from university but were to serve an apprenticeship in a major spending department; similarly establishment and finance officers were to be planted in every ministry, and all permanent secretaries appointed departmental accounting officers, to ensure that throughout the service due regard was paid to economy and efficiency. By such means, it was hoped, policy could be formulated in the light of national budgetary constraints and co-ordinated in its objectives. Treasury control would at last be both well informed and effective.

The reformed civil service achieved many of its objectives: wartime waste and duplication were eradicated, corruption forestalled and an *esprit de corps* based on public service established. Throughout the inter-war period, however, the service was subjected to a series of attacks which historians have since repeated. These concerned its escalating power, its inefficiency, its enervation, and, above all, the failure of Treasury control. The history of the Ministry demonstrates that, whilst the last of these attacks was justified, the others were not.

The charge most easily refuted, that of the inter-war service's bureaucratic lust for power, was one especially favoured by lawyers and given particular force by the Lord Chief Justice, Lord Hewart, in his book *The New Despotism* published in 1929. It was based on the growth of such expedients as delegated legislation and administrative discretion by which civil servants (mainly in the new social service departments) became the sole legal authority for the drafting, interpretation, and revision of the detailed regulations needed to implement parliamentary legislation. Common law, the lawyers asserted, was being supplanted not by administrative law (as on the Continent) but by administrative lawlessness: the bureaucrat was seeking to 'clothe himself in despotic power'.[8]

This attack was insubstantial and was, in fact, little more than a thinly disguised bout of professional self-interest. Bureaucratic power, particularly in relation to the extension rather than the restriction of state intervention, was always more potential than real during the inter-war period; and, to the extent that it did exist, was the unavoidable consequence of either the unprecedented com-

---

[8] Lord Hewart, *The New Despotism* (1929), p. 14.

plexity of government (of which the lawyers displayed little appreciation) or political vacillation. Delegated legislation, for example in such areas of the Ministry's responsibilities as unemployment insurance, was inevitable, as parliament had neither the time nor the expertise to debate anything other than the general principles behind legislation. Similarly, administrative discretion was unavoidable so long as politicians refused to determine the criteria by which scarce resources should be apportioned and statutory regulations had to be sufficiently flexible to meet the particular needs of individual clients.[9] Some senior officials, it is true, did display a certain enthusiasm for apolitical administration, especially in the 1930s when the attempt was made to take key policies such as unemployment relief 'out of politics'; but this was largely an expression of sheer relief that ministers were at last prepared to take the hard decisions necessary for the proper implementation of existing policy. Their enthusiasm, in any case, was markedly less than that of outside reformers (seeking speedier action) or Conservative politicians (fearful of the consequences of the Labour Party's rise to power at both a national and local level). Inter-war civil servants had, without doubt, little bureaucratic lust for power. Beveridge's maxim of 1920 still rang true: 'democracy, if it knows its business, has no reason to fear bureaucracy.'[10]

Specific attacks on the inefficiency of the inter-war civil service, especially those made at the end of the First World War and the start of the Second, can also be easily refuted. For instance, the real target of the businessmen whose anti-waste campaign in the early 1920s culminated in the Geddes Committee on National Expenditure, was the political expansion of government not its administration. The attack, moreover, was anachronistically focused on wartime extravagance (for which they, as temporary civil servants and government contractors, had been in no small way responsible) and ignored subsequent administrative reforms.

---

[9] See, for instance, M. Hill, *The Sociology of Public Administration* (1972), p. 76: 'Discretion will survive ... so long as politicians insist upon a rigorous rationing of resources for the poor whilst at the same time remaining unable to settle upon any hard criteria upon which to base such rationing.' Hewart's concern was such that he failed to find the time to appear before the Committee appointed to investigate his, and others', fears. See D. G. T. Williams, 'The Donoughmore Report in retrospect', *Public Administration*, 60 (1982), 281, which also notes the rejection by lawyers of Sir Ivor Jennings's appeal to move with the times.

[10] Beveridge, *Public Service*, p. 63.

Similarly, the vitriolic press campaign of the early 1940s, spearheaded by the publication of Cato's *Guilty Men*, was directed less at the administration of peacetime policy than at deficiencies in the preparation for war, to which public opinion, vested interest, and political vacillation had contributed as much as official advice.

More general charges of enervation are, however, harder to rebut if only because all large organizations are guilty of such a weakness. Even H.E. Dale, the most persuasive apologist for the inter-war civil service, acknowledged an increasing negativism amongst inter-war officials. As a result of open competition, Dale argued, independent zealots (on whom nineteenth-century administration had depended for its innovatory reputation) were being gradually replaced by officials of lower social status whose 'animal spirits' had been extinguished by the continual need to pass exams. Attracted not by any reforming ideal but by the security of the profession and lacking, in the main, both financial independence and a social rapport with ministers, these new recruits had neither the vitality nor the self-confidence to challenge convention.[11] Accordingly they interpreted their role as 'political advisers' to ministers in a narrow sense (the avoidance of parliamentary embarrassment) rather than the more positive sense of the promotion of policies by which a minister might make his reputation; and when the opportunity arose, as in the Anderson Committee on All-in Insurance in 1924 or in the Wilson Committee on Special Areas Legislation after 1935, they failed to stamp their personality on policy in a positive manner.

However, even so authoritative a testimony as Dale's can be qualified if the alleged negativism of inter-war bureaucracy is placed in its true political and cultural context. As Dale himself admitted later:

Timidity, rigidity, slowness of decision and action, red tape, evasiveness, fear of responsibility—such imputations are the convex ... of the concave represented by close obedience to the law and the will of Parliament, loyalty to Ministers ... (and) the desire to meet the varying demands of the public and the House of Commons.[12]

Thus administrative negativism was the consequence not so much of bureaucratic failings but of general political pressures such as

[11] Dale, *Higher Civil Service*, ch. 4, 5 and conclusion.

[12] H.E. Dale, *The Personnel and Problems of the Higher Civil Service* (1943), p. 6.

ministerial indecision and parliamentary convention: if, for example, at question time in the House of Commons, any MP on behalf of any constituent could question the consistency of any administrative decision, then caution and a resort to precedent became decided virtues not vices. Moreover, it really was impossible, as Dale should have acknowledged, for inter-war officials to emulate nineteenth-century zealots because such behaviour would have challenged the essence of twentieth-century parliamentary democracy and substantiated Hewart's otherwise unfounded charge of bureaucratic despotism. Consequently inter-war officials were prevented by political pressures from formulating policy with the cold logic of leading Edwardian pro-consuls. Instead they adopted a 'stoical realism', which respected parliamentary and public opinion, however apparently ill informed.[13] Such opinion, as has been seen, was opposed to further extensions of state intervention and so, even had the civil service wished to endorse bold initiatives such as the 'new deals' of Mosley and Lloyd George, they would have been constrained. Political and cultural pressures, in short, discouraged bureaucratic initiative and encouraged a liberal belief in the market and self-help. For the civil service, the welcome corollary of such a philosophy was that, if policy failed, the ultimate responsibility lay not with it but with the community as a whole.[14]

It is possible, therefore, to defend the inter-war civil service against the charges of escalating power, inefficiency, and enervation. The one specific charge that cannot be dismissed is the failure of Treasury control. The Treasury, inevitably, is not without a powerful defence. First, even its bitterest critics acknowledge that the civil service had to be modernized after the First World War, that the Treasury alone could undertake such a task, and that, given the political vacillation and economic depression of the inter-war years, the task was awesome. Secondly, modernization was not without its major successes: a unified service, free of

[13] Dale, *Higher Civil Service*, pp. 92–4; C. K. Munro, *The Fountains in Trafalgar Square* (1952), p. 138.

[14] See the summary of the philosophy of administrative-class officials by M. E. Dimmock in R. Thomas, *The British Philosophy of Administration* (1978), p. xii–xv: 'Theirs has been a liberal view. It has trusted democracy and distrusted the expert. It has placed confidence in reserved power and not in concentrated power. It has believed in improvisation and self-reliance .... Their ideal [has been] to encourage common citizens to govern themselves by learning as much as their leaders, and applying it in their daily pursuits.'

patronage and motivated by a common philosophy based on a commitment to public service, was swiftly developed. Thirdly, some managerial inflexibility was inevitable and even desirable, for, as Michael Hill has argued, not only did the increasing size of the civil service 'make formalism necessary but equally formalism ... made growth possible'.[15] Fourthly, the Treasury should not (as so often in the past) be judged solely on its record in the early 1920s because, like every other department, it evolved: after its own internal reforms had taken effect and recruits from major spending departments gained influence, it became relatively less rigid. Finally, it could be argued—as has already been argued in defence of the rest of the civil service—that, since policy was ultimately determined by ministers within given political constraints, Treasury officials should not be held responsible for all the failures of Treasury control.[16]

Such a defence, however, is disingenuous because Treasury officials—not ministers—had *de facto* power in the reform of the civil service and the exercise of this power signally lacked the breadth of vision demanded by the advent of democracy. In the first place, as one of the many reactions to Lloyd George's premiership, politicians after 1922 kept largely aloof from administrative matters thereby giving Treasury officials their heads. In the second place, if a new *esprit de corps*, based on a commitment to public service, was fostered, then both the nature of that commitment and the definition of public service were extremely narrow. Moreover, the 'new professionalism' that developed, rather than encouraging much-needed specialist expertise, merely reasserted the out-dated virtues of 'muddling through—or the cult of the privileged and well-born'.[17] Given the opportunity to pioneer a twentieth-century 'revolution in government', designed to meet the needs of a greatly expanded state, the Treasury seemed bent on the anachronistic fulfilment of the 1852 Northcote-Trevelyan Report, drafted to satisfy the very different requirements of a night-watchman state.

Reformers during the First World War had been alert to such an eventuality. Hence the 1918 Haldane Report, whilst advocating an extension of the Treasury's authority, had insisted that a vital

---

15 Hill, *Sociology of Public Administration*, p. 43.

16 For the Treasury view of Treasury control see its evidence to the 1943 Machinery of Government Committee (Prem 4/8/6).

17 Dimmock in Thomas, *British Philosophy of Administration*, p. xxi.

precondition was the radical revision of traditional Treasury philosophy. Treasury officials should, above all, recognize the need for wide ranging 'investigation and thought as a preliminary to action' and 'an obligation not to assume a negative reaction in the first instance towards suggestions for improving the quality of a service and the efficiency of ... staff'.[18] Neither condition was met. The Treasury in its management of the civil service continued to take the restricted view of a ministry of finance, resisting instinctively all proposals that entailed increased public expenditure.[19] Its officials also acted with a narrow-minded arrogance which, in its hostility to new ideas, was strikingly similar to that of its ideological opponents. In 1919, the permanent secretary of the Ministry of Labour attacked syndicalist shop stewards on the grounds that any trade union leader

who as a result of the additional education which close contact with the employers and with economic facts afford him, has the courage to advise his members in the light of this further information, is looked upon as a 'lost soul' and told he is no longer in touch with workshop life.[20]

Treasury officials, despite their supposedly superior upbringing, similarly treated as a 'lost soul' out of touch with the economic facts of life anyone who had the courage to question economic orthodoxy after close contact with the unemployed. Such attitudes destroyed all chance of an enlightened management of the civil service.

The Treasury's managerial failings were particularly damaging to those new departments, such as the Ministry of Labour, which were attempting to adjust both policy and the machinery of govern-

[18] Cmd. 9230, PP (1918), xii, 1, pp. 6, 20.
[19] See, for example, Beveridge's complaint on 10 June 1940 to Attlee that there was a 'tendency of the Treasury to claim for itself the functions that should be performed by an Economic General Staff and then not to perform them' (Beveridge papers, II b 39, part IV). This letter contains allegations similar to those of Keynes (see above, p. 9) of the damage caused by the excessive promotion of people 'either of Treasury experience or of the Treasury type of mind'.
[20] Lab 10/64. Treasury arrogance was epitomized by the dismissal of Keynes by Leith-Ross in 1929 on the grounds that he lived in 'a little economic world of his own up at Cambridge and he is pleased to consider the group of theorists up there as representing the sole exponents of "modern economic thought". In fact, the rest of the universe treats their theories with much scepticism and their general acceptance is in reverse ratio to the dogmatism with which they are expressed' (T 161/303/S 40504/04).

ment to the challenge of democracy. In respect of policy, the narrow financial focus of the Treasury (dominated by its obsession to balance the budget annually) not only placed these departments in an economic strait-jacket but also denied them the positive leadership in the development of responsible long-term policy which they might reasonably have expected from the senior economic ministry. This is well illustrated by the history of unemployment insurance. Here the Ministry of Labour officials (as the new *esprit de corps* required) were no less committed to economy than Treasury mandarins; but they defined 'economy' rather differently. Convinced that, politically, government could no longer evade responsibility for unemployment and that insurance was the most cost-effective form of relief, they strove to devise a permanent scheme that would clearly define exchequer liability within limits that were both realistic and publicly acceptable. In the 1920s, this meant agreement between the three contracting parties (the state, employer, and employee) to contribute equally to an Unemployment Fund whose liability was clearly defined. Treasury officials, however, throughout the 1920s fought vigorously to reduce the exchequer contribution to an absolute minimum and, after the return to the Gold Standard, even tried to disengage the state totally from an area which was 'after all primarily a trade matter'.[21] They made, in other words, no attempt to establish any realistic formula on which unemployment relief could be permanently based and, 15 years after its introduction, were still disputing the very principle of unemployment insurance.

This nihilism was not an aberration of the 1920s but continued into the 1930s, when pressure on the budget had eased. In 1935, for instance, the Unemployment Insurance Statutory Committee (UISC) sought (under Beveridge's prudent chairmanship) to be virtuous by building up a reserve to secure the solvency of the Unemployment Fund over an eight-year trade cycle. The Treasury, despite its earlier advocacy of such a policy, produced its traditional wet blanket. Its representative (unfortunately an ex-Ministry of Labour official) informed the Committee:

[21] For the clash of policy, see the letters of Churchill (20 Mar. 1927) and Steel-Maitland (3 May 1927) to Baldwin (Baldwin papers, vol. 7, fols. 388 and 397). Such criticism of the Treasury might be equated with blaming a goalkeeper for not scoring goals. However, it is a strange team that makes its goalkeeper captain and manager. With its 'penny-wise, pound-foolish' policy, the Treasury also had a weakness for scoring own goals.

The Treasury would be disinclined at the present stage of economic and political development even to attempt to look forward for seven or eight years.... The Treasury thought a hand-to-mouth policy was better. One could not see far enough ahead to make long-term forecasts.[22]

In the actual management of the civil service, the Treasury displayed a similar lack of appreciation for the needs of new departments. It failed both to encourage the necessary heterogeneity of talent and to recognize the need to promote not just generalists (experts in the machinery of government) but also specialists (experts on policy) and men of 'push and go'. On the one hand, it discouraged the research and external contacts considered by the Haldane Committee to be essential to good government. Its recruitment policy, as has been seen, also increased the percentage of entrants from Oxbridge at a time when other universities (particularly London) had far greater expertise in the social sciences. It was a strange paradox, as Ernest Barker noted, that 'a group of subjects which should, if anything, be specially encouraged [were] specially rebuffed'.[23] On the other hand, the promotion of specialists was actively discouraged. 'Let us guard ourselves against the idea', Sir Warren Fisher instructed the Tomlin Royal Commission on the Civil Service in 1930, 'that the permanent head of a department should be an expert: he should be nothing of the kind:'[24] and the convention was duly established that none of the senior departmental positions on which Treasury advice was sought by the prime minister (particularly permanent and deputy secretaryships) should be filled by internal promotion. As a result, Treasury control reinforced not only economic but also administrative orthodoxy—and it did so both formally and insidiously. Few ambitious young officials would have failed to notice that promotion was reserved almost exclusively for men in the Treasury mould and that, almost from their very entrance into the profession, they crossed the Treasury at their peril.

It might appear paradoxical that, whereas the inter-war civil service as a whole can be successfully defended against its detractors,

---

[22] Minutes of the UISC, 20-1 June 1935 (Beveridge papers, VIII, 4, i). The culprit was Sir Alan Barlow whose qualities were those of a generalist rather than a specialist.
[23] E. Barker in W. A. Robson (ed.), *The British Civil Servant* (1937), p. 37. For recruitment figures, see above, p. 8.
[24] Quoted in G. K. Fry, *Statesmen in Disguise* (1969), pp. 57-8.

the department which dominated its reform stands so roundly condemned. The solution is quite simple: despite the Treasury's very best efforts, uniformity was never imposed throughout the service. Some departments were able to reap the benefits of the new professionalism without suffering from its worst excesses, as the more detailed administrative history of the Ministry demonstrates.

The Ministry and Treasury Control

Administratively, the Ministry of Labour evolved from wartime chaos, through a period of restrictive orthodoxy, to a decade after 1927 of gradual expansion and experiment punctuated only by the economic crisis of 1930-2. Immediately after the war, a despairing permanent secretary could describe the Ministry as a

juxtaposition of a number of separate and self-contained Departments— some of them dating from before the War and manned by Civil Servants, each with its own traditions and its own organizations; others being the creations of the war with no traditions, with impoverished organizations and manned by a heterogeneous personnel consisting of Civil Servants (mostly on loan from other Departments), Naval and Military officers, discharged or remobilized officers, professional and businessmen, and clerical staff recruited on a temporary footing from the outside market.[25]

In the early 1920s order was quickly imposed and the Ministry, at some cost, fashioned by Treasury control into a standard civil service mould. Then, in the late 1920s, with the eventual recognition of unemployment as a long-term problem, the Ministry at last had the opportunity and the confidence to surmount Treasury restrictions and to develop its own peculiar character.

As far as its premises were concerned, the Ministry never fully recovered from its improvised beginnings. Its London headquarters, Montagu House, was the former property of the Duke of Buccleuch and the last aristocratic town house in Whitehall to be commandeered by government. It was hardly an appropriate setting for the state's new 'embassy' to the working class for, as Richard Church recalled, 'every ceiling [was] treble lacquered and insulated with sea-shells, all the doors rosewood. ... The entrance hall was wide, paved with coloured marble ... The staircase rose to a landing ... then parted in right and left curves up to the salon

[25] Lab 2/1718/CEB 186, pt. 1.

floors.'[26] A valiant attempt was made to disguise this splendour by the erection in the grounds of numerous bungalows. Indeed, as late as 1932, only 95 of the 1,259 headquarters staff had actually gained residence in Montagu House, whilst a further 472 squatted in the bungalows and the rest were distributed among six other buildings. Office efficiency and economy inevitably suffered. In the provinces, conditions were just as difficult. A survey in 1932 classified only 99 of the 410 employment exchanges as satisfactory, and 170 as 'definitely bad'.[27]

The Ministry's organization and staffing, however, recovered more successfully. During and immediately after the war, both had been the subject of some embarrassment. Given few well-defined wartime responsibilities, the Ministry had become constantly embroiled in debilitating administrative battles with other departments (most notably the Ministries of Munitions and National Service) which stunted its development.[28] The quality of its personnel was also suspect. As a minor wartime department it was able to attract few able officials and, when asked to expand rapidly after the Armistice, it was bound by government commitments to recruit only ex-servicemen and officials made redundant by the war departments. These weaknesses were compounded by the appointment as the first permanent secretary of a trade-unionist, whose expertise lay in an area other than the administrative; and by the sudden imposition on the Ministry, for the first nine months of peace, of a temporary Civil Demobilization and Resettlement Department headed by former Ministry of Munitions officials. These officials had not only been recently at war with the Ministry but were also uninterested in its long-term needs. The new department absorbed the majority of the Ministry's staff, including its largest permanent department (the Employment Department), most officials transferred from the war departments and a further 16,000 temporary staff recruited to handle demobilization; and yet its

---

[26] Church, *Voyage Home*, p. 27. Church, the novelist, was one of the Ministry's many artists-in-residence. Others included Humbert Wolfe and F. S. Flint (the poets) and C. K. Munro (alias Macmullan) the playwright.

[27] Cab 27/479/EC 32 (16) for Whitehall and EC 32 (12) for the employment exchanges. Departmental morale, however, was normally high, being fostered by staff clubs such as the one patronized at the Kew Claims and Record Office: the Kew Klerks Klan.

[28] See R. Lowe, 'The Ministry of Labour 1916-1919: a still small voice?', in K. Burk (ed.), *War and the State* (1982), pp. 108-34.

controller-general (Sir Stephenson Kent) obstinately maintained that 'it was no concern of his, in view of his temporary position, to tackle staff problems'.[29] Consequently, there was considerable confusion and unrest, especially amongst the permanent staff, who were incensed at their sudden subordination to temporary businessmen and ex-colonial administrators seeking indoor relief.

In these circumstances, it was hardly surprising that Lloyd George—under pressure from the anti-waste campaign and the Treasury—should have concluded in 1920 that 'the organization of the place is very imperfect and there is a lack of grip'.[30] Consequently a new permanent secretary, Sir James Masterton-Smith, was appointed to cast a 'fresh official eye' over the Ministry. The appointment, however, was unnecessary for, as both Masterton-Smith and the Cabinet's all-powerful Finance Committee were soon to recognize, the Ministry had, between the summer of 1919 and the spring of 1920, independently achieved a remarkable degree of reorganization under the direction of its second secretary, E. C. Cunningham.[31] Unfortunately for the Ministry, this achievement was recognized too late. On his appointment, Masterton-Smith froze all new appointments and later found that, owing to the Whitley reorganization and then the questioning by the Geddes Committee of the Ministry's future, he could not unfreeze them. In 1920 77 per cent of the Ministry staff had been temporary and 80 per cent had been working above their official gradings.[32] To the detriment of departmental morale, these conditions prevailed until December 1923 when, on the eve of the first Labour Government, the Ministry was at last granted the status of a permanent department.

By 1924, therefore, the permanent staffing needs of the Ministry had been finalized; so too had its organization layout. The Ministry was divided into three major policy-making departments—the Em-

[29] Lab 2/1800/CEB 103/94/1920.
[30] Lloyd George papers, F 9/2/22.
[31] Austen Chamberlain papers, AC 25/4/37; *Report of the (Peel) Committee on the Staffing and Methods of Work of the Ministry of Labour* (Cmd. 1069), PP (1920), xxv, 265, para. 16. Cunningham, a former colleague of Fisher at Customs and Excise, received no real help from the Treasury, which was undergoing its own internal reform.
[32] The problem was no mere technicality, for it affected seniority within the service and pension rights and so made it even harder for the Ministry to attract well-qualified recruits. For the organizational layout of the Ministry, see Appendix I, B.

ployment and Insurance, the Industrial Relations, and the General Department (the latter co-ordinating the work of the International Labour, Trade Boards, and Statistics divisions); three common services departments—the Establishments, Finance, and Solicitor's Departments; and two temporary departments—the Appointments, and the Training and Civil Liabilities Departments. The only major subsequent developments were to be the inclusion of the Industrial Relations Department within the General Department and the contraction of the temporary departments. The one temporary responsibility to be made permanent, training, was linked first to the employment responsibilities of the Ministry (to form in 1929 two new departments, the Unemployment Insurance, and the Employment and Training Departments) and then to its responsibilities for juveniles (to form in 1938 the Employment, and Training and Juveniles Departments). These changes reflected major developments of policy—the permanent commitment to industrial transference in the late 1920s and to special areas legislation in the mid-1930s.

If the reorganization of the Ministry was complete by 1924, it had not been achieved without considerable costs, and the manner in which these costs were incurred epitomized both the dangers and the insidiousness of Treasury control. The two most serious blows sustained by the Ministry were the destruction of both the administrative means by which the Ministry's predecessor, the pre-war Board of Trade, had maintained its innovatory character and the Ministry's own wartime ideal of devolution. On the one hand, the Treasury in 1919 banned the use of section 4 of the 1859 Superannuation Act (the technique by which the Board had recruited mature experts such as Llewellyn Smith and Beveridge) and then contracted the Ministry's Intelligence and Statistics Department to a size at which it could not undertake wide-ranging 'investigation and thought as a preliminary for action' but only routine administration.[33] The compilation of important sources of information, such as the *Weekly Report on the Labour Situation* to the Cabinet (by which ministers and permanent secretaries were kept informed of trade union developments), had consequently to be abandoned, as did major statistical enterprises such as the Z8 returns on employment and the revision of the cost-of-living index. For the sake

---

[33] Treasury bloodhounds were also trained especially to sniff out 'thinkers and those who apply information and statistics to problems and indicate policy'. See T 162/6/E 372.

of easy, short-term economy, the Treasury was prepared to sacrifice the statistical foundations of policy-making—in direct defiance not only of the Haldane Committee but also of its own mentors, Northcote and Trevelyan, who (in the true tradition of the mid-Vietorian middle class) had sought out 'fact' as an antidote to prejudice. Prejudice was again, apparently, to be an acceptable substitute for reason. On the other hand, the Ministry's local services, by which wartime planners had set such store to encourage industrial self-government and to 'humanize' the social services, were also seriously curtailed. Local officials responsible for conciliation, trade boards, and the encouragement of joint industrial councils were savagely cut, whilst rapport with the public was further impaired by the abandonment in 1919 of 10 advisory Divisional Councils ('because "the best in our view" is too costly')[34] and of the Publicity Department. Not until the appointment of a press officer in 1936 did the Ministry again have, as all departments dealing directly with the public should have, specialist expertise in public relations.

This emasculation of the Ministry was to a considerable extent achieved—as prescribed by the service's new *esprit de corps*—by agencies within the Ministry: the permanent secretary working in conjunction with the new Establishments and Finance Departments. After Masterton-Smith's retirement, the permanent secretary from 1921 to 1930 was Sir Horace Wilson, who was a willing collaborator with the Treasury. Admittedly he fought hard in 1924 to secure the Ministry's permanent status and, soon after his appointment, attacked the 'impertinence' of a junior Treasury official who had questioned his own good faith. 'I do not know Mr Graham's age', he minuted,

but I think he might at least have given some of us credit for having studied both the nature of the work to be done by conciliation staff and the qualities required in the officers ... It is very disappointing to find that at this stage anybody in the Treasury should think it necessary to try to teach us ... the most elementary principle on which the Department can be conducted.[35]

[34] Horne to Lloyd George, 19 Oct. 1919 (Lloyd George papers, F 27/6/25). The contraction of the Ministry is fully documented in R. Lowe, 'The demand for a Ministry of Labour, its establishment and initial role, 1916-24' (unpublished Ph.D. thesis, London University, 1975), especially ch. 5.

[35] Lab 2/1719/CEB 166/1923; Lab 2/1930/CEB 154/1927.

Such outbursts, however, were rare. Despite the permanent con-traction of his own specialist department (the Industrial Relations Department) to a size which he once denounced to Sir Warren Fisher as being 'down to, if not well below, the minimum which is really necessary', he stood out before the Tomlin Commission on the Civil Service as a leading advocate of Treasury control, claim-ing that:

Since I have been in charge of the Department I have experienced no difficulty at all in carrying the Treasury with me ... If they differed from me then it would be my duty to go to my Minister ... My minister is then at liberty to approach the Chancellor. That has not in fact happened in the last nine years.[36]

Such a claim demonstrated Wilson's willingness (at best) to close official ranks in public or (at worst) to sacrifice departmental and arguably public interest to personal advancement.

The Establishments Department, under a fierce ex-Indian civil servant (A. W. Watson), was no stooge of the Treasury, but it nevertheless restricted the Ministry's development. First, its whole ethos was at odds with the original spirit of the Ministry. Un-orthodox appointments, especially of trade-unionists, were readily banned and a stiffening of university graduates sought (though definitely not 'long-haired intellectuals of the Bolshevik type'[37]). Secondly, it caused serious delays because, as a new formal buffer between the Ministry and the Treasury, its very existence invited delay and because 'establishment policy' on occasion conflicted with the expeditious execution of social policy. At the time of the Geddes Committee, for instance, the filling of sanctioned posts was delayed out of 'consideration primarily of the interests of the men themselves and not of the Department which ... undoubtedly re-quires additional staff ... if [it is] to attain the requisite degree of efficiency'.[38] The proper administration of policy sanctioned by parliament was therefore delayed for fear that new appointments might exceed eventual requirements. Calculated risks taken in the interest of good government had come to be discouraged.

The third and most formidable internal agency of Treasury con-trol was the Finance Department, headed between 1919 and 1933

---

[36] Lab 2/1822/CEB 537/2/1921; Lab 2/1983/S & E 229/1930.
[37] C. G. Dennys to Tribe, n.d. 1919 (Tribe papers).
[38] Lab 2/ 1822/ CEB 537/4/1921.

by the puritanical F. W. Bowers. Bowers's appointment had been
rapturously received in the Treasury because he was 'very Treasury
minded ... and very useful for the Treasury interest'[39] and it provoked between 1923 and 1925 a major policy-battle within the
Ministry. The attack was initiated by T. W. Phillips, then head of
the Employment and Insurance Department, who argued:

Broadly, two quite different views of the functions of a Finance Department are possible:

(1) The Finance Department, as such, is not concerned with the settlement
of policy but only with seeing that no expenditure is incurred without due
authority, that there are proper safeguards against misappropriation and
that all money received and expended is properly accounted for.
(2) The Finance Department is responsible not only for the work specified
under (1) but also for taking part in the settlement of policy, in order to
ensure that that policy is framed with due regard for economy.

(1) was substantially the system of the Employment Department under the
Board of Trade.
(2) is the system now in vogue.[40]

As an ex-Board of Trade official, Phillips clearly preferred the first
option. The second, he claimed, merely duplicated the work of
administrative officials, who had explicit responsibility to ensure
'public economy', and provided, moreover, no guarantee of either
cost-effectiveness or good policy. In particular he resented the delay
involved in the double-checking of policy before it was submitted
to the Treasury and the need for administrative departments to
exaggerate their financial requests in the foreknowledge that the
Finance Department, like the Treasury, would inevitably demand
reductions.

Bowers naturally resented the suggestion that his department
should be restricted to mere accountancy. In line with the
Treasury-backed Council of Finance Officers, he insisted on his right
to be consulted during the formulation of policy so that he could
'assist in framing proposals still malleable rather than engage on
destructive criticism after they have been crystallised': he further

---

[39] T1/12386/41565/1919. The Treasury did refer to the common services departments as the 'lines of least resistance' within departments (T1/12394/4401/1919).
[40] Lab 2/1907/CEB 649/1922. This and the succeeding paragraph are based on
this file.

demanded the right during the implementation of policy to vet all administrative regulations in case they raised financial matters 'not in contemplation and decided when the general policy was under discussion'. Since the final departmental court of appeal for the dispute was Wilson, the verdict was never in doubt. Indeed Wilson's 'lifting' of large sections of Bowers's memoranda (including the quotations cited above) in his final minute shows how close his instincts were to those of Bowers. The Finance Department was thus able to establish itself firmly in the Ministry's policy-making process, to the long-term detriment of departmental initiative.

The Ministry's reorganization in the early 1920s, therefore, was achieved largely by its officials, fulfilling their part of the bargain under the post-war conventions of Treasury control: as members of a major spending department, they exercised self-restraint and acted with administrative and financial 'responsibility'. Inevitably, the Treasury officials failed to honour their obligations. In their dealings with the Ministry, they continued to display all their traditional talent for delay and a readiness to confuse their economic and administrative functions. Accordingly, as has been seen already in the case of unemployment insurance, they failed to provide the Ministry with any positive administrative or economic lead.

The Treasury's ability to transform delay into an art was, of course, legendary, but its scope was immeasurably increased by the creation of establishments and finance departments as buffers between it and zealous administrative departments. 'The truth is', lamented A. W. Watson in 1919, 'if you do not tell the Treasury the reasons for your demands they refuse them on that account. If you do, they reply that your letters are so long that they take months to answer.'[41] The Treasury showed no appreciation of the fact that, if its traditional checks were to be performed within each department, it should trust departmental decisions and use the time thus released to develop new techniques of administrative management. On the contrary, it used the extra layer of bureaucracy as an additional excuse for delay which, as its junior officials admitted, led to unjustified 'unpleasantness' and 'scandals' in the administration of other departments.[42] Senior officials, being essentially unsympathetic to the needs of the new interventionist ministries, condoned these scandals. As officers of a non-executive department,

[41] Lab 2/1730/CEB 158/1925, part v.
[42] T 162/55/E 43301; T 162/320/E 7110/1.

they never really grasped (in the 1920s at least) the fundamental link between the formulation and implementation of policy or the difference between the needs of administrative class officials in Whitehall and hard-pressed, low-paid officials in the provinces. In the immediate post-war years, for example, they tried to group the Ministry's administrative-class (university-educated) officials into a small secretariat around the minister, while leaving the running of departments to executive-class officials (school-leavers). It took Masterton-Smith some time to convince them—and himself—that policy was not a 'Heaven-sent gift to be acquired by ruminating on the general problems of employment and unemployment' and that 'policy emerged from day to day study and handling of problems peculiar to the department'.[43] Mismanagement of the outstations was not so successfully parried. An imaginative training scheme for counter staff in the employment exchanges was permanently vetoed in 1920 on the grounds that 'civil servants should have sufficient interest in the work to be performed and in their prospects of advancement to ensure a sufficient number will be willing to avail themselves of instruction offered to them gratis, without the additional inducement of overtime pay'.[44] Such a pronouncement revealed a total ignorance of administrative reality outside Whitehall and of the urgency with which the working conditions of the most public members of the civil service had to be improved, if the popular image of bureaucracy were ever to be enhanced.

The Treasury's attitude towards the Ministry reflected not just managerial ignorance but also economic dogma. The 'Treasury view' identified public expenditure with lost investment and hence as an obstacle to the restoration of high employment; when such expenditure disrupted market forces, it was deemed doubly obnoxious. The Ministry's industrial relations and trade board service fell into this latter category, for it was believed that, by strengthening trade unions and establishing minimum wages, they prevented the reduction in wages which was necessary if the economy were to return to equilibrium at a high level of employment. Accordingly, the existence of both services was challenged. In September 1919, for instance, the appointment of local conciliation staff was rejected on the incredible grounds that there was no

[43] Departmental Whitley Council, 7th meeting, Feb. 1921. The Treasury master plan is in T1/12610/24460/1920.
[44] Lab 2/1727/CEB 256/1925.

specific Cabinet authority for the Ministry to intervene in 'industrial disputes arising up and down the country', a doubt which five months later (and after Masterton-Smith had frozen new appointments) was admitted to be groundless.[45] Trade boards were attacked with equal vigour. Since the Ministry had statutory authority to establish trade boards wherever industrial wages were low or organisation weak, the Treasury had first to restrict their operations by reducing investigation and enforcement staff. That the Treasury was prepared thus to use its administrative powers for political ends was made quite explicit by the head of its Establishments Division (S. R. Scott) who minuted that there was 'no power to prevent the Ministry of Labour setting up Trade Boards in every industry ... *except* the check which the Treasury or Cabinet may apply to the "heavy expenditure" on *staff* thereby entailed'.[46] Having successfully checked expansion, the Treasury then sought the reversal of policy by a royal commission; and when the Cave Commission failed fully to endorse its wishes, its recommendations were swept aside. As Scott again minuted: 'on the assumption that the Ministry of Labour must ... ensure that the rates of remuneration prescribed by Trade Boards are actually paid, there is a clear case for strengthening the inspectorial staff. But *pace the Cave Committee* I do not see why this should be the assumption.'[47] Thereafter he vetoed any new appointment of staff although it was conceded by his junior officials that this would defy 'accepted government policy'.

Such defiance by the Treasury of parliamentary legislation was not confined to the depression of the early 1920s but continued throughout the inter-war period. In 1938, for example, when the Treasury lost the political battle against the extension of special areas legislation, the Chancellor immediately wrote to relevant departments:

I think there was general agreement that on merits the case for expansion was not strong.... I am therefore writing to you with the Prime Minister's

[45] Lab 2/1779/CEB 109/5. The real political motive was revealed in 1922 when the Financial Secretary (Hilton Young) advised the Cabinet: 'The Industrial Relations Department was a new Department and was regarded outside as constantly interfering between employers and work people. It was staffed by officials carrying in the main high salaries and this was precisely the kind of Department which the public thought should be suppressed.' See Cab 27/165/GRC(CSD).

[46] T 161/133/S 11261.

[47] T 162/74/E 7113.

agreement to ask your cooperation in trying to limit, so far as may be possible by administrative action, further large commitments by the Commissioners.[48]

This incident is of considerable importance for three main reasons. First it is proof, if further proof were needed, that the Treasury (despite frequent denials) was ever prepared to use its establishment powers for political ends. Secondly, in defence of Treasury officials, it does demonstrate that Treasury control was not solely the preserve of the civil servant; even when reversals of 'accepted government policy' were sought, it often had the covert support of prime ministers. Most significant, however, was the incident's denouement. Having received the letter, the Minister of Labour (Ernest Brown) consulted the Special Areas Commissioners and then replied to the Chancellor expressing general sympathy with his budgetary problems but reminding him that 'having regard to the Commissioners' statutory duty, I do not see how they can be expected to curtail their activities unless the Government make an unequivocal statement to the effect that it is their intention to restrict and contract the work for the Special Areas'.[49] Such a statement both he and the Chancellor knew to be politically impossible and so regional policy continued unchecked. Treasury control, therefore, could be defeated given administrative determination and political support.

This victory over the Treasury is proof of the administrative muscle and self-confidence that the Ministry had attained by the 1930s. In the 1920s it had never been wholly tamed by Treasury control and in the 1930s, when the Finance Department had been downgraded and—in contradiction to the Treasury's veto on internal promotion—officials such as Sir Thomas Phillips and Humbert Wolfe (neither of whom was noted for excessive obeisance to the Treasury) had been appointed respectively permanent secretary and establishment officer, it seized the opportunity to develop its own character. It successfully 'humanized' its local offices so that observers as diverse as Ernest Bevin and Quentin Crisp, PEP and the Miners' Federation could praise the courtesy and constructive help, beyond the immediate calls of duty, offered by officials.[50] It also

[48] Scottish Record Office (SRO), DD 10/178.

[49] Ibid., E. Brown to Simon, 23 Dec. 1938.

[50] Bevin papers 4/7/110; Q. Crisp, *The Naked Civil Servant* (1977), p. 57; PEP, *Report on the British Social Services* (1937), p. 98; PRO 30/69/5/163.

made good Treasury negligence by pioneering new administrative methods. It improved the implementation of policy, by innovating administrative tribunals and codifying administrative regulations. It was also the first department to organize a coherent training scheme for its administrative-class recruits and to decentralize its regional organization which, accordingly, not only 'spread the Ministry's testicles over the whole country' (in the words of one apprehensive trade union leader) but also helped to broaden attitudes in Whitehall.[51] Above all, the Ministry remained ever open to new ideas, thereby avoiding the pockets of reaction which still characterized other departments. The association of its officials with organizations such as the International Labour Organization (ILO), Toynbee Hall, and the Workers' Educational Association, and their participation in ginger groups such as the Romney Street group (under Tom Jones) and the Tate Gallery group (under R. C. Davison) prevented undue rigidity. In the 1930s, in short, the Ministry was able to benefit from the discipline of Treasury control without being castrated.

Administrative Personalities

The escalating vitality of the Ministry was clearly dependent on the personality of leading officials which, despite the conventions of official anonymity, no administrative history can properly ignore.

Two officials dominated the inter-war Ministry: Sir Horace Wilson and Sir Thomas Phillips, permanent secretary respectively between 1921 and 1930 and between 1935 and 1944. Of the two, Wilson is the more notorious because of his later role during the Munich crisis and as head of the civil service during the virulent press campaign of 1939-42, when he was described as the most powerful British official since Cardinal Wolsey:

If you put a Cardinal's hat on Wilson you would see the typical priest politician of an earlier age. Tireless, caring of nothing but power, conscientious and hard-working, free from the failings of greater men, patient of rebuff and rising again after every reverse, he rose because he had to.[52]

He had certainly risen from humble origins, as has been previously mentioned. His first major opportunity had occurred during the

[51] P. H. St. J. Wilson (very private information). In the 1920s, the Ministry had also been the first to develop a 'departmental' as opposed to a 'Whitley' class.

[52] W. J. Brown, *So Far* (1943), p. 221. For Wilson's origins, see above, pp. 9-10.

First World War when he was appointed secretary of the government's arbitration service, the Committee on Production, and by 1919 he had displaced his former chief (Sir George Askwith) as head of the Ministry's Wages and Arbitration Department. There, during a period of intense industrial unrest, his physical vitality and staying power, his encyclopaedic knowledge of trade-unionists and employers, his mastery of detailed briefs, and the clarity of his vision made him indispensable to ministers and the Cabinet alike. Within three years he had become (symbolically at a reduced salary) permanent secretary. As permanent secretary, Wilson had considerable strengths and serious weaknesses. Despite a shy and somewhat humourless personality, he secured from other departments many talented officials (thus enabling the Ministry to overcome both its wartime shortcomings and the limitations of Treasury control) and he was considerate to those who fell on hard times. His friendship with Sir Warren Fisher helped to secure the Ministry's future and his knowledge of industry also protected him from the worst excesses of economic orthodoxy. As he wrote to Baldwin in 1925: 'We cannot be sure that improvement is in sight and will come in the happy way that it did after the smaller depressions of the pre-war period; we cannot afford to sit still and hope for the best.'[53] However, his vision—although clear—was very restricted. In 1919, seeking to put more 'fight' into the employers, he was involved in the creation of the NCEO which was later so to circumscribe government action;[54] he also reimposed economic and (as has been seen) administrative orthodoxy on the Ministry, thus restricting the extent of the radical influence it might initially have had on government. His tragedy was that, having had the courage to face problems others evaded, he was unable to suggest any lasting remedies. He was not an original thinker, nor, in the nineteenth-century sense, a 'zealot'. He was a compromiser, seizing on policies not for their inherent worth but because they temporarily satisfied the bargaining positions of the interests involved. In this way he was, as even *Guilty Men* admitted, 'a man of integrity ... with a single purpose, the welfare of the State';[55] but in neither economic nor administrative policy did his efforts meet with permanent success, because neither would employers voluntarily compromise with trade-unionists (and

[53] Baldwin papers, vol. 28, fol. 4.   [54] Lab 2/696/15 and see below, pp. 82-4.
[55] Cato, *Guilty Men* (1940), p. 87.

economic reality) nor the Treasury with the Ministry (and political reality).

Sir Thomas Phillips was far less public a figure. Superficially, indeed, he was the quintessence of the faceless, negative bureaucrat. Shy, like Wilson, he had no driving ambition to make him socialize with the powerful, his preference (derived from a brilliant classics career at Oxford) being to lunch in Lyons tea-shops with Euripides. He had risen to prominence in the Board of Trade as a leading draftsman of the 1911 Unemployment Insurance Act and was thereafter continually responsible for insurance legislation. A lack of wider experience perhaps intensified his 'bureaucratic' resistance, which was most noticeable in his leadership of the revolt against the Civil Demobilization and Resettlement Department and his quarrel with the Finance Department. He had, however, 'an acute brain and compassionate heart' which made him seek bold answers to fundamental problems such as the breakup of the Poor Law.[56] He was also fired by a hatred of Wilson. The origins of the conflict are obscure; but the enmity was cemented during Wilson's second-ment to the office of the Lord Privy Seal in 1929-30 when Wilson asked Phillips's (and his own former) private secretary to spy on the department and when Phillips, having been acting permanent secretary, was passed over for the permanent appointment. Phillips thereafter used his ability as the 'best politician in Whitehall' to resist Wilson's policies (in particular the creation of an unemploy-ment relief agency independent of parliament);[57] and, as an expert drafter of replies to parliamentary questions, he parried Treasury attempts to pin on the Ministry sole responsibility for employment policy. Phillips was perhaps not a 'zealous' permanent secretary but, as a specialist, he understood fully the complicated adminis-tration of the Ministry and was thus able to achieve the remarkable feat of saving even Ernest Brown from regular parliamentary em-barrassment. He was, indeed, as Bevin to his surprise was to dis-cover after 1940, the perfect foil for a strong minister.

Wilson and Phillips overshadowed the three other permanent secretaries appointed to the Ministry before 1944. The first, Sir David Shackleton, was a tall, teetotal, and non-conformist Lancas-

---

[56] Butler, *Art of the Possible*, p. 62; Lab 2/502/ED 27444/1919.

[57] The phrase is that of Phillips's private secretary, Sir John Walley. This portrait leans heavily on private information supplied by Sir John, Sir Harold Emmerson, and P. H. St. J. Wilson.

trian who had entered a mill at the age of nine and had risen via the Weavers' Amalgamation to be chairman of the Labour Representation Committee (1904-6) and President of the TUC (1908-9). By keeping the industrial and political movements separate at such a critical time he has been credited with as personal an influence over the development of the TUC as Broadhurst, Bevin, and Citrine.[58] As a government official, he progressed through the Home Office, National Insurance Commission and Ministry of Munitions to the permanent secretaryship in 1916, because Hodge wanted someone 'who had inside knowledge of the Trade Union movement ... who had the confidence of the work people in that movement, and who also, because of his character, had a standing in the eyes of the employer'.[59] His character certainly won him respect in Whitehall and his expertise in conciliation earned him, in 1920, the post of 'chief labour adviser', with the continuing status of permanent secretary. This change, however, was an admission that his original appointment had been a mistake. An unorthodox appointment at an unorthodox time, he had not the administrative ability to establish the Ministry on an orthodox footing; responsibility for the wartime chaos must consequently be placed largely on his shoulders. Moreover, like Hodge and Roberts, he had the cautious conservatism of an early Labour pioneer and thus proved an unwitting ally to the Treasury in its scaling down of the Ministry's role. His immediate replacement was Sir James Masterton-Smith, 'a miracle of efficiency' who had reformist leanings, especially concerning the equality of women.[60] His stay was too brief to make any great impression. Of the third permanent secretary, Sir Francis Floud (1930-5), the best his officials could say of him was that he was 'distinguished-looking'.[61] The doyen of generalist administrators, his appointment symbolized the inappropriateness of Treasury promotion policy to the new specialist ministries.

Beneath the rank of permanent secretary, four officials had an exceptional influence on policy: Harold Butler, Humbert Wolfe, Frederick Leggett, and Wilfrid Eady. Butler (a fellow of All Souls, and later director of the ILO and the first warden of Nuffield

[58] R. M. Martin, *TUC: The Growth of a Pressure Group* (Oxford, 1980), p. 328.
[59] J. Hodge, *Workman's Cottage to Windsor Castle* (1931), p. 179.
[60] E. H. Marsh, *A Number of People* (1936), p. 242.
[61] P. H. St J. Wilson (private information).

College) was a man of high intellect, administrative ability, and charm whose appointment had been demanded in 1917 by the parliamentary secretary (and fellow Etonian), W. C. Bridgeman, in order to give the Ministry an authoritative administrative lead. His contribution to policy was vital because the circumstances of the Ministry's establishment had estranged from it two of the Board of Trade's leading labour experts, Beveridge (head of the Employment Department) and Askwith (the Chief Industrial Conciliator). The reasons for the estrangement were partly personal. Both Beveridge and Askwith were prima donnas who had been used to an exceptional freedom under the loose organization of the Board and they consequently resented closer control, especially when it was imposed by a minister and permanent secretary who were former trade-unionists. Askwith even went so far as to sustain a personal feud with Lloyd George throughout the war, which led eventually to a formal Cabinet reprimand.[62] Behind the personal friction, however, there was also a major clash of policy. Both men, as archetypal Edwardian pro-consuls, believed in the impartiality of the state above vested interest and in aggressive bureaucracy—Beveridge to cure unemployment by the rationalization of the labour market and Askwith to defend the 'public interest' in industrial disputes. Their concept of impartiality, however, was suspect to the Labour movement (with some reason, as Askwith's formation of a Middle-Class Union after his resignation revealed) and their concept of bureaucracy was also identified with the spectre of a 'servile state'. Butler's task was to redefine the long-term role of the state in labour administration and so to repair, through the Ministry, the state's relationship with the trade union movement.

Butler totally rejected the old philosophy of the Board of Trade. 'It is the strong belief of the Department', he wrote in 1918,

that the great problems of industrial reorganization which were looming ahead before the war and which have now been brought definitely to the front by war conditions, can only be successfully solved by a policy of decentralization. It is clear that no system of bureaucratic control of industry is ever likely to succeed in this country. There are two reasons for this (a) that state interference is foreign to the whole temper and outlook of the British people, who have always been bred in the belief that they

---

[62] Cab 23/4. W. C. 288(15), Nov. 1917. Beveridge was obliged to move to the Ministry of Food in 1917, Askwith to resign in 1919. See R. Lowe, 'Review article', *British Journal of Industrial Relations*, 13 (1975), 115-120.

are competent to manage their own affairs and (b) that no system of centralized administration is likely to produce such good results as a system by which the people concerned are themselves interested in the working out of their problems and the success of the scheme adopted to solve them.[63]

Whilst maintaining the impartiality of the state, therefore, Butler developed a policy of 'home rule for industry' with the state adopting a positive role only to encourage devolution and to safeguard minimum standards. He developed two new unorthodox departments, whose officials shared a 'driving conviction rather than a bureaucratic sense of duty':[64] a Labour Intelligence Division to educate government, through its *Weekly Report* to Cabinet, in trade union politics, and a Joint Industrial Council Division to promote industrial self-government. His major achievements were the Trade Board Amendment Act (which enabled the Ministry, on its own initiative, to protect the ill-organized) and the creation of the ILO (in which, uniquely, employers and trade unions had independent representation on the Governing Body).His secondment to the ILO in 1919 was a major blow to the Ministry.

Humbert Wolfe (successively head of the General Department, 1920-9, of the Services and Establishments Department, 1929-33, and of the Employment and Training Department before promotion to deputy secretary in 1938) was the most charismatic of the Ministry's officials. Of Italian–Jewish extraction, he had been educated at Bradford Grammar School and Oxford, and became a best-selling poet and society figure in his own right. He had been Lloyd George's private secretary at the Ministry of Munitions and the characters of the two men had marked similarities: Wolfe had a versatility of mind which permitted him to dictate simultaneously three letters on different subjects and, at the ILO, to interrupt the interpreter to translate his own speech into two different languages in order to achieve the correct nuance. His wit was legendary. He commiserated with the non-conformist Bowers, on his late arrival at a committee, for his 'immaculate misconception' and, when Margaret Bondfield disrupted his lunch hour to redraft a reply to a parliamentary question, he simply answered a later en-

[63] Lab 2/218/16.
[64] R. Charles, *The Development of Industrial Relations in Britain, 1911-1939* (1973), p. 210.

quiry after her health 'virago intacta'.[65] His effusion of talent, and especially his iconoclastic humour, led both to his being mistrusted and to a certain dissipation of his administrative ability. In policy matters, he urged adherence to principle. Macnamara, in 1922 for instance, when tempted by political pressure to abandon his statutory obligation to the trade boards, was recommended to do what was 'right'; and in 1932, when the fundamental principles of unemployment relief were again under discussion, he minuted: 'I suggest that what is needed is the courage of our convictions.... Again and again in the last few years the Insurance scheme has been jeopardized by a failure at a critical moment to speak out. I strongly urge we should not repeat this failure.'[66] On both occasions he was defeated. Despite an openness of mind (which led him to resist economic orthodoxy in the 1920s and to advocate in the 1930s a rebuilding programme for exchanges both to help claimants and to provide a Keynesian boost to effective demand), he was not a zealot. He mistrusted statistics (a favourite party piece at the ILO being to prove statistically that white lead alone was a healthy diet for children) and he never pursued a matter of principle to the point where a decisive breakthrough could be achieved. As director of establishments, he successfully reformed the Ministry's local and regional offices and, in his recruitment policy, he held fast to a belief that 'people who showed talent and originality, in any direction, could apply that ability to the work and development of the Ministry'.[67] Unorthodox though this was, it significantly did not have the concentrated purpose of the pre-war Board of Trade to attract committed reformers.

Wolfe's successor as deputy secretary in 1939 was Frederick Leggett who, like Wilson, had entered the pre-war Board of Trade as an executive officer and was a graduate of London University. He dominated industrial relations policy after Wilson's departure and triumphed in many disputes, often as a result of his superhuman ability to defy the needs of nature. On general policy, he was

[65] Beveridge's obituary in *The Times*, 9 Jan. 1940; Church, *Voyage Home*, pp. 29-31, 82-4; private information supplied by N. Singleton. The favourite office example of Wolfe's humour was his rather more obvious reply to Bondfield's request to see her about the facilities provided for women at employment exchanges: 'at your convenience'. An alternative and in some ways more plausible 'virago intacta' was Margaret Lawrence.

[66] Lab 2/831/TB D100/A/43; Pin 6/46/2F 816/1932.

[67] Church, *Voyage Home*, p. 107.

committed to keeping politics out of industrial relations. Richard
Crossman for once was right when he described Leggett as being
'strongly suspicious of state intervention in industrial affairs, his
basic political principle [being] the freedom of the individual and
of the group to work their own problems out for themselves'.[68] He
resisted outside interference in disputes (be it by ministers or national organizations like the Labour Party, NCEO, or TUC) and
was especially critical of attempts to revive the NIC of 1919–21
which, he maintained, would be 'an obstacle to [the] reasoned consideration' of industrial facts which employers and unions indivi-
dually were prepared to acknowledge.[69] His fanatical defence of
free collective bargaining led him to resist any move by the state to
give an industrial lead unless it had the full backing of both sides
of industry—a condition which, in view of the attitudes of inter-
war employers, was outwith the realms of practicality. His reply,
for instance, to a prospective member of a trade board who confessed that he was 'strongly laissez-faire so that he might find himself out of sympathy with what he was doing' was that his beliefs
were 'a strong reason for offering him an appointment'.[70] Accordingly, both in industrial relations and economic policy (on which
he was regularly consulted), his influence was conservative.

The fourth major influence on policy was Wilfrid Eady (educated at Clifton College and Cambridge), an ambitious man of
quicksilver mind and administrative ability who rose to prominence
as secretary of the Industrial Transference Board in 1928, was
appointed secretary of the UAB in 1934 and finally joined the
Treasury in 1942. He had radical instincts, being a close friend of
Tom Jones and a stalwart of the Romney Street group of left-
wing public figures; he was also one of the first officials to appreciate the structural problems of the British economy, calling in
1926 for a 'novel' involvement by the state in capital expenditure
to ensure 'proper industrial development'.[71] His weakness (as one

[68] R. Crossman, *Palestine Mission* (1946), p. 24.
[69] PRO 30/69/1/359(12), appendix III.
[70] Beveridge papers, 11b 31–2, Leggett to Beveridge, 7 Nov. 1932 and 17 Jan.
1933. He was nevertheless admired by Bevin, the trade-unionist, for the way he
'fondled' disputes. He fell foul of Bevin, the minister, owing to his chaotic administrative style and his open hostility to state intervention in the catering trade.
[71] Lab 2/1215/ED 48401/1926. Having been sympathetic to Keynes's evolving
views in the 1920s, Eady's awareness of Britain's structural problems made him
suspicious by the 1930s of easy macro-economic solutions to unemployment, see
below, pp. 219–20.

member of the UAB noted) was a readiness to play the politician rather than the statesman. 'His mind', complained Violet Markham, 'is too subtle amd it veers about too much.'[72] She despised his devious manoeuvrings to keep policy firmly in official hands and his regular collapses, no doubt for career reasons, before Phillips whenever the Board and the Ministry clashed. He was, indeed, a prime example of Dale's 'stoical realism'. He confessed he had been conditioned to 'serve that curious but helpful God, Pragmatic Sanction' and, when he quarrelled with his old friend, Tom Jones, over the need for greater strictness in unemployment relief, he argued:

Historically assistance to the poor has always reflected the average temper of the times.... Our proposals do little more than this—even if they do as much. If we, or anyone else, were in a position to offer employment to those applicants, we could afford to be stiff and to stand out against current sentimentality. But we are not. They must live on ... what we choose to give them ... I do not like to have on my conscience an insistence that they shall, for some social philosophy of my own, be compelled to live less reasonably than public opinion is clearly prepared to pay for.[73]

Admirable though those sentiments may have been, they lacked the perspective and the principle of a committed reformer. His ultimate failure to realize fully his undoubted talent was perhaps the result of his being too clever and his lack of, in the eighteenth-century meaning of the word, 'bottom'.

Beneath these major figures, two other officials had for a time considerable personal influence: F. G. Bowers and John Hilton. They were very different characters. The role of Bowers (another graduate of London University) as accountant-general has already been noted. He was a profoundly religious man, whose sense of duty drove him to seek out economy and efficiency in the true spirit of the Charity Organization Society. His foremost principle was self-help and he strongly supported any agency that would promote it. He was not, however, blindly opposed to state intervention. He supported the expansion of industrial training, for example, as a cost-effective and speedy means of restoring self-respect to the unemployed; and he vigorously castigated the Treasury for its failure to appreciate that, by doing nothing to encourage mobility

[72] Tom Jones diary, Markham to Jones, 3 Nov. 1935 and 3 Apr. 1936.
[73] Ibid., Eady to Jones, 29 Sept. 1935 and 3 July 1936.

from the depressed regions, it was increasing the ultimate cost of unemployment relief.[74] In 1933 he left the Ministry to become comptroller-general of the London County Council. In 1931, Hilton also left the Ministry to become Professor of Industrial Relations at Cambridge. A self-taught Lancashire mill mechanic, he was a radical wartime protégé of Butler whose appointment as head of the Intelligence and Statistics Department in 1919 was the occasion for the Treasury ban on the use of clause 4 of the 1859 Superannuation Act. In the true radical spirit of nineteenth-century 'statesmen in disguise', he was a leading debater at the Royal Statistical Society (equally suspicious of economic orthodoxy and the 'unproven magic' of Keynes) and had a spirit of adventure, which led to his dressing as an unemployed man to experience employment exchanges from the other side of the counter.[75] The Treasury's contraction of the Statistics Department, however, prevented him from fully emulating his nineteenth-century peers.

Supporting this hierarchy of officials were two particularly distinctive groups of officials: the former employees of the Board of Trade and the new men recruited to the Ministry once open competition was resumed in 1925. The ex-Board of Trade officials included men of considerable talent such as R. C. Davison, who, after his resignation in the early 1930s, wrote the two standard works on unemployment policy and became a leading influence on relief policy through the columns of *The Times*. They included also the exceptionally acrimonious, such as C. F. Rey (who lay at the root of much of the friction between the Ministries of National Service and Labour during the First World War) and J. S. Nicholson (who maintained the tradition by fighting a rearguard battle against the UAB in the mid-1930s). This group also contained many 'characters', such as Commander Adams, a Polar explorer who had held Churchill, as president of the Board, spellbound during an interview and secured his appointment by admitting that, to him, the most impressive feature of Beveridge's *Unemployment: A Problem of Industry* was the price. In the 1930s, as North West Divisional Officer, he confessed his admiration for Mussolini and

[74] See above, pp. 50, 58-9 and Pin 6/86. Bowers also considered unemployment insurance a justifiable form of self-help and attacked the Treasury for its short-sightedness, see Pin 6/60, minute of 21 Dec. 1932.

[75] A full résumé of Hilton's later views is incorporated in this report which led to the repeal of the 'genuinely seeking work' clause, see Steel-Maitland papers, GD 193/94/2.

was responsible for the suspension of the Durham and Rotherham Public Assistance Committees.[76] Another 'character' was C. E. M. Joad, later lecturer in philosophy at London University and a member of the Brains Trust. A self-confessed revolutionary, the distinguishing features of his official career were lack of influence and idleness. He never appeared for work on Saturday, ordering his clerk to hang up and then remove his coat from behind his door at the appropriate times, a tactic which deceived nobody, because 'the apparel was green with age and covered in a thick bloom of dust'. The distance of his office from the nearest lavatory led to other equally undesirable habits.[77]

The influence of the second group of officials was felt most fully during and after the Second World War, but as junior administrators they had some impact on the implementation of inter-war policy. Their virtues were epitomized by F. N. Tribe, whom many acknowledged as their mentor. Educated at Clifton and Oxford, Tribe entered the Ministry in 1919 and eventually became secretary to the English Commissioner for the Special Areas in 1934 and, after a spell at the Treasury, deputy secretary in 1940. He was not an original thinker (as he was the first to admit), felt more at home with employers than trade-unionists, and was ever attentive to economy, as befitted a future comptroller and auditor-general. However, as a member of a leading congregationalist Bristol family, with a long tradition of charity, he had a firm commitment to social reform and public service. As an administrator he never admitted defeat but employed a 'sympathetic but sane' approach to any problem, however seemingly intractable.[78] In this way he was a leading exponent of the art of pragmatic experiment by which British society in peacetime can alone be gradually steeled to change.

The Administrative Account

The administrative response of the Ministry, as of the civil service as a whole, to the advent of democracy was by no means flawless. It was guilty of frequent delay and inefficiency, albeit often for reasons outside its control. It was guilty also, as two major policy

---

[76] F. A. Norman, *Whitehall to West Indies* (1952), p. 29; Markham papers 9/3, Adams to Markham, 7 Feb. 1935.

[77] For full details see Church, *Voyage Home*, p. 100.

[78] Tribe papers, Forbes Watson to Tribe, 21 Dec. 1934.

developments illustrate, of the cardinal bureaucratic sin of goal displacement. In 1917 all reservations about the principles behind Whitleyism were dropped with indecent haste once the prospect of a Ministry of Reconstruction threatened its authority in this area, and, in 1934, the character of the ÜAB was unduly influenced by a battle with the Ministry of Health and the need to satisfy the frustrated ambitions of its own officials. The Board, so it was rumoured, was created to provide 'for the poor and Eady and to keep the Wolfe from the door'.[79] In the provinces, also, an observer for Mass Observation was first amused and then angered by the length to which an insurance officer went to explain the difficulty of his own position, whilst seemingly oblivious of the needs of the claimant who was in danger of losing his benefit.[80] Nevertheless, within the political and cultural constraints of the time, the Ministry in both the formulation and implementation of policy did act with an open-mindedness and vigour which defy traditional criticisms of inter-war bureaucracy.

Apart from the greater pervasiveness of Treasury control, the most telling difference between the Ministry and its much-lauded predecessor, the Board of Trade, was the nature of its officials' reforming zeal. Those who did have a zealous commitment to an ideal were men, like Bowers and Leggett, who wished to minimize the role of the state; whereas the initiative of officials, such as Hilton, Wolfe, and Eady, who might have emulated such Edwardian pro-consuls as Llewellyn Smith, was gradually sapped by what Dale has termed 'stoical realism'. C. W. K. Macmullan, the head of the short-lived Intelligence Department and one of the Ministry's most gifted officials, left the most evocative description of this attitude. He summarized his experience in inter-war Whitehall thus:

I learnt that one ought to make up one's mind on the issues ... and express one's views ... as clearly and as shortly as possible. I learnt that these views should be based on reason into which one's own emotions did not enter, yet should take account of the feelings of those members of the community who might be affected ... I learnt also that they should take account of, and be in harmony with, the general policy of the Government of the day. I learnt that many problems were of such a nature as to admit of a variety of views as regards their solution, and that one's own views,

[79] Lab 2/212/16; private information supplied by Sir Harold Emmerson and P. H. St. J. Wilson.
[80] Mass Observation, W 26/D.

therefore, though they might be rational, were not necessarily right. I learnt that, once my superior had given his decision, that was the end of my own view ... I learnt that my own personal interest had nothing to do with my official work ... Finally, I learnt that peculiar neutrality as regards political issues which is the hall-mark of a Service which has to serve all Parties alike. I learnt that the whole nation might be rent with political controversy ... yet ... civil servants are so much concerned with the practical problems involved in implementing the policy of any Party that, if they discuss politics at all, it tends to be in terms of the practical and impractical, a subject about which cool argument is possible, rather than right or wrong which only leads to heat and denunciation.[81]

Such an ethos naturally precluded any dramatic radicalization of policy by bureaucrats, as in the Edwardian period; but Ministry officials, like other inter-war civil servants, were only too aware that aggressive, centralized bureaucracy had been publicly rejected during the First World War. It had three further strengths. First, it respected the pluralistic constraints of democratic government and, instead of seeking to impose solutions from Whitehall, sought to encourage personal responsibility, private charity, and private enterprise. As one of the inter-war recruits, whilst serving as a regional officer during the war, remarked: 'It is for us alleged bureaucrats who are supposed to be depressing private initiative to encourage it, and to discourage people from unduly relying on bureaucrats.'[82] Secondly, it made a mockery of Lord Hewart's obsession with the rise of bureaucratic despotism. Finally, and most importantly, it did not preclude the Ministry—as a new department with a vigorous regional organization in daily contact with human problems—from a constant, pragmatic questioning of received administrative and economic orthodoxy. Consequently, the Ministry was able, as the succeeding chapters show, to achieve a quiet but permanent revolution in government policy.

[81] Munro, *Fountains in Trafalgar Square*, pp. 200–1. Munro was the alias of Macmullan.

[82] P. H. St. J. Wilson in Northern Region circular, R. O. Circ. Minute 17/1944 supplement (privately supplied).

CHAPTER 4

INDUSTRIAL RELATIONS

INDUSTRIAL relations were the kernel of the Ministry's responsibilities. Politically, the Ministry had been created during the war expressly to appease the Labour movement; and the social and economic policies for which it became responsible may be seen, at root, as attempts to forestall political and industrial unrest. Administratively, it was responsible for the institutional and legal framework in which industrial relations were conducted and for the day-to-day resolution of disputes.[1] These responsibilities had a pervasive, if sometimes unconscious, influence throughout the whole Ministry. Within Whitehall, policy was framed by officials who, whilst no mouthpiece of the TUC, were fully alive to its views. At Westminster, as has been seen, the political partisanship of successive ministers was qualified by their role as conciliator of last resort (a qualification which one post-war minister—inevitably a lawyer—took to its logical but absurd conclusion by refusing to address his party conference).[2]

The importance of industrial relations policy was not reflected in the Ministry's administrative structure. The number of industrial relations officials was always relatively small and, after 1922, their status within the Ministry became increasingly anomalous. In 1919 they were divided among five departments: the Wages and Arbitration Department under Horace Wilson, which had the major responsibility for policy and administration; a central conciliation staff first under Askwith and then under Shackleton; a Labour Intelligence Division, responsible for the study of long-term policy and the compilation for the War Cabinet of the *Weekly Report on the Labour Situation*; and finally a Joint Industrial Council and a

[1] The Ministry's authority was not total. During the war, contracting departments, especially the Ministry of Munitions, had the initial responsibility for handling disputes in relevant industries as, in peacetime, did such departments as the Ministry of Agriculture and the Mines Department of the Board of Trade.
[2] E. Wigham, *Strikes and the Government, 1893–1974* (1976), p. 107. The minister was Sir Walter Monckton.

Trade Boards Division, respectively charged with the promotion of Whitley councils and minimum wages. At their maximum, the staff in the first two of these departments numbered 229 (112 at headquarters, 117 in the provinces) and in the other three, 174. Numbers, however, were rapidly reduced by Treasury retrenchment and political objections to state intervention in industrial relations. By 1924 the Industrial Relations Department had been reduced to an effective strength of 28 (13 at headquarters, 15 in the provinces), the Labour Intelligence and Joint Industrial Council Divisions disbanded, and the expansion of Trade Boards staff halted.[3] By 1935, the staff of the Industrial Relations Department had declined further to 23 (13 at headquarters, 10 in the provinces) and that of the Trade Boards Department to 66 (7 plus 59).

This decline threatened to undermine the authority of the industrial relations establishment which had presented itself to the Geddes Committee in 1921 as the Ministry's 'general staff'.[4] As unemployment insurance began to dominate the Ministry, so its officials began to assert themselves with the result that, by 1935, both the permanent and deputy secretary (Phillips and J. F. G. Price) had risen from their ranks.[5] However, while Wilson was permanent secretary and later, when Leggett shrouded conciliation in mystery, the industrial relations staff continued to enjoy an influence which belied their numbers. Throughout the 1930s Leggett was automatically consulted on economic policy and no legislation was considered in the Ministry, at either a political or an administrative level, without due consideration of its industrial acceptability—a matter on which the industrial relations staff were the acknowledged authority.

The development of industrial relations policy, especially in the immediate post-war period, underwent considerable change according to the evolving perception of political and industrial priorities and, within that perception, the personalities of leading officials. The major political change occurred after the autumn of 1919 when first inflation and then depression undermined the establishment's

---

[3] See above, pp. 60-1.   [4] Cab 27/167/E (Labour) 2.

[5] The Employment Department scored a notable victory in 1940 when local conciliation officers were made responsible to the Ministry's divisional officers and thus lost their right to report direct to headquarters; the dominant influence of inter-war industrial relations officials has, however, been constantly reiterated in interviews.

willingness to accept and the Labour movement's ability to promote social reform. This change was reflected by administrative developments. On the Ministry's creation, the sitting tenant as chief industrial commissioner had been Sir George Askwith. During the war, however, he had fallen increasingly into disgrace for challenging the competence of both the Cabinet and the conciliation officers in the wartime production departments; his influence had been gradually assumed, in long-term planning, by Butler and, in day-to-day conciliation, by Shackleton.[6] After the war, from under his own tutelage, there then emerged Horace Wilson to supplant first Askwith himself as head of the industrial relations staff (in November 1918), secondly Butler as strategist (in the autumn of 1919), and finally Shackleton as permanent secretary (in 1921). Wilson's progress was of the greatest significance. He was too knowledgeable to swallow the current Treasury obsession that an industrial relations staff caused rather than reduced industrial unrest (on the self-evident analogy, as Humbert Wolfe remarked, that the fire brigade created fires).[7] He did, however, accept the economic orthodoxy that in a depression public expenditure should be reduced and that wages should reflect solely the value of work done, so that anything that offended both canons (such as the active promotion of trade boards) should be immediately curtailed. Politicians, confident in the reassertion of this orthodoxy, were thereafter largely prepared to withdraw from detailed involvement in industrial relations. Indeed, they were eager to do so, if only to emphasize their distance from the opportunism of Lloyd George.

Although few in number, therefore, industrial relations officials throughout the inter-war period were able to exert considerable influence not only over their colleagues but also over policy. This influence they used to champion two conflicting policies. First, under Butler, there was a positive attempt (in Marxist terms) to 'humanize' or 'moralize' capitalism. As has been seen, Butler was a committed adherent of industrial devolution but, in the last resort, he was prepared to countenance state intervention in order to remedy organizational weakness and to maintain minimum standards.[8] His ultimate objective was that of the wartime, liberal advocates of a ministry of labour and industry, who had planned to use the authority of central government to achieve a 'regime of

---

[6] For a full account of Askwith's decline and fall, see Lowe, 'Review article'.
[7] Lab 2/1822/CEB 461/2/1922.   [8] See above, pp. 67–8.

ordered freedom' in which (by such reforms as industrial democracy and a greater equality of income) the conditions and status
of the work-force could be permanently enhanced. 'All this is not
Socialism,' the wartime liberals had argued; 'it is simply Democracy
... it is a means of preserving the greatest possible measure of
individual freedom with a tolerable social existence.'[9] After 1919,
however, such idealism was received with increasing scepticism by
officials, such as Shackleton, Wilson, and Leggett, steeped in the
practical experience of industrial relations. Leggett was its most
outspoken critic. He maintained that, since 'the preservation of
order in a democracy depends on a personal sense of responsibility', it could not be imposed from above by a small minority but
had to develop from below. The state should show the utmost
respect for the traditions and the autonomy of each industry, and
its constructive role should be limited to encouraging—as unobtru-
sively as possible—both sides of industry to accept practices which
would foster self-restraint and responsibility. In the last resort,
strikes and lock-outs were even 'desirable' if they confronted both
employers and the work-force with the hard 'economic facts' and
thereby resulted in stable, lasting agreements.[10]

Both these strategies shared certain basic assumptions, such as
a belief in voluntaryism and the need, within a capitalist framework, to promote reform; but, for the practical purpose of guiding
short-term policy, they were in fundamental disagreement. They
disagreed over the extent to which working-class acceptance of
capitalism could be assumed or had to be fostered. They disagreed
over whether reform should be concerned solely with pay and conditions or whether it should challenge the traditional preserves of
management (industrial democracy) and the market (income equal-
ization). Consequently they disagreed also over the speed at which
reform could be achieved and the government's ability to pioneer
change. It is the purpose of this chapter to examine in some detail
the nature and significance of these conflicting strategies; but, first,
the overall record of inter-war industrial relations and the general
factors influencing it must be summarized.

[9] Tom Jones papers, C 19; Jones, *Whitehall Diary*, vol. I, p. 13.
[10] F. W. Leggett, 'The settlement of labour disputes in Great Britain', in E.
Jackson (ed.), *Meeting of Minds* (New York, 1952), p. 674; Lab 10/248.

The Record

Any comparison of industrial unrest at the start and conclusion of the inter-war period immediately suggests that the Ministry's industrial relations policy was remarkably successful. The following table contrasts the annual average of strikes, workers involved in strikes (directly and indirectly), and working days lost in four-year periods before and after the Ministry's creation and prior to the Second World War:[11]

	Strikes	Workers involved (m.)	Days lost (m.)
1911–14	1,034	0.88	17.7
1919–22	1,075	1.72	41.8
1935–38	844	0.36	2.1

Wartime comparisons are equally dramatic. During the Second World War, the number of strikes admittedly exceeded that for the First World War, but (from a larger work-force) the annual number of workers involved was never as great as in 1917 or 1918 and the total number of working days lost was under half. Moreover, as a legacy of inter-war industrial relations, both sides of industry acted throughout the Second World War as 'trustees on behalf of the state'[12] and accepted for a further six years compulsory arbitration—a commitment which, as the strike record between 1919 and 1922 shows, could not have been further from the trade union leaders' minds after the First World War.

Such comparisons, however, can be misleading for a number of reasons. On the one hand, peacetime comparisons should take account of mass unemployment in the export industries, which discouraged unrest in traditionally militant areas, and of both rising living standards and political incorporation (through the franchise, Labour Party and government propaganda) which affected the rest of the country.[13] On the other hand, wartime comparisons should allow for prompt government action in 1940 to counter the two major causes of unrest (inflation and excess profits), the different relationship between Britain and Russia (which obliged Com-

[11] See Appendix 2, A.   [12] Lab 10/434 (Aug. 1942).

[13] There is, however, no clear statistical correlation between a decrease in strikes and an increase in either national or sectional unemployment. See K. G. J. C. Knowles, *Strikes—A Study of Industrial Conflict* (Oxford, 1954), p. 246 and chapter 5, appendix A.

munist shop stewards in the Second World War actively to support the war effort), and the election in 1945 of a Labour Government committed to full employment and social security (which realized many of the objectives of earlier militancy). There were also, throughout the inter-war period, three more subtle influences favourable to industrial peace. Occupational change increased the relative number of clerks and professional workers (decreasing militancy), of semi-skilled workers (diluting craft pride), and of female workers (weakening organization). The geographical shift in industrial location resulted in a greater proportion of migrant workers within 'new' industries which had no tradition of militancy. Finally, the growth of trade unions' central bureaucracies signified a greater ability to control local strikes and a greater willingness to negotiate. The true test of the Ministry's policy, therefore, is not simply the decrease in formal, large-scale disruption, but the translation of favourable underlying trends into constructive new relationships on the shop-floor.

In seeking these improvements, inter-war conciliators—confronted with the friction generated by falling money wages and sheer desperation within the structurally defunct staple industries—may, with some reason, have failed to recognize any favourable trends. Certainly in many key industries industrial relations appeared utterly unamenable to reason. In coal-mining, for example, the miners (clinging obstinately to demands which they knew the exporting section of industry could not afford) made an irresistible claim to be the stupidest men in England and would have succeeded had it not been, in Lord Birkenhead's incomparable phrase, for the mineowners (whose managerial incompetence had been fully exposed by the Sankey Commission in 1919). In the cotton industry of the early 1930s, outside observers were dumbfounded by the apparent death-wish of price-cutting employers and the 'barnacles of tradition' that prevented union members from acknowledging the need to revise pre-war agreements in the light of changed economic circumstances.[14] Rearmament also revealed the sterility of relationships in the engineering industry, where innovation (in the 'national' interest) was eschewed by the employers for fear of restoring to unions some of the bargaining strength that had been denied them since the 1922 'right to manage' lock-out—a lock-out described by the employers' own historian as 'among the most

[14] Lab 2/1258/4.

high-handed operations in the history of industrial relations'.[15] In the 'new' industries, industrial relations were little better. Sir Alfred Mond of Imperial Chemical Industries (ICI), at the very time he was attempting nationally to involve the TUC in responsibility for rationalization policy, was seeking to stifle any germ of independence in his own work-force.[16] Sir William Morris, whose Nuffield Trust provided the most significant private source of economic aid to the depressed regions in the late 1930s, was also an outspoken opponent of the trade unions.

Confronted by such sectional enmities, conciliation officers (owing to their reduced numbers) could only hope to improve shop-floor relations by working through central employers' organizations and trade unions which, it was hoped, would exercise a beneficial influence over their members. This hope, however, went largely unrealized. Informally, the national representatives of both sides of industry displayed increasing goodwill. Regular meetings at the ILO, for example, nurtured friendships which bore fruit on occasions, such as the Amulree Committee in 1938 when both sides reversed roles and argued with the utmost conviction their opponents' case for and against statutory holidays with pay.[17] Formally, however, this mutual understanding, to the frustration of the Ministry, did not mature until the Second World War.

This failure was due largely to the negative attitude of the employers. At a national level, the Ministry had to deal with them almost exclusively through the NCEO—an organization founded in 1919 by hardline engineering employers expressly to cauterize the liberal impulses of another national organization (the Federation of British Industries (FBI)) dominated by financiers and monopoly capital.[18] The NCEO's negativism, which it duly admitted during the Second World War, had three main causes.[19] First, it was never

---

[15] E. Wigham, *The Right to Manage. The History of the Engineering Employers' Federation* (1973), p. 119; Lab 8/213.

[16] W. J. Reader, *Imperial Chemical Industries*, vol. 2. (1975), pp. 64-70.

[17] A. V. S. Lockhead, 'The use of advisory bodies by the Industrial Relations Department of the Ministry of Labour', in R. V. Vernon and N. Mansergh (eds.), *Advisory Bodies* (1940), p. 296. Again, interviews stress the informal achievements of the ILO, which the formal record fails to convey.

[18] S. Blank, *Government and Industry in Britain* (Farnborough, 1973), pp. 17-18; T. Rodgers, 'Work and welfare: the National Confederation of Employers' Organizations and unemployment problem, 1917-36' (unpublished Ph.D. thesis, Edinburgh University, 1982), ch. 1.

[19] 'Reconstruction Policy' by Sir Henry Brand, Sir Ralph Wedgwood, and Basil Sanderson, Oct. 1942 (Lithgow papers, 34).

able to secure the support of more than one-seventh of its potential membership (of 350) and in the depressions of 1920–3 and 1930–4 was heavily in debt: to conserve its strength it had to be 'as die-hard as its most die-hard member'.[20] Secondly, a more broad-minded policy was discouraged by the division of responsibility for economic and labour policy between the FBI and the NCEO (parallel to the artificial division in central government between the Board of Trade and Ministry of Labour and, in international agencies, between the League of Nations' Economic Secretariat and the ILO). Thirdly, the small-scale employers in the staple exporting industries (which the NCEO particularly represented) adopted, owing to their economic predicament, an essentially pessimistic and undynamic concept of the economy. They equated depression not with changed world demand, structural imbalance, or bad management, but with high costs generated by high wages and high taxation. State intervention was consequently attacked both for undermining the rights of management and for the disastrously high levels of public expenditure. On the one hand, it was claimed, employers were shackled by red tape, and by the strength of trade unions which, after the 'fortuitous circumstance' of the war, was artificially maintained by state intervention; on the other, impractical sentimentalists 'saddled the export trades with unbearable charges' and deprived industry of much-needed investment capital.[21] The NCEO was prepared to acknowledge neither the permanency of new working-class aspirations nor the reality of democratic government. Government departments were castigated for their 'socialistically inclined attitude towards all employers' problems' and politicians for their spinelessness.[22]

The NCEO accordingly provided a formidable obstacle for the Ministry. In the settlement of disputes, the known views of its leaders—the dreaded Scottish triumvirate of Sir Allan Smith, Lord Weir, and Sir James Lithgow—were hardly conciliatory. Smith, to Baldwin's intense displeasure, insisted on referring to trade unions

[20] Ibid.

[21] The particular spleen is Sir James Lithgow's in Lithgow papers, 74 (June 1925, Dec. 1926, Oct. 1930).

[22] Lithgow to Lord Blanesburgh, 28 June 1927 (Steel-Maitland papers, GD 193/94/2). Lithgow's balanced view was that, 'in the present state of democratic Government in Britain', politicians axiomatically based policy on 'the instincts of greed, laziness and ignorance ... not ... the real ideals of the British public'. See Lithgow papers, 74 (1931).

as 'the enemy'; Weir, having been responsible for the deportation
of agitators from Clydeside in 1915, clashed violently with building
workers in the 1920s over the erection of steel houses; and Lithgow
had a tendency to reflect in public that there was 'nothing wrong
with the British worker except his trade union'.[23] In relation to
more fundamental issues, the NCEO was equally unhelpful. Steel-
Maitland angrily denounced its 'obstructive inertia' during his
attempt to construct an 'industrial concordat' after the General
Strike; and, at the height of the economic crisis of 1931, one of the
most degrading episodes in British industrial relations took place
when the NCEO and the Labour Cabinet bandied insults about
lack of political and industrial leadership.[24] The bitter irony was
that, although it had in no small way been created by the Ministry
and continued to depend on the Ministry's patronage (especially
the right to select the employers' representatives at the ILO) to
ensure the allegiance of members, the NCEO was an outspoken
antagonist. It singled out the Ministry as one of the most extravagant and 'socialistically-inclined' departments, whose abolition was
essential to national revival. Relief was therefore considerable
within the Ministry when, as a result of its behaviour during the
1931 economic crisis, the NCEO's credibility with both government
and its own constituents was seriously weakened.

In its formal policies the TUC was able to offer the Ministry
rather more comfort although, as an organization, it shared many
of the NCEO's weaknesses. It had a relatively small membership
(never representing more than one-third of the work-force after
1921), no executive authority over its members, and was equally
ambivalent towards the Ministry. Despite its pre-war demand for
the Ministry and the continuing need for recognition in order to
validate its status, the TUC clashed repeatedly with the Ministry,
never more so than during Labour governments. If the Ministry
was uncertain of its ambassadorial role to the working class, then
the TUC was equally uncertain about its proper relationship to the
medium which stood between it and the rest of the government
machine. Between 1916 and 1926, the relationship was particularly
barren because the Labour movement displayed at times a 'con-

---

[23] R. R. James, *Memoirs of a Conservative* (1969), p. 106; Lithgow papers, 74.
Weir virtually demanded the abolition of trade unions after the General Strike (Cab
27/326/5), a strange ambition for an instigator of the Mond–Turner talks.
[24] Cab 24/189/CP 285(27); Weir papers, 12/1 (19 Feb. 1931).

tempt for parliamentary democracy which stopped short only at deposing the Government'.[25] In 1919, moreover, the year most favourable to radical reform, it was—in the words of the president of the FBI—'not only too suspicious but too irresponsible and had tried to move too fast'.[26] Suspicious of every reform offered by government and employer, irresponsible in its refusal to match concession with concession, and too fast in seeking ultimate ideals (such as nationalization), it had furthermore been unable to present a united front or to translate its slogans into practical policy. This period had damaging long-term consequences for, whenever reforms such as nationalization or shorter working hours were demanded in the future, they could be rejected on the pretext that experience proved they would not be reciprocated.

The formal policy of the Labour movement was transformed by defeat in the General Strike. The central bureaucracy of the TUC had been gradually developing since the appointment of a General Council (in 1921) and of a full-time general secretary (in 1923) and, as soon as the policy of direct action was exposed as 'empty rhetoric', this bureaucracy (under the guidance of Ernest Bevin and Walter Citrine) swung the TUC in a constructive 'new direction'.[27] Whilst never forgetting the long-term objective of socialization or the fact that bargaining power depended on industrial organization, the new policy sought to defend living standards in the short term (be they dependent on an industrial or a social wage) by regenerating industry within a capitalist framework. A policy of co-operation was substituted for conflict, the concept of industrial interest for class warfare.

The corollary of this new policy for the Ministry was the TUC's willingness to co-operate with employers, to discourage militancy within its own ranks, and to adopt a 'responsible' attitude towards state intervention. Conflict on the shop-floor was officially discour-

[25] V. L. Allen, *Trade Unions and the Government* (1960), p. 147. Even the 'labourist' wing of the trade union movement was obliged to demand a fundamental restructuring of capitalism and to condone the use of industrial strength for political ends. See, for example, the TUC submission to the NIC, PP (1919), xxiv, 21, appendix 1.

[26] Blank, *Government and Industry*, p. 23.

[27] G. A. Phillips, *The General Strike* (1976), p. 294. This and the following paragraph have been greatly influenced by Martin, *TUC*, and M. Jacques, 'The emergence of "responsible" trade unionism: a study of the "new direction" in TUC policy, 1926–1935' (unpublished Ph.D. thesis, Cambridge University, 1976).

aged, militant action against either wage cuts or unemployment opposed, and rival sources of militancy (such as trade councils, the unemployed workers' movement, and the Communist Party) wherever possible emasculated. State intervention, although still regarded as a potential threat to independent bargaining strength, was in the last resort accepted as a means of counteracting the economic ascendancy of employers—Citrine replying to those who continued to demand a policy of non-cooperation that it was 'far better to exert our influence to control ... things ... than to stand aside and have to take the consequences'.[28] Open confrontation between the TUC and the Government on matters of principle (as in the early 1920s) was thus exchanged for reasoned, and often secret, discussion on matters of detailed administration. The Ministry could not but benefit from this new, intimate relationship. Indeed Bevin exactly mirrored official attitudes when he remarked to the TUC conference in 1928 that 'the difference between a politician and an industrial leader is this: that our party is working for change, but the industrial leader has every day of his life to deal with facts as they are'.[29]

The one drawback to this essentially sympathetic if frequently uncomfortable relationship was the question of its consummation. In the 1930s, the National Government remained ever distrustful of a body allied to (indeed dominant over) the Labour Party and committed to dubious long-term objectives such as socialization. Employers mistook restraint for weakness and, as has been seen, rejected the fundamental purpose of consensus—the ending of cuts in wages and public expenditure. The TUC itself, moreover, was only as strong as its divided membership. As Bevin (when minister of labour) wrote during a bitter argument with Citrine in 1941: 'I have been perturbed at times at what I think, rightly or wrongly, is unwillingness to come to decisions and accept responsibility and the desire to refer back and then at the same time to hear criticism of our lack of speed.'[30] If a trusted ex-colleague, in the emergency of war, was unable to obtain prompt action, how much more hopeless was the task of peacetime officials. Indeed, the instances of TUC impotence were legion. In social policy, for example, the TUC campaigned throughout the 1920s for ratification of the Washington Hours Convention, yet found itself unable to support the rele-

[28] TUC, *Annual Report*, 1938, p. 311.   [29] Ibid., 1928, p. 448.
[30] E. Bevin to W. Citrine, 1 Oct. 1941 (Bevin papers, 3/1, fols. 85-6).

vant legislation in 1930 owing to internecine warfare between the National Union of Railwaymen and the Transport and General Workers' Union. In industrial relations, the frequency of unofficial strikes (reflected in the continuing high numbers of disputes) exposed the precarious hold that central union bureaucracies had over the shop-floor.[31]

Despite the impressive statistical record, therefore, inter-war industrial relations were fraught with tension. The underlying trend (supported by national culture) was undoubtedly towards industrial co-operation, but much surface bitterness was generated by depression and structural economic change. New national organizations of employers and workers developed which were dependent on government recognition for the legitimization of their status, and yet both became outspoken critics of government. With its small conciliation staff, the Ministry was dependent on these organizations for, as *The Times* confirmed on 26 November 1924, the success of a minister of labour was determined 'less by what he does himself than by what leaders of industry, employers and union officials, can be induced to do'. Unfortunately, throughout the inter-war period the employers (who were economically in the ascendant) could be induced to do little, whilst the TUC (which in theory at least was more sympathetic towards the Ministry) lacked the necessary influence over its members. The Ministry's response to this challenge fell into three distinct stages.

Failure to Maximize Consent, 1916–1922

For six years, until Lloyd George's fall from office in 1922, the Ministry strove with varying degrees of vigour to force the pace of industrial change. In accordance with the campaign for its establishment, it sought to redress the government's perceived bias against Labour, to improve industrial organization, and to nurture industrial responsibility. During the war the political revolution was attempted by the three leading figures drafted in from the trade union movement—Hodge, Roberts, and Shackleton—whilst the administrative planning was masterminded by Butler. Butler's objective, as has been seen, was to strive for a 'peaceful revolution in industry' through a reversal of the pre-war momentum towards bureaucratic control. Better organization, combined with a devo-

---

[31] TUC archives, box 234. Less than a quarter of recorded strikes in 1936, for example, were known to be official, see Knowles, *Strikes*, p. 33.

lution of power from government to industry and from national to district organization, was to be the key; and at the hub of the new, ideal industrial world was to be the Ministry. As the War Cabinet was informed:

A properly constituted ML will have divisional and local offices in all important industrial areas, and these offices will be for that area the common resort for employers and employed on all questions which are related to the activities of the State. The ideal for such an office would be a central building in the town, in which was situated the local Employment Exchange and the local office of the Factory Inspector, and at which the meetings of the District Committee of Trade Boards would be held and disputes which were to be settled locally were heard by the appointed Court of Arbitration. In connection with this office would be a local Advisory Committee of employers and workmen, representative of the local industries, who would thus be in a position to keep in constant touch with the action of the Ministry and to stimulate it by criticism and suggestion.[32]

Four major pitfalls threatened the realization of this ideal. First, as Butler himself acknowledged, both the representation of Labour within government and the devolution of power to industry were in potential conflict with government perception of 'the national interest'. 'The State', admitted Butler,

must always remain vitally interested in the development and regulation of industry as constituting the backbone of the national welfare, and also because the State, as the representative of the whole people, is concerned not only with the well-being of every section of the community, but also is interested to secure that the interests of any section are not set above the interests of the whole.

Secondly, as Butler again acknowledged, devolution assumed industrial consensus because 'home rule for industry' could succeed only if industry spoke with one voice and was prepared to act in order to achieve the necessary reforms: 'If no-one else acts,' he insisted, 'the State will, not because it wants to, but because someone must.' Thirdly, the Ministry's role as the central industrial authority presumed an integration of social, industrial, and financial policy which the Ministry's separation from the Board of Trade had, if anything, discouraged. Finally, the reform of established industrial institutions and the temporary extension of bureaucracy

[32] Lab 2/212/13. Butler's convictions are also expressed in three other Lab 2 files: 1804/1, 212/7, and 454/1. The last two are respectively the source of his reservations noted in the following paragraph.

(even if its ultimate object was the diminution of state intervention) anticipated a degree of political consensus and goodwill towards government which the wartime record did little to justify. The experience of the Ministry after 1916 was indeed that each of these pitfalls gaped open, as can be illustrated by its failure to achieve, first, a political understanding with Labour, then industrial devolution, and, finally, a rational wages policy.

The first of the Ministry's ideals to crumble was the special political relationship with Labour. Initially Hodge, Roberts, and Shackleton repeatedly protested their allegiance to the ideals of the pre-war Labour movement. Hodge's simple reply to an early TUC request for the enactment of its 1911 Trade Union (Amalgamation) Bill was: 'The Labour Party might be asked for a print and then I could ask the War Cabinet to adopt it.' Roberts confided to his first deputation from the TUC: 'I may tell you that I am motivated here with the same spirit as a member of the TUC and the ordinary trade union movement.' Shackleton likewise confessed: 'I have no interest except the State, but if I have any bias it leans towards those with whom I have always worked.'[33] Very quickly, however, the unresolved ambiguities in the pre-war Labour demands for the Ministry made themselves felt. Allegiance to pre-war policy became anachronistic as working-class aspirations expanded in wartime; to Shackleton's despair, all trade-unionists who collaborated with government continued to be regarded as class traitors;[34] and the realities of office soon revealed the frequent incompatibility between the demands of Labour and other vested interests. Consequently, traditional professions of impartiality started to proliferate. Hodge sportingly pronounced: 'If one is going to make the Ministry of Labour a success it can only be done ... by playing cricket, that is we have got to be fair to both sides.' Roberts confessed to the TUC in 1917: 'It is extremely difficult to require that state machinery shall be used on behalf of one section of the community only.' Similarly, in 1921 Shackleton urged on a trade union deputation 'the neutrality of the Department and the futility to put forward a proposal for legislation on the representation of one party and where there was no measure of agreement'.[35]

[33] These professions of faith are in Lab 2/218/16 and Lab 10/399 (deputations on 23 Nov. and 21 Sept. 1917).

[34] See above, p. 49.

[35] Recantation is recorded in Lab 2/212/7, Lab 10/399 (deputation on 23 Nov. 1917), and Lab 2/647/2.

This erosion of personal commitment was mirrored by administrative change. In 1917, for instance, a Labour Intelligence Division
had been created to provide the War Cabinet with an accurate and
sympathetic account of weekly Labour developments, but post-war
retrenchment first emasculated its *Weekly Report* (November 1919)
and then caused it to be abandoned (April 1920).[36] At the same
time, the traditional means by which labour administration had
maintained its close contact with Labour—the recruitment of
trade-unionists and mature Labour experts—was banned. The
Treasury had long sought to end such 'outside' appointments and,
despite the resistance of Askwith, Shackleton, and Wilson, it was
at last able to succeed by arguing that the needs of expanding
labour administration should be subject to those of an otherwise
contracting civil service. Consequently, in 1920, when central
government's first permanent local conciliation officers were
appointed, none was appointed directly from industry.[37] Trade
union leaders, despite their vilification of colleagues who entered
government service, were characteristically affronted by such a development. As one leading pre-war advocate of the Ministry complained:

The Labour Ministry had started off with some enthusiasm ... Men of
great experience were appointed ... but since Sir Robert Horne has been
appointed some of the experienced men have been dispensed with, and
University men are being pushed into offices and the experienced men are
being rejected.... He did not know of any greater scandal.[38]

The Ministry's return to the establishment's political and administrative embrace did not automatically mean the reinstatement of
pre-1916 assumptions. In a revealing confession, a leading official

[36] The Division was created specifically to challenge the disinformation of the
Ministry of Munitions. For their differences of interpretation, see in particular Lab
2/254/13.
[37] For the initial hostility of the Treasury in 1917 and its mellowing by 1936, see
T 1/12220/43042/1918 and T 162/551/E 4315. Of the first 17 local conciliators
appointed, four came from the employment exchange service and 10 were former
officials of wartime departments who had already been transferred to the Ministry.
In equal proportions they had had earlier experience in management, the professions, and skilled unions. None seemingly hailed from south of Potters Bar and, as
with the NCEO leadership, there was an unhealthy preponderance of Scots (Lab 2/
1819/CEB 892/1920).
[38] Tillett in Dockers' Union, *Minutes of the Recalled Triennial Delegate Meeting*,
1919, pp. 44–5.

from the most aggressively bureaucratic department of the Board of Trade (J. F. G. Price of the Employment Department) admitted in 1917 that the war had fostered 'a greater understanding of the functions of unions' and that he was now convinced that unions were 'far too important a factor in our industrial life to be relegated to the background after the war is over and [that] it should be frankly recognized that the trade unions are national institutions ... becoming more and more involved in the whole system of departmental and voluntary associations of which the State consists'.[39] Politically, the Cabinet for the first time was regularly presented—even after 1920—with well-informed assessments of labour issues which could not but dispel earlier suspicions bred of ignorance. Labour's sectional interests were also championed. During the war, Roberts's memoranda had reiterated the justifiable causes of labour unrest and (despite later lapses) Horne in 1919 discharged 'his self-appointed function ... to see the government as the workers saw it and to spur his colleagues by unpleasant reminders of their own shortcomings'.[40] The enactment of the Restoration of Pre-War Practices Bill in 1919, despite the bitter hostility of those committed to higher productivity such as Lloyd George and Churchill, was a token of the Ministry's good faith; and even under the erratic leadership of Macnamara, the Ministry encouraged the Cabinet to provide a lead similar to that given during the signing of the Treasury Agreement in 1915. 'Just as at that time the Government tempered the play of economic forces,' the Ministry argued in 1921, 'so should they now appeal to employers not to exercise to the full the economic advantage which they possess by reason of the slump in trade.'[41]

The tenor of ministerial advice, however, did undoubtedly start to change in 1919 following the political disappointment of the first two ministers, official disillusion with the disunity and 'irresponsibility' of the trade unions, and the revival of Treasury control. The trend was completed by the winter of 1921, when Macnamara excised from a draft statement of industrial relations policy the observation that:

The trade unions believe that arbitration cannot deal with the fundamental problems of the structure of industry, and that to accept compulsory

---

[39] Lab 2/218/16.
[40] P. B. Johnson, *Land Fit for Heroes* (Chicago, 1968), p. 479.
[41] Cab 24/121/CP 2792.

arbitration would mean a recognition of the permanence of the existing system. These ideas are usually subconscious, though they are latent in the minds of even the most moderate trade unionists, and it would be unwise to neglect their existence or minimize their importance.[42]

After 1921, the sympathetic appreciation of such unspoken assumptions was minimized, so that, although well-reasoned memoranda continued to be submitted to Cabinet and the *Weekly Report* was partially revived in the shape of 'industrial memoranda', the added dimension of earlier advice was lost. Certainly the Labour movement was denied the positive discrimination which it had originally sought.[43]

The second of the Ministry's ideals to founder was industrial devolution, in particular the organization of industry into joint industrial (Whitley) councils. The object of this reform was to 'minimize the chances of friction and to maximize the opportunity for co-operation'[44] by the organization of each industry into a council which had a hierarchy of national, district, and works committees designed to fuse 'industrial interest' at the most appropriate level. It was an ideal initially advocated with a 'driving sense of conviction rather than a bureaucratic sense of duty' at all levels within the Ministry;[45] but the results were disproportionate to the energy expended. At their peak, there were only 106 councils and by 1939 the number had declined to 87 (65 in private industry and the rest in local and central government), covering some three million workers. No major industry had been affected.

The Whitley system, as the Ministry itself recognized at an early stage, was fatally flawed. It was the brainchild of a reconstruction committee, appointed in 1916 before the Ministry's establishment, about which both Butler and his chief lieutenant (the economist,

[42] Lab 2/921/7. Mounting disillusion within the Ministry was noted by a contemporary American observer, A. Gleason, *What the Workers Want* (1920), p. 21.

[43] As confirmation of the continuing anti-Labour bias in government, Askwith on leaving office founded a Middle-Class Union, while the chairman of the new Industrial Court (Lord Amulree), during a Ministry-sponsored mission to the USA in 1926, likened Bevin's enquiries on the shop-floor (rather than in the boardroom) to seeking information 'in the gutter'. See p. 37 of the unpublished memoirs of the secretary to the mission, Sir Harold Emmerson.

[44] Lab 2/218/16. The phrase was actually used in support of another attempt at positive reform, the 1917 Trade Union (Amalgamation) Act, designed to speed the transformation of Britain's 1,100 trade unions into larger, more efficient units. It again only enjoyed modest success. By 1939 there were still 1,019 unions.

[45] Charles, *Development of Industrial Relations*, p. 210.

Henry Clay) had initially expressed serious reservations. Indeed the Cabinet was warned by the Ministry that the whole reasoning of the Whitley Report rested on the unproven premiss that 'there is in each industry a common interest which needs a special organization to express itself and which will be strengthened by giving the opportunity to expression'.[46] Such reservations, however, were instantly swept aside when the Ministry of Reconstruction was established in the autumn of 1917 and threatened to assume total responsibility for industrial reconstruction. Whitleyism was embraced not just to save industry but also to save the Ministry.

Goal displacement alone, however, could not spirit away industrial obstacles to reform or resolve the compromises which had been purposely left because all the Report's signatories had realized that 'in order to preserve a precarious agreement, it was wise to avoid all precision'.[47] Foremost amongst the obstacles was the resistance of well-organized trades to the disruption of established procedures by model rules imposed from outside. Such resistance might have been overcome had national leaders given a positive lead, but this they declined to do. The TUC, which had refused to nominate representatives for the committee, was suspicious of the long-term effect which Whitleyism might have on trade union organization and was wary of so open an accommodation with capitalism. The employers, led by the Engineering Employers' Federation (EEF), whose secretary (Allan Smith) was on the committee, adopted their traditional stance of passive resistance, suspicious of any encroachment on managerial prerogatives and of so open a recognition of trade unions.[48] These reservations themselves were based on the four major areas of conflict on which the Report had deliberately remained silent: the conflicts between skilled and unskilled unions, shop stewards and trade union bureaucracies; the concepts of workers' control and workers' participation; and vested and national interest.

Local union resistance to Whitleyism was based on fears concerning the representation of specific groups of workers on the councils, in particular the apprehension of craft unions that semi-

[46] Lab 2/212/18 and 11; Lab 2/229/7. The Ministry speedily relented in Lab 2/212/16.

[47] E. Halévy, *The Era of Tyrannies* (1967), p. 110.

[48] Ministry conferences with the engineering industry throughout 1918 revealed the discouraging views of the EEF (Lab 2/816/9).

skilled unions and employers might combine to break their traditional, privileged position. This resistance was complicated by the
second conflict of interest, that between shop stewards and the
central bureaucracies of the trade unions, which centred on the role
of the projected works committee: was this, or the district committee, to be the future centre of authority? Shackleton, as a former
president of the TUC, fought hard and successfully for the supre-
macy of the district committees as the only answer to the 'crucial
question' of how trade union control could be preserved.[49] The
third conflict reflected the rival purposes to which trade unions and
employers might put the councils. During the First World War, the
Labour movement had become increasingly committed to the concept of workers' control (a share by Labour in the management of
industry), whereas progressive employers had embraced only the
concept of workers' participation (mutual co-operation to raise
productivity and an equitable distribution of the resultant profits).
If anything, the Whitley Report favoured the latter concept and
consequently became increasingly isolated from trade union aspirations. As the Ministry warned the Cabinet in 1919:

The situation has developed since the Whitley Report was written. The
Report provides machinery for enabling the workman to have some control over the conditions under which he shall work; that is to say, given
that so much has to be expended in aggregate, he has some control in how
it is to be expended; but in the matter of how much is to be allotted to
him, the position is left vague ... the assumption [being] that things in this
sphere will remain more or less as they are for the moment. But it is just
this question of 'how much' on which all the big organizations are concentrating.[50]

Even the limited ambitions of the Report, however, were not without controversy for, as the *New Statesman* pointed out, collusion
on the councils between employers and employed might raise prices
and thereby exploit the consumer. Roberts had to be regularly
restrained by his officials from promising councils too ready an

---

[49] Lab 2/254/12. Shackleton was not totally 'a lost soul'. His stand was determined not only by his suspicion of the revolutionary shop steward but also by the
fear that employers might use works committees, especially in a recession, to drive
a wedge between the work-force and professional union negotiators (who were not
so dependent on the employers' goodwill).

[50] Cab 24/81/GT 7420.

acceptance of their proposals, in case such promises jeopardized the 'public interest'.[51]

The Ministry's attempt to implement the Whitley Report was undermined by these conflicts and dogged by the passive resistance of industry, which emanated from the very suspicions which Whitleyism was intended to resolve. Its enthusiastic campaign continued for three years, employing considerable ingenuity to encourage industry to organize by means of either promises (that the councils would be the sole avenue of communication with the government) or threats (that more inflexible machinery, such as trade boards, would be imposed). Finally, the campaign was destroyed by political betrayal and retrenchment. The summoning of an NIC in February 1919 was a betrayal (not, as some observers believed, an affirmation) of Whitleyism because, of necessity, all leading trade-unionists attended and dominated the proceedings. The Ministry was thus no longer able to cajole industry into Whitleyism by the promise that the councils would be the sole avenue of communication with government. Soon afterwards, in November 1919, the campaign staff were subjected to internal scrutiny by the Finance Department, whose report epitomized Treasury attitudes to industrial reform. 'I can quite imagine that a well-equipped and adequate Joint Industrial Council branch may be a potent factor in averting a social revolution,' opined the inspector, 'on the other hand it is no less necessary that these results shall be attained with the utmost regard to economy. An industrial revolution may equally result from national extravagance.' The staff was cut and the Ministry's enthusiasm duly wilted.[52]

The failure of Whitleyism was part of a wider failure by the Ministry to pioneer change through industrial devolution in which two other experiments, the National Industrial Conference (NIC) and the International Labour Organization (ILO), were also involved. After the war, 'industrial parliaments', either to provide governments with expert advice or to promote industrial legislation, temporarily became fashionable throughout the industrialized

[51] Lab 2/454/1.

[52] Lab 2/1717/CEB 109/15/1920. Shrinkage, on the part of the Ministry, was reflected by its total lack of support of the movement's own 'industrial parliament', the Association of Joint Industrial Councils; on the part of the movement, by the failure of Whitleyism in Whitehall. The Treasury, having been forced to admit in 1919 that its powers of veto would have to be modified, then used Whitleyism to stall reform with all the finesse of a Dickensian circumlocution office. See Lab 10/67 and Citrine in Lab 10/56.

world.[53] In Britain, a conference of 600 trade-unionists and 300 employers was summoned in February 1919; it immediately elected a Provisional Joint Committee (PJC) which drafted a 26-point programme of reform. However, little permanent reform resulted, the Conference never met after April 1919, and the PJC resigned in July 1921. In the same month, the Government also defaulted on its first major commitment to the ILO (the ratification of the Washington Hours Convention). The ILO was largely the creation of the British delegation to the Paris Peace Conference—in particular of two Ministry officials (Butler and Phelan)—and its purpose, as a rival to the Communist Third International, was to demonstrate that industrial co-operation could flourish under capitalism. It provided also a unique opportunity for 'industrial responsibility' because the national representatives of employers and trade unions both had an independent vote on the Governing Body and at conferences. In 1919, however, the ILO suffered—in the eyes of the British government—the double calamity of the withdrawal of the USA and the appointment as director-general of a French socialist, Albert Thomas (with all the extravagant extremism which that, it was assumed, would guarantee). It survived, with Butler as first deputy-director and then director-general (1932–8), but its pioneering role was strictly limited.[54]

The Government in general and the Ministry in particular were blamed for the failure of both these experiments in devolution. G. D. H. Cole, the secretary to the trade union side of the PJC, accused Lloyd George of keeping 'the trade unions amused by vain discussions' until the threat of revolution had waned; and George Barnes, the first government representative at the ILO, likewise denounced the Ministry which 'as regards the Labour Office evaded all that it could evade and did only what it was forced to do by pressure and publicity'.[55] Unquestionably there were elements of

[53] A summary of international experiments was prepared for MacDonald in 1934 (PRO 30/69/1/359 (12)). For a full exposition of the evidence on which the following comments on the NIC are based, see R. Lowe, 'The failure of consensus in Britain: the National Industrial Conference, 1919–21', *Historical Journal*, 21 (1978), 649–75.

[54] The Treasury quibbled at the excessive cost of £30,000 p.a. to the British taxpayer but, more seriously, a bipartisan policy evolved after 1925 that the Organization's sole purpose should be to raise international standards of welfare and industrial practice to Britain's relatively high standard. See, in particular, Cab 27/272 and Cab 24/172/CP 198 (25).

[55] G. D. H. Cole and R. Postgate, *The Common People* (1938), p. 538; G. N. Barnes, *From Workshop to War Cabinet* (1923), p. 244.

duplicity in governmental attitudes, which will be examined later, but this duplicity was no more fatal to devolution than lack of industrial and international trust and the absence of common ground on which practical reform could be based. The reform programme of the PJC, for example, was largely hollow, for it had been agreed only by the shelving of major issues such as underconsumption (the trade unions' foremost explanation for unemployment) and productivity (the employers' foremost remedy); and, even when agreement was reached on specific issues such as hours of work, there were, as the Ministry discovered when trying to draft the requisite legislation, 'mental reservations' on both sides which in effect precluded their practical realization.[56] This hollowness reflected the reality of industrial politics. Smith (the employers' leader) was an acknowledged expert in the art of delaying unpopular decisions until the blame could be laid elsewhere, whilst Henderson (the leader of the trade union side of the PJC) for all his sincerity was unable to disguise either the gulf between the labourist and syndicalist wings of the Labour movement or the fact that major unions (including the Triple Alliance and the Amalgamated Society of Engineers) had disassociated themselves from the negotiations. The preconditions, in short, did not exist for industrial consensus.

The ILO, for its part, never attained its declared purpose of acquiring sufficient technical knowledge 'to draw up international labour standards in such detail as would enable them to be practically applied'.[57] Its conventions were often too inflexible to allow either implementation in Britain (as the TUC discovered in 1930 with the Washington Hours Convention) or widespread ratification abroad. The NCEO rapidly developed a formal antipathy towards ILO conferences, which they characterized as 'log-rolling competitions accompanied by the blowing off of sentimental steam'.[58]

In the actual working of the NIC and the ILO, therefore, industry displayed neither the consensus nor the readiness to act which Butler had declared to be the essential prerequisites of successful

---

[56] Lab 2/677/TB(Gen)106/10; Lab 2/821/13.

[57] The hope of practicality was expressed by E. J. Phelan, 'The peace conference: British preparations', in J. T. Shotwell (ed.), *The Origins of the International Labour Organisation*, vol. 1 (New York, 1934), p. 109 and disabused by Leggett in Lab 2/1389/IL 119/2/1922.

[58] Lithgow papers, 74 (address to the Imperial Conference, 1930).

devolution. Government, however, did little to remedy the situation and indeed, by its own duplicity, added to the atmosphere of distrust. After the autumn of 1919, its collaboration with the PJC was half-hearted and its enthusiasm for the ILO evaporated once Albert Thomas had adopted a policy of 'navigation rather than drift' in the search for 'social justice'.[59] Such Government negativism exposed a basic, political ambivalence towards devolution. In 1919, the Ministry's *Weekly Report* to Cabinet had advocated an industrial parliament as the means of ensuring expert examination of industrial legislation and of relieving parliament of onerous duties. Horne had also submitted draft legislation to the NCEO and TUC with a frequency which the latter was wistfully to recall when denied similar treatment by Labour governments. However, in September 1919 Horne himself effectively destroyed the NIC by declaring that it was 'impossible for the Government to surrender its freedom to any body of people however eminent'; and in 1920 the Government similarly resisted an attempt to give the ILO a measure of legislative initiative.[60] Industrial leaders, understandably, were not prepared to tolerate taunts of collaboration unless they were guaranteed in exchange a real share of political power.

Within the Ministry, the opinion of officials was divided over the devolution of power to the NIC and ILO. Some, like Wolfe, were committed supporters of international co-operation and industrial home rule and supported government policy only reluctantly on the grounds, earlier conceded by Butler, that government must always reserve its right to defend its particular concept of the national interest. However, others, less sympathetic to change, welcomed the collapse of Butler's more grandiose ideals. Shackleton, concerned for the independence of the TUC, welcomed the demise of the NIC. So too did Wilson, who admitted that he had felt the Ministry to be 'to some extent embarrassed' by such independent authorities.[61] Leggett was the most outspoken. His distaste for the

[59] E. J. Phelan, *Yes and Albert Thomas* (1949), pp. 242, 250.

[60] Cab 24/92/CP 25 and 68; Lab 10/1 (1924); Lab 2/556/13. The Home Office (in a rare moment of radicalism doubtlessly inspired by the formal loss of its pre-war responsibility for international labour negotiations) argued that the 'spirit' of the Peace Treaty demanded that draft conventions should be laid before parliament, for it and not the executive to decide upon ratification. The Ministry successfully opposed the suggestion (Lab 2/774/5).

[61] Lab 2/775/3 and 2; Lab 2/841/TB 165/5/1921. Later, Wilson described the NIC more graphically as an 'abortive futility' (see PRO 30/69/1/359(12)).

ILO was surpassed only by his contempt for the NIC. When its revival was canvassed by Macnamara in 1922, he was vehement in his opposition. First, he argued, national bodies only served to emphasize political differences whereas sectional discussions cemented mutual understanding. Secondly, the Labour movement was prone to use such opportunities to press for political objectives 'without the responsibility for any results which might follow' and to publicize the failures of reform, whilst ignoring its achievements. Thirdly, Treasury retrenchment precluded any really significant change in policy.[62] Under his influence, and that of Wilson, official opinion hardened against devolution with important consequences for policy in the 1930s, when conditions were again favourable to corporatist experiment.

The final and perhaps the most important failure of the Ministry to pioneer change concerned wages. There were three related issues: the establishment of a national minimum wage, the expansion of the pre-war system of trade boards, and the rationalization of wage settlements under free collective bargaining. A national minimum wage was a long-standing ideal which had been revived by the NIC. The Ministry opposed the idea, arguing that, as there could be no scientific definition of need applicable to the whole country, the level of the wage would be inevitably determined by political compromise. Were it to be low, little would have been gained at the cost of great inflexibility (especially for 'abnormal' groups such as part-time workers) and, possibly, of a reduction of wages (should the new minimum be interpreted as a 'standard' rate). Were it to be high, it would result either in unemployment or evasion. The Ministry consequently strove secretly to thwart the NIC, ignoring a Cabinet decision and censoring a draft letter from Lloyd George to the PJC which accepted the principle of a 'family wage'.[63]

The Ministry, led by Wolfe, was nevertheless positively committed to the raising of low wages. Its major wartime achievement had been the enactment of the Trade Boards (Amendment) Bill, which had both streamlined the pre-war procedure for the establishment of minimum wages in selected industries and extended the power

[62] Lab 2/775/3.
[63] Lab 2/934/TB 155/2/1925 part 13; Lloyd George papers, F 27/6/19. For a detailed examination of the Ministry's attitude towards wages policy, see R. Lowe, 'The erosion of state intervention in Britain, 1917-24', *Economic History Review*, xxxi (1978), 270-86.

of the Ministry, so that it could help all grades of workers in poorly organized industry (not simply the lowest paid workers in notoriously 'sweated' trades). The reform was originally intended to forestall a heavy fall in wages, especially amongst women, at the end of the war; but its implementation was greatly accelerated in November 1919 to pre-empt the findings of an anticipated royal commission on minimum wages. As Horne advised the Cabinet:

It is only by convincing the Commission that Trade Boards have found, and are finding, a fair solution to this problem on lines which adequately reward labour without endangering trade, that the risk can be avoided of a flat minimum wage having no relation to the ability of trade to bear the increase thus forced upon it. A flat minimum, fixed without regard to what trades could bear, might seriously cripple unfortunate sections of industry, or alternatively might involve the State in demands, difficult to resist, for subsidies in support of uneconomic wages.[64]

By December 1921, the number of boards had increased from the pre-war figure of 13 to 63 and the workers involved from 500,000 to 3 million. The peak of achievement, however, had been reached. With rising unemployment and falling prices, employers and public opinion turned against the boards. In March 1921, the Cabinet forbade further expansion and, in June, the Ministry (with the Cabinet's sanction) evaded its statutory responsibility to confirm minimum rates in the grocery trade.[65] A Committee, chaired by Lord Cave, was appointed to review the Trade Boards Acts and, although it recommended that the boards should be retained, it recommended also that they should revert to their limited pre-war purpose—the prevention of sweating. No amending legislation ensued, but the Ministry implemented the 'spirit' of the Cave Report through administrative discretion.[66] Only six new boards were created after 1921 and by 1939 the numbers of workers covered had declined to $1\frac{1}{4}$ million.

The abandonment of trade board expansion followed the failure of the Ministry's third initiative in wages policy, the rationalization of wage settlements under free collective bargaining. Officials had laid store by several expedients including sliding-scale agreements varying with the cost of living, the legal enforcement of negotiated

[64] Cab 24/93/CP 129.
[65] Lab 2/841/TB 227/5/1920; T 162/42/E 2811; Cab 26/3/HAC 91 (2).
[66] Lab 2/1029/TB 357/1924. The Cave report was Cmd. 1645, PP (1922), x.

agreements, and the development of a code of agreed principles by arbitration settlements under the Industrial Court. The first expedient did not long survive the steep fall in prices after 1920, so that by 1939 only 1½ million of the original 3 million workers were still covered. The second was rejected by the TUC in 1919, because the corollary was the suspension of strikes against arbitration awards. The third foundered owing to the Industrial Court's inability to determine a fixed set of principles on which to base awards and, later, the steep decline in the number of cases submitted to it.[67] The failure of the Industrial Court coincided with the increasing 'stoical realism' of Ministry officials. In March 1920, Wilson had not been above having an 'informal' discussion with the 'independent' chairman of the Court to encourage him to adopt 'the value of work done' rather than social need or industrial profitability (the two other most common bases for arbitration awards) as his guiding principle. This bore immediate dividends in the notorious Award 180 which, to the annoyance of the employers, forced the engineering industry to pay not a small wage increase based on the cost of living, but a larger one based on the price of the finished goods which (owing to buoyant demand) was high. Wilson's intervention, however, was not inspired by a desire to discriminate positively in favour of Labour (which stood to suffer once demand declined) or permanently to dictate wages, but rather to revert to the market mechanism in a time of rapid inflation. As the Ministry advised the Cabinet: 'In the long-run, the country will more quickly revert to a normal condition if "supply and demand" in regard to labour are allowed to operate freely than if an attempt is made by the State to regulate the one or the other.'[68] Even the Intelligence Division, in a brief which anticipated the disillusion of planners after the Second World War, was forced reluctantly to admit that 'the Industrial Court cannot apply principles of justice to what is in effect a conflict of forces'.[69]

The Ministry's failure to devise a positive wages policy and, in particular, the collapse of its trade board policy illustrated the full range of external constraints and internal weaknesses which broke

[67] PEP, *British Trade Unionism* (1948), p. 75; Lab 2/689/9; Lab 2/758/19. See also Appendix 2, B.

[68] Cab 24/105/CP 1232; Wilson's informal chat was incidentally recorded in Lab 2/696/15.

[69] PEP, *British Trade Unionism*, p. 70; Lab 2/758/18.

the Ministry as a pioneer of change. The external constraints were four: Britain's cultural resistance to bureaucracy, employer hostility and trade union ambivalence towards state intervention, Treasury retrenchment, and political vacillation. In the case of trade boards, public opinion, as represented by parliament, the press, and the courts, was hostile to the Ministry because of both the ease with which the boards were erected by bureaucratic fiat and the (incorrect) identification of the board's insensitivity to local and cyclical wage-variations as a major cause of unemployment. The NCEO attacked the boards' independent members (appointed by government to represent the public) for a bias towards Labour and, after 1920, the boards' alleged encouragement of high wages; even after the Cave Report, it continued to seek the system's abolition.[70] The TUC, for its part, failed to support unreservedly a system of which it approved in principle, partly because it feared it would weaken union organization and partly because expansion had led to a bureaucratic anonymity which pre-war pioneers resented. It consequently became the NCEO's dupe when, in accordance with the policy of 'home rule for industry', a joint demand was made for the translation of policy-making powers from the Ministry to an independent Trade Boards Advisory Committee—a demand which the NCEO privately boasted was the first step in its abolition campaign.[71] Government discouragement took the form (as has been seen) of the Treasury's use of its establishment powers to arrest trade board expansion and the Cabinet's condoning of such action. Even more ingloriously, the Cabinet also reneged on its statutory obligation to the Grocery Trade Board.

The Grocery Board was, admittedly, not the most likely venue for a major political dispute; but it rose briefly to prominence in 1921 because, as the first incursion into the retail trade (where both the workers' need for and employers' resistance to minimum wages were at their greatest), it provided an acid test of the Government's integrity. In the fixing of its wage-rates, deadlock was reached between the employers' and workers' representatives and so the final decision rested (as was the intention of the Trade Boards Act) with the board's independent members. They sided with the union. The agreed rates were duly forwarded to the Ministry which, at the employers' prompting, referred them back (as was its right). After

[70] NCEO papers, NCO 86; Lab 2/935/TB 155/2/1925 part 18.
[71] Lab 2/841/TB 165/7/1921. For government discouragement, see above, pp. 60-1.

further discussion, the board resubmitted identical rates which the Ministry then refused to confirm (as was its statutory duty), on the grounds that economic conditions were too volatile for the determination of fixed wage-rates. Instead the dispute was submitted to Cabinet by Macnamara who, having been urged by Wolfe to 'choose the course ... which is right in principle', clearly wished to do otherwise. The Cabinet supported him.[72]

Faced with so comprehensive a range of external constraints, the Ministry's pioneering role was further compromised by three major internal weaknesses. The first was administrative incompetence. Trade boards, for instance, were not expanded with sufficient rapidity to realize their original objective (the maintenance of wages during demobilization) and, when they were expanded in 1919 for a very different reason, the Ministry antagonized the Treasury (by exhausting its grant without establishing the promised number of boards), employers (by insufficient investigation and definition of industries), and unions (by insufficient inspection and enforcement of minimum rates). As was admitted in 1924, the Ministry had laid itself open to 'serious and deserved criticism' and had done nothing to allay popular hostility towards bureaucracy.[73]

Secondly, the abandonment of trade board expansion together with the dispute over the basis of Industrial Court awards reflected a critical division of opinion between officials over economic principle. The rival philosophies were most forcefully represented by Hilton (as head of the Statistics Department) and Wilson (as permanent secretary).[74] Hilton fought for the retention of the cost of living as a major 'element in wage determination' on the grounds that it provided for a greater equality in wage-bargaining and hence social justice. On the issue of the trade boards, he rejected the economic assumptions underlying the Treasury view, arguing (in accordance with the formal trade union submission to the NIC) that unemployment was essentially the result not of high costs but of underconsumption: abolition of the boards, therefore, could not cure but would actually aggravate unemployment by depressing wages and thus the home market from which, given the state of international markets and credit, British industry could alone expect sufficient increased demand to stimulate production. Wilson, in contrast, was disillusioned with wartime wage regulation and

[72] Lab 2/831/TBD 100/A/43.   [73] Lab 2/1038/TB 145/1924.
[74] The battle was joined in Lab 2/758/2 and 831/TB 102/7/1921.

sought an immediate return to the determination of wages by market forces. He also fully accepted the Treasury view. Thus, in contrast to Hilton's anger, his response to the formal Treasury letter demanding economies in trade board administration was:

It was not easy to see the reply to the suggestion that, for the time being, particularly having regard to the financial position, no fresh trades should be dealt with and the outstanding investigations ... should be left over and the whole scheme proceeded with in a more leisurely manner.

Since it was Wilson's views that prevailed, the Ministry's pioneering role duly contracted.

The third internal weakness was a gradual decline in the personal commitment of officials to reconstruction. Two incidents illustrate this decline. First, as J. J. Mallon (a friend of Hilton and the leading Labour expert on trade boards) angrily perceived in 1920 when, at the prompting of employers, the Wages (Temporary Regulation) Act—the last vestige of wage control—was repealed, the policy of industrial devolution could become the perfect excuse for ministerial prevarication. Officers insisted that the Act had to be repealed as they could not intervene in industry without the consent of both sides, to which Mallon tartly retorted:

Though the consent of the employers ought to be sought, yet I think the policy of the Ministry ought not to depend on whether the consent is given or not. The Ministry have a policy, and it is their duty, if the rates of wages are threatened with serious collapse, to take appropriate action.[75]

Secondly, as revealed by a dispute during the preparation of evidence for the Cave Commission, there could be significant differences of opinion over the exact time at which industrial devolution (carefully monitored) should be abandoned in favour of state intervention (to maintain standards and to safeguard the national interest). Shackleton argued that the Ministry should merely be a neutral registrar of trade boards' decisions, whereas Wolfe, mindful of the Grocery Board's fate, maintained that the Ministry could not absolve itself from all responsibility for wage-rates and should therefore become openly a court of appeal. As he argued:

The objection to this course is that it appears to involve bureaucratic interference with trade. The answer to this criticism is that it is always possible for enemies to describe the whole Trade Board system in this

[75] Lab 2/647/2. Mallon wished to retain the Act to safeguard women's wages.

terminology ... The simple truth is that Trade Board policy involves an Act of Government; that Acts of Government can only be performed by and through Ministers and that any attempt to evade that obligation is in effect an attempt to get away from the principle of the Trade Boards Acts.[76]

Wolfe was defeated, although the logic of Shackleton's position was that the Ministry itself was a 'bureaucratic interference with trade' and so—as in fact the NCEO wished—ought to have been abolished.

Between 1916 and 1922, therefore, the attempt by the Ministry to force the pace of industrial change was defeated. From the start, it had been bedevilled by internal inconsistencies and, especially after the economic collapse of 1920, a host of factors without and within the Ministry did little to assist their resolution. After the secondment of Butler to the ILO in 1919, individual officials such as Hilton and Wolfe fought for the retention of the Ministry's pioneering role, but they were overruled by more senior officials such as Wilson and Shackleton (who, consciously or unconsciously, assisted the Treasury in imposing greater orthodoxy on the civil service) and by successive ministers (who thus exposed the essential conservatism of the Lloyd George coalition).

Minimizing Dissent, 1922-1930

Throughout the rest of the 1920s the Ministry was, superficially at least, on the defensive. In 1922 the Geddes Committee challenged the very principle of state intervention in industrial relations (and indeed the continuing existence of the Ministry), whilst the Trade Disputes and Trade Unions Act of 1927 gave vent, in the aftermath of the General Strike, to the anti-union bias latent within the industrial and political establishment. The Geddes proposals, however, were quickly dismissed as politically naïve by the Cabinet and the industrial clauses of the Trade Disputes Act were of little more than symbolic importance.[77] Other developments favoured the Ministry. Industrially, as has been seen, there was an underlying trend towards conciliation. Politically, the election of two Labour Governments hastened acceptance of the implications of the 1918

---

[76] Lab 2/935/TB 252/1925.

[77] Cab 27/165/GRC(CSD), 2nd conclusion. A. Anderson, 'Political symbolism of the labour laws' and 'The labour laws and the Cabinet Legislative Committee of 1926-7', *Bulletin of the Society for the Study of Labour History*, 23 (1971), 14-15 and 39-52.

Reform Bill and, in Barlow and Steel-Maitland, the Ministry enjoyed two Conservative ministers who (unlike Horne) sought a
genuine *rapprochement* with Labour. In the late 1920s, moreover,
Baldwin's instinct for conciliation was matched by the TUC's 'new
direction', whilst NCEO intransigence was challenged at the
Mond–Turner talks. The 1920s were, therefore, a period of fluc-
tuating fortunes for the Ministry; and throughout it was dominated
by its permanent secretary, Horace Wilson.

During the war, as secretary of the Whitley Committee and of
the Committee on Production (the central arbitration tribunal),
Wilson had developed extensive contacts throughout industry and
was consequently sensitive to its jealous independence and to the
dangers of state intervention. Nevertheless, he had been convinced
by the anarchy of wartime industrial relations that the state could
not absolve itself of all responsibility. The Ministry itself had been
a symbol of wartime weakness, unwilling to wrest from production
departments responsibility for day-to-day negotiations and unable
to impose upon them an overall strategy as envisaged by the Cabinet's Barnes–Milner memorandum of 1917. As a result, government (as the final paymaster) had been at the mercy of collusion
between employers and employed, conflicting awards had intensified unrest, and the Cabinet had been inundated by labour problems with which it was incompetent to deal.[78] In 1919, Wilson
attempted to remedy the situation by drafting the Industrial Courts
Act, which established Britain's first permanent arbitration tribunal
(in the vain hope, as has been seen, of securing an 'agreed and
rational' wages policy) and also empowered the Ministry to establish courts of inquiry (to fulfill Askwith's long-standing desire to
mobilize public opinion in national disputes). However, in the end,
the Industrial Courts Act was significant more for what it excluded
than what it included. At the TUC's request, the Court's power to
compel the attendance of witnesses was dropped, the Ministry undertook not to intervene until all voluntary procedures had been
exhausted, and the permissive power to legalize voluntary agreements was withdrawn.[79] Accordingly, its power to promote reform
was extremely limited.

[78] For a fuller discussion of the Ministry's wartime antics, see Lowe in Burk,
War and the State, pp. 111–19.

[79] The most revealing papers on the drafting of the Industrial Courts Act are
Lab 10/64 and Lab 2/689/9. Both sides of industry were equally conservative in the

In framing a permanent peacetime policy, Wilson had, as a result of this débâcle, little faith in legislation; but simultaneously he resisted Treasury and NCEO demands for total non-intervention. He agreed with Leggett that the cost of industrial relations staff was not wasteful but 'productive expenditure' since its purpose was the 'conservation of national wealth';[80] 'the greatest economy to the nation', both asserted, was not marginal staff cuts but 'the avoidance of industrial disputes and the consequent loss of production and efficiency'. Moreover, non-intervention was a 'hypothetical laissez-faire doctrine' since all governménts, as trustees for the community, had to intervene in disputes in which 'the public may suffer more severely than the disputants and where public opinion may profoundly affect the course and result'. Hence the abolition of an expert conciliation staff would be the 'reverse of economy' because the only alternative was (as under Lloyd George) 'the most wasteful and mischievous form of intervention, namely intervention decided upon ... hurriedly in response to public clamour'. But what was this permanent conciliation staff actually to do? Initially Wilson had stressed its active defence of the 'public interest', but in time he characteristically trimmed his beliefs to political necessity. 'The efficacy of the State's action', he had concluded by 1922, 'depends very largely upon the care with which the responsible Department ordinarily refrains from active intervention.' Accordingly, officials were directed to

strive to the utmost to avoid active intervention while at the same time maintaining just sufficient contact with the progress of affairs to let those in authority know, as and when necessary, what is happening or is likely to happen by way of industrial conflict ... to be acquainted with matters of importance without anyone concerned knowing that they are acquainted.

Overtly, it was hardly a heroic role for the Ministry.

use of the Wages (Temporary Regulation) Act of 1918–20. Designed to provide a breathing-space in which voluntary understandings might be renegotiated after war-time disruption, they were used merely as an excuse for inaction.

[80] This paragraph is based on the preparation and presentation of the Ministry's evidence in relation to the Geddes Committee (Lab 2/1822/CEB 461/2/1922 and Cab 27/167/E(Labour)2) and the file in which the principles of inter-war policy were permanently settled (Lab 2/921/7). Additional material comes from the following Lab 2 files: 978/TB 213/6/1923, 1779/MHEstab.1012/2/1918 and 933/21. Courts of Inquiry were the one formal initiative the Ministry had in the conduct of industrial relations and it was used increasingly sparingly except under the first Labour Government. See Appendix 2, B.

The Ministry's heroics in the 1920s were in fact reserved for a covert battle to defend trade-unionism against attack from employers' organizations and the right wing of the Conservative Party; and the measure of its success was, rather perversely, the 1927 Trade Disputes and Trade Unions Act. After the General Strike, the Ministry had initially been opposed to all legislation, especially legislation designed to 'punish' trade unions, and so the Act can hardly be described as an unqualified success. It duly outlawed sympathetic strikes designed to coerce government, strengthened the law on picketing, threatened Labour Party income by obliging trade-unionists to contract in rather than out of the political levy, and forbade the affiliation of central and local government workers to the TUC. More draconian measures, however, were successfully resisted. Criminal law was not substituted for civil law in industrial relations (as demanded by the Lord Chancellor); the 1906 Trade Disputes Act was not repealed nor the 1875 Conspiracy Act extended (as requested by the employers); and neither strike ballots nor arbitration were made compulsory (as demanded by Conservative Party Central Office). The Act, indeed, 'failed to satisfy the employers on most important issues and was the very minimum that was acceptable to the Conservative Party after the General Strike'.[81] In the defeat of these more vindictive demands, Horace Wilson played a crucial part thwarting, for example, Neville Chamberlain's pet scheme of compulsory arbitration.[82] Considerable political courage was also displayed by Steel-Maitland. In October 1926, he sought to steel Baldwin's resolve by warning him privately that 'responsible trade-unionists may at this moment still believe in the Prime Minister. But I know they are suspicious if not of him yet of some reactionary "hidden hand" or other that may overbear him.... The most fatal fault for a party is not to stand up to its own extremists.' A month later he openly ridiculed the Cabinet's 'self-delusion' that, in drafting new legislation, it was acting to defend individual freedom and would accordingly win the support of rank and file trade-unionists. 'The policy of the Conservative Party', he argued, 'should be in substance, and not merely in profession, constructive.' In the detailed drafting of the Act he also swept aside, with all the confidence of a past chairman of the

---

[81] Anderson, *Bulletin of Labour History*, 15 and 39.
[82] Neville Chamberlain papers, NC 2/22, 25 Mar. 1927.

Party, the evidence of constituency associations on the grounds that 'if Central Office had undertaken a proper enquiry very different conclusions might have been reached'.[83]

The Ministry's determined opposition to the reform of industrial relations law was based on three main premisses: the impracticality of specific suggestions, the irrelevance of legal sanctions against a large body of aggrieved men, and the self-defeating nature of any measure that undermined 'responsible' free collective bargaining. These arguments were most clearly expressed in opposition to two reforms designed to delay strikes and thus provide a 'cooling-off' period in which the strikes might be settled: compulsory strike ballots and compulsory arbitration (along the lines of the Canadian Lemieux Act).[84] First, as the agency which would have to implement the reforms, the Ministry raised such practical questions as how small a vote would have to be before a ballot became unrepresentative. Secondly, mindful of the fate of the 1915 Munitions of War Act and the relative failure of international strike legislation (including the Lemieux Act, which, between 1917 and 1924, was invoked in only 30 per cent of relevant cases), it rejected demands for compulsory arbitration on the grounds, reminiscent of Leggett's attack on the ILO, that it was 'repugnant to British ideas and legislation to place upon the statute book enactments which it is not seriously intended to enforce'. Governments, it argued, would not enforce the law because, aware that the right to strike was ultimately determined not by law but by the action of the rank and file, they dared not risk mass non-compliance. Finally, the Ministry rejected compulsory arbitration because it would make a mockery of free collective bargaining (as both sides would jockey for position rather than seek genuine agreements) and secret ballots (because they would undermine industrial leadership). Rather than standing up to their extremists, trade union leaders would be encouraged by a ballot to follow a 'new line of least resistance' and would then find themselves in the position not of leaders but of delegates, bound by the 'embarrassment of a written

[83] Baldwin papers, vol. 2, fol. 51; Cab 24/182/CP 394(26); Cab 27/326/L(26)7.

[84] The clearest exposition of the Ministry's views are in the memoranda to the Cabinet's Legislative Committee of 1926–7 (Cab 27/327). Earlier rejection of Askwith's proposals and of secret ballots are in Lab 2/880/9 and 921/7. In the 1926 memoranda there was some dispute between Steel-Maitland and his officials over whether, respectively, it was just local leaders or the whole membership that were more extreme than the national leadership.

vote ... cast without full appreciation of the facts'. Secret ballots
would thus encourage rather than discourage strikes, especially as,
in the opinion of officials if not Conservative politicians, the rank
and file or at least the local shop steward (who had his name to
make and was unaware of the wider, national issues) was more
militant than the national leaders.

The obvious weakness of the Ministry's determined opposition
to detailed legislative change, let alone the wholesale revision of
industrial relations law, was, as Neville Chamberlain (amongst
others) quickly pointed out, its negativism.[85] The one legislative
reform the Ministry championed after the General Strike was the
restriction of legal immunities to registered trade unions, a move
designed to improve long-term industrial relations both by enabling
the Registrar of Friendly Societies to impose minimum rules of
conduct and by encouraging unions to appoint more efficient local
officials. The Cabinet, however, quickly dropped the proposal for
fear of being seen to infringe union autonomy. Consequently the
Ministry, when faced with such pressing issues as the need to
protect the public interest in national disputes or the rights of
individual workers, had few positive suggestions to make. In 1924
Askwith (himself a zealot for the defence of the 'public interest'
by a 'neutral' civil service) accused the Ministry of having 'forgotten
the public'; and the charge seemed fully justified when such claims
were made, as by Steel-Maitland in his rejection of compulsory
arbitration, that 'it is all very well to say that the public are the
biggest sufferers and most need protection, but neither the public
nor even the House of Commons can judge as well as industry how
the thing will work'.[86] Government action was even rejected by
Ministry officials as the means of fulfilling Baldwin's pledge that
no worker should be victimized by his union for having stayed at
work during the General Strike; their alternative policy was that
non-strikers should pay the requisite union fine and then exhaust
the union's own appeals machinery. The overt justification for this
policy was that it would least harm the worker's relationship with
his fellows. The suspicion remains, however, that in this, as in most
other instances, the Ministry opposed legislative change not simply

[85] See Cab 27/326/11, 31 Jan. 1927: 'If the only alternative to acceptance of his
proposals was to do nothing, he would prefer to give his proposals a trial.'

[86] *Parl. Deb.* (Lords), 1924, 57, col. 188; Cab 24/186/CP 101(27), 22 Mar. 1927.
Victimization policy was discussed in Lab 2/1206/24.

on merit but because 'provocative action' might have compromised departmental neutrality and the minister's position as the conciliator of last resort.[87]

The Ministry's 'weakness' extended to its role as a conciliator and especially to its conduct during and after the General Strike, when both Steel-Maitland and Wilson became national figures. Steel-Maitland was (with Baldwin and Birkenhead) one of the 'big three' during the negotiations of April 1926, a focus for peace moves during the Strike, and thereafter a leading figure in the search for a settlement to the coal dispute. Wilson, too, was an important intermediary in successive negotiations and the acknowledged expert on the nuances in every communication. He drafted, for instance, the formula designed to call off the Strike on 1 May, advised the Cabinet that the *Daily Mail* incident provided a pretext for its withdrawal, drafted Baldwin's 'man of peace' broadcast of 8 May, and finally opened the door to the TUC deputation when it surrendered unconditionally to the Prime Minister.[88] The Ministry also supplied the Cabinet with realistic if unwelcome information, stressing, during the Strike, that (whilst not revolutionary) the workers were uninfluenced by government propaganda about unconstitutional behaviour and, afterwards, that (although exhausted) the trade unions were neither demoralized nor repentant. The Ministry's importance, however, was not as great as its strategic position permitted. Before the Strike, it failed to use both its extensive contacts within industry to build up trust and its expert knowledge to guide the Government to a 'more enterprising or Machiavellian' policy which, even if it could not have weakened the miners' resolve to commit *hara-kiri*, might at least have prevented the TUC from joining the pact. Afterwards, in the attempted settlement of the miners' dispute, its representatives epitomized the classic Conservative dilemma of an 'intellectual recognition of the need for change versus the emotional aversion to implementing it'.[89]

The explanation of the Ministry's ineffectuality is partly political

[87] For the protests of Barlow, see above, p. 39; of Shaw, Cab 24/173/CP 222(24); and of Steel-Maitland, Baldwin's papers, vol. 2, fol. 89. The Ministry was not even represented on the Cabinet committee appointed by the second Labour Government to draft the repeal of the 1927 Act.

[88] Jones, *Whitehall Diary*, vol. 2, pp. 24–53. For the Ministry's intelligence during and after the Strike, see Cab 27/261, Cab 24/184/CP 28(27) and Lab 10/5.

[89] Phillips, *General Strike*, pp. 127, 131.

and partly strategic. Politically, the Ministry was dependent on
Baldwin who, as a negotiator, was not as incisive as either the
situation or Wilson demanded. More particularly, Steel-Maitland
lacked the essential qualities of leadership to capitalize on official
expertise. He was replaced by Churchill as the Government's
leading parliamentary spokesman during the Strike and as the chief
negotiator with the mining industry thereafter; he was thus reduced
to a supporting role which was valued largely because his car, club,
house, and wealth were ever at the Government's disposal. Strateg-
ically, the Ministry—like most of the other participants—lacked
consistent short- and long-term policies for the mining industry. In
the short term, the economic and psychological need for a fair and
lasting settlement was realized; hence the miners were urged to
make concessions over pay or hours, and the owners to accept
some form of national agreement. The dilemma was over the role
of government. 'The general principle of action', Steel-Maitland
wrote to Baldwin, 'should be to let the miners weaken as far as
possible ... and then at the last moment deal firmly with the owners', by either withdrawing the Eight Hours Act or (in the spirit of
1918–19) threatening the imposition of a trade board.[90] In the
event, however, he shied away from coercing the owners. In the
long term, the Ministry argued, government should neither under-
write a settlement by a temporary subsidy nor assume coercive
powers (as recommended by some progressive employers and
adopted in 1919 on the railways) to force rationalization. Government, in other words, 'should get out of the position of controlling
the industry and as far as possible work to the position that on any
future occasion it should not be so predominantly involved as a
mediator'. After years of decline and bitterness in the mining industry, the trouble with such a policy was that it held out little
hope of success. Churchill indeed was as scathing of the Ministry
as a conciliator as Chamberlain had been of it as a legislator:
'without active government help involving serious risk and labour,'
he warned, 'no progress will be made.'[91]

[90] Steel-Maitland's views are best expressed in two letters to Baldwin in Aug.
and Sept. 1926 (Baldwin papers, vol. 15, fol. 296 and Steel-Maitland papers, GD
193/94/2); his waverings in Jones, *Whitehall Diary*, vol. 2, pp. 89–90.
[91] Jones, *Whitehall Diary*, vol. 2, p. 75. The Ministry's knowledge of the industry
was admittedly limited since the Mines Department of the Board of Trade had
prime responsibility even for its industrial relations.

As both a conciliator and a legislator, however, the Ministry was by no means as negative as it sometimes appeared. It did have a positive policy (even if it lacked the drama of the solutions proposed by Askwith, Churchill, and Chamberlain) and, after 1926, it did not lack the determination both to foster industrial co-operation and to seek remedies for the fundamental economic and social causes of unrest. The Ministry rejected the bland assumption that legislation or government fiat could secure industrial progress. New laws, it argued, could not create a new will, nor could new machinery guarantee co-operation. Legislative panaceas such as compulsory arbitration had been tried during the war and failed; improvements to free collective bargaining had been attempted in the Industrial Courts Act and had been equally unsuccessful. Genuine progress, therefore, could be achieved only by a new spirit on the shop-floor; and this could be attained only by forcing both sides of industry to recognize or resolve their own problems.[92]

After the General Strike, the Ministry encouraged industrial co-operation with renewed vigour. It quickly recognized the structural weakness of British industry and sought, as later chapters will show, to remedy its economic causes (through industrial transference and training). Steel-Maitland, until his physical collapse in 1928, was also exceptionally active behind the scenes helping to inspire the Mond-Turner talks. Immediately after the General Strike, an industrial mission (including Bevin) was dispatched to the USA to prove that industrial co-operation and not wage-reductions was the remedy for depression; and Lord Weir was provided with an agenda for the House of Lords speech of 14 December 1926 in which he called for a meeting of 'a few men capable of concentrating on the industrial necessities of the time, apart entirely from political considerations'.[93] Discussions between the interested parties were interrupted by the parliamentary passage of the Trade Disputes Bill but, after its enactment, Steel-Maitland urged their

[92] It was for these reasons that the Ministry (to the surprise of many) had opposed the coal subsidy in 1925 and had welcomed an 'educative' confrontation between miners and owners. See Neville Chamberlain papers, NC 2/22, Aug. 1925.

[93] Weir papers, 4/14/6; Steel-Maitland papers, GD 193/9412. Characteristically Steel-Maitland promised in his letter to Weir to make three points and then made two. For detailed evidence, see especially G. W. McDonald and H.F. Gospel, 'The Mond-Turner talks, 1927-33: a study in industrial co-operation', *Historical Journal*, 16 (1973), 807-29.

immediate resumption. Hicks's presidential address to the TUC
followed, with its call for effective co-operation with the employers,
and, in response, Sir Alfred Mond formed his group of progressive
employers. The resultant Mond-Turner talks were closely monitored by the Ministry, especially in January 1928 when each leading
employer was privately interviewed and encouraged; and their progress was the Ministry's justification for its rejection of more
glamorous but insubstantial policy-initiatives such as the renewal of
the NIC (as demanded by Arthur Henderson and the Liberal Party)
and co-partnership and profit-sharing (as advocated by moderates
within the Conservative Party).

The Ministry's association with the Mond–Turner talks was significant for three reasons. First, it revealed Steel-Maitland's irresolution for, having prostrated himself in the arrangement of the
talks, he then panicked at their reality. He became terrified (no
doubt at Allan Smith's instigation) that naïve industrialists would
be ensnared by wily trade-unionists and make impractical commitments which the NCEO's seasoned negotiators would then, to the
permanent souring of industrial relations, have immediately to dis-
own. Secondly, as the increasing discomfort of the Minister's principal private secretary (Tribe) suggested, a rift opened between
ministerial and official policy. Steel-Maitland—albeit reluctantly—
wanted, like Butler before him, to hasten the pace of industrial
co-operation. As he wrote to Baldwin in September 1926:

We have reached a stage at which it is possible for a concordat to be
reached between the two sides in industry. But the initiative will not come
from within. If only it would so come, it would be a much healthier
development. The more that the alignment of political parties is economic
the more suspect the intervention of politicians in an industrial question.
But failing initiative from within, there should be an attempt from without
and it is probably only the Government that can make the endeavour.[94]

He also wished to use economic concessions, such as safeguarding
legislation, to force industry to accept improved negotiating procedures. Horace Wilson, as his political adviser, cautiously supported this policy, but Leggett, as a practising conciliator, deferred.
He acknowledged that the Mond–Turner talks could not be
actively discouraged because their spontaneity conformed to the

[94] Baldwin papers, vol. 11, fol. 49; for Tribe's tribulations, see Steel-Maitland
papers, GD 193/94/2.

Ministry's policy of 'home rule for industry'; but he doubted their success and openly opposed any legislative initiative. As he warned Steel-Maitland in 1928:

It is difficult to have faith in any other course than the building up of organization and knowledge and goodwill. Others may see quicker methods of reforming industrial relations but ... [we] cannot afford to adopt such devices. The facts are very stubborn because they concern human beings in an individualistic world.[95]

Finally, the Mond–Turner talks were significant because their ultimate failure disappointed the cautious optimism of Steel-Maitland and Wilson whilst justifying Leggett's greater pessimism. Although an interim report was published, advocating (amongst other things) trade union recognition, the establishment of an NIC, and co-operation over industrial rationalization, its implementation was assigned in 1929 to new tripartite talks between the FBI, NCEO, and TUC. These talks were barren, although extreme views on both sides of industry were modified and the NCEO was brought—if fleetingly—round a table with the TUC.

The suspicion remains that more could have been achieved through the Mond–Turner talks, especially had the Conservative Government threatened more convincingly to legislate in the event of industry failing to put its own house in order.[96] Similar suspicion surrounds the whole of the Ministry's policy in the 1920s. Under Wilson's stewardship, the worst excesses of reaction were averted and the ground prepared for cautious progress, but were all the opportunities for improvement to industrial practice and conditions seized? During the Geddes Committee, the Ministry's foremost justification of its existence had been the defence of the public interest. How far was it, in fact, actively defended? If inaction could be excused, as on occasion it was, by the maxim that 'you cannot pass ultimately effective legislation which is in advance of the spirit of your people', were 'the people'—as opposed to the vested interests of the NCEO and the TUC—ever actually consulted? Did officials sufficiently recognize and stress to ministers the dangers of legislative

[95] PRO 30/69/1/359(12), appendix II; Steel-Maitland papers, GD 193/319.

[96] The chances of success were not exactly enhanced by economic recession and a general election; on the other hand, employers seemed set in their opposition. Even Mond himself was suspected of having no intention of applying the Interim Report to ICI, and major organizations, such as the EEF, threatened secession from the NCEO if even the bland commitment to union recognition was endorsed.

inaction as well as legislative action? After the defeat of Butler's reconstruction idealism, Wilson's policy of 'positive voluntaryism' had, of necessity, to be finely balanced.[97] It depended for its success on the building-up of co-operation from below and the correct judgement of the precise moment at which to apply moral and legislative pressure; it was constrained, moreover, by lack both of resources (owing to Wilson's early surrender to the Treasury) and of room for manoeuvre (owing to the Ministry's early encouragement of the NCEO). Wilson failed to find the correct balance but, in his defence, it must be admitted that more than just administrative expertise was needed. Political leadership of the highest quality was also required and this neither Baldwin nor Steel-Maitland was able to provide.

Stoical Realism, 1930–1939

The 1930s were the apogee of the Ministry's policy of 'divide and conciliate'. The quality of ministerial and Cabinet leadership precluded bold political initiative and simultaneously left the formation of policy to officials who, after the appointment of Wilson as the Government's chief industrial adviser in 1930, were headed by Leggett. Leggett, as has been seen, had long been the leading opponent of ambitions experiments, such as the NIC and ILO, and was zealously committed to a policy of developing slowly within each industry mutual understanding and responsibility. Hence, although central government grew economically more influential (through its increasing management of the economy and rearmament), the Ministry discouraged the use of its power both as a legislator and an employer to pioneer change; and, as both sides of industry became more amenable to pressure (through the 'new direction' of the TUC and increasing disarray of the NCEO), it also discouraged corporatist experiment. A corollary of this policy, as this section will faithfully demonstrate, was to make the activities of the Ministry exceedingly dull.

The depression of the early 1930s saw one potentially revolutionary development which, with a due regard for the dramatic, was entitled the Cotton Manufacturing (Temporary Provisions) Act of 1934. The cotton industry epitomized the structural defects of inter-war staple industries, and both Wilson and Leggett had

[97] *Parl. Deb.*, 1919, 120, col. 1713. The term 'positive voluntaryism' was coined by Roger Davidson, 'Social conflict and social administration', in T. C. Smout (ed.), *The Search for Stability and Wealth* (1979), p. 194.

been heavily involved in its problems since 1929. When Wilson left the Ministry to concentrate further on the industry's economic restructuring, Leggett assumed responsibility for the resolution of its immediate labour problems and achieved a major breakthrough with the signing of the Midlands Agreement of 1932, by which both the weaving and spinning sections of the industry agreed to modernize their bargaining procedures by the establishment of new joint conciliation committees. Because of the legacy of distrust and uncertainty bequeathed by earlier conflicts, however, the weaving committee was unable to make any significant progress. Individual employers, faced with bankruptcy, in desperation continued to break agreements on production, prices, and wages and neither the employers' association nor the Weavers' Amalgamation was able to bring them to heel. The consequences were serious: a general disillusion with written agreements, organizational chaos (as both employers and workers deserted their respective associations), an intensification of the industry's financial plight (as falling wages and prices failed to increase the volume of production) and rising social unrest. In order to halt this vicious spiral, both sides of industry requested from government the power to make their collective agreements legally binding.

This request reopened a debate that was as old as the concept of the Ministry of Labour itself.[98] The legalization of voluntary agreements had been under regular consideration since the 1891-4 Royal Commission on Labour and had been endorsed by the Industrial Council in 1913, the NIC in 1919, and the Balfour Committee on Industry and Trade in the 1920s. Throughout the 1920s, there had also been repeated parliamentary demands for the granting of legislative powers to Whitley councils, to prevent their undercutting by non-federated firms. But since the TUC and NCEO normally opposed such demands, so too did the Ministry. Officials accepted that the reform would assist 'good' employers and help to rationalize industrial relations; but they doubted both the practicality and ultimate desirability of legislation. It would, they argued, be extremely difficult to define the scope of industries covered by agreements, let alone to impose penalities on the recalcitrant. In the longer term it was feared that government might supersede industrial self-discipline as the guarantor of agreements and that

---

[98] The fullest history of the debate on the statutory enforcement of collective agreements is in Lab 10/276.

there might be undesirable economic consequences such as monopoly and low wages (as new firms found it impossible to match the
standards of established companies and established companies hesi-
tated to raise standards from which there was no legal retreat). In
1934, however, traditional fears were swept aside as Betterton and
Leggett piloted the Cotton Act through Cabinet against the determined resistance of the Board of Trade.[99] The Cabinet agreed that
statutory force should be given to conciliation board agreements
once they had been approved by an independent board of inquiry
and that the agreement should then be irrevocable for three
months. The Act initially was to last for only a year but, if the
experiment were to prove successful, it could be extended both
within and beyond the cotton industry.

The Act was hailed (especially by the Whitley council movement)
as a major breakthrough in principle; but in fact it was not.
Although the experiment proved successful, in that it remained
operative within the weaving section of the cotton industry until
after the Second World War, it was not extended (as promised) to
any other industry. Indeed, the Ministry, under NCEO and TUC
pressure, reverted to its earlier opposition so that, when the Board
of Trade decided in 1938 to extend the experiment throughout the
industry in its Cotton Industry (Reorganization) Bill, it was, ironically, challenged and again defeated by the Ministry. This contradiction can be explained by the peculiar industrial and political
circumstances of 1934. Industrially, the Ministry, like the cotton
employers and trade unions, was not interested in any fundamental
reform but was merely reacting to an emergency—the fear (as expressed by Leggett) that 'the days of voluntary collective bargaining
in the cotton trade were over'.[100] Organizational weakness was
seen to be seriously threatening the industry's economic future, for
unions were impotent to enforce voluntary agreements against
maverick employers who, by cutting wages, lowered price and thus
undercut 'good' employers who honoured agreements and sought
profitability through rationalization. The Act's purpose, therefore,
was simply to provide a breathing space in which the industry
might regain its faith in voluntaryism and economic co-operation.
State intervention, in other words, was being invoked to preserve,

[99] The papers of the Cabinet Committee on the Cotton Trade are in Cab 27/566
and the dispute over its conclusions recorded in Cab 24/248/CP 72, 87, 90 and 92.
[100] Cab 27/566/CT(34)2. Betterton's later intervention is recorded in CT(34)4.

not to change, the status quo. In a year preceding a general election, the Act also had an explicit political purpose. There was concern for the political balance of Lancashire. As Betterton warned the Cabinet:

The real trouble was that the whole system of collective bargaining in the manufacturing section of the cotton industry was in jeopardy. If it crashed there would not only be industrial chaos, but the situation would be one that would play into the hands of the left wing who were opposed both to the trade unions and the employers. If they thought the trade unions were bodies that ought to be suppressed, then he would say: do not accept the procedure now being advocated. But the present state of the industry was such that something must be done to prevent it crashing.

Under the pressure of depression, therefore, the Ministry reverted to its wartime commitment to defend trade-unionism in order to safeguard industrial self-government and social peace. The experience of 1916–22, however, had clearly left its mark, for neither politicians nor officials now enthusiastically endorsed the new initiative. At no time during the drafting of the Act were the positive virtues of the philosophy of 'home rule for industry' advocated; nor was the application to the cotton industry of model schemes such as Whitley councils or trade boards ever seriously entertained.[101] There were two major reasons for this evasion. First the imposition of model machinery in an industry with proud traditions would have generated antagonism; in addition, an application of the trade board system (with its association with low pay) to a major exporting staple during a world slump might have undermined confidence in the cotton industry and in the British economy as a whole. Secondly, past experience (such as the fracas over the Grocery Trade Board in 1922) had fully alerted politicians and civil servants to the complexity and potential embarrassment of state intervention. The Act accordingly went to great lengths to minimize state responsibility. The unions, not Ministry inspectors, were to enforce the law; the Ministry was shielded from adjudicating a split vote (as in 1922) by the need for employers and trade unions to reach agreement before independent endorsement was sought; and the consideration of the 'national' interest was made explicit by the

---

[101] Cab 27/566/CT(34)4. Later attacks on low pay were similarly channelled not into trade boards but into the fully independent London Theatre and Retail Distribution Trade Councils.

separation of the independent board of inquiry from the joint conciliation committee. The Act, therefore, was not a bold initiative,
but a faithful embodiment of the Ministry's new policy of minimizing state responsibility (and embarrassment) and maximizing industrial freedom (and self-discipline).

Throughout the 1930s, government maintained this low profile
both as an employer and a legislator on industrial conditions. As
an employer it had considerable influence directly (through the civil
service) and indirectly (through its contracts with and its subsidies
to private industry); and this influence, as the TUC realized, might
have been of use to pioneer model codes of industrial practice.
Such a lead, however, was rejected. Policy was one of complete
agnosticism, well summarized in a Ministry memorandum on
wages policy: 'Government wages policy is a "fair wage" policy i.e.
to take wages as they are in outside industry, to take no responsibility for fixing wages and, in the expenditure of public money, to
do nothing calculated to disturb the level or influence the course of
wages in outside industry.'[102] Whether such a policy was practical,
given the increasing scope of government influence, and whether
indeed it was desirable, were questions that gave rise to mounting
debate within the Ministry.

Controversy over the government's role as a direct employer of
labour reached its peak at the start of the rearmament boom in
1936 when the TUC requested the Government to reduce the working week of civil servants to 40 hours. Officially, the demand was
never seriously considered, but Phillips, wishing to make some
positive gesture, drafted a reply stating that the Government fully
recognized that it 'should treat its employees not less favourably
than outside industry and should in proper cases set an example'.[103] However, the Treasury, under Wilson's influence, objected
and finally secured the non-committal form of words that 'the
Government should treat its employees not below the general standard observed by the good employers in comparable outside industry'. That this was not purely a private Ministry–Treasury
battle, nor indeed a continuation of the Phillips–Wilson vendetta,
was demonstrated by the attitude of Leggett. Conveniently drop-

---

[102] Lab 10/73.
[103] This paragraph is based on Lab 10/56. Phillips's commitment to precision
would not have permitted him to overstate actual practice, but the Treasury did not
want to acknowledge even that.

ping his assertion that pay and conditions should be determined solely by the particular circumstances of an industry, he argued:

The General Council, like the Government, must accept the fact that wages and hours possible either for Government or other employees are dependent upon general economic conditions. Those conditions would not be changed by putting the conditions of Government employees on a much more favourable basis than those of other employees ... The more that has to be paid for houses or for Government, the less is the chance of improving the standard of living of other employees.... For the sake of the millions of workpeople concerned, there should be no self-deception.

The Treasury, abetted by Leggett, was in other words resolutely opposed to any attempt to turn government into a 'model' employer.

The government's position as a contractor was dominated by the 1909 Fair Wages Resolution, which again came under attack from the TUC in 1936.[104] The Resolution specified that contractors should 'pay rates of wages and observe hours of labour not less favourable than those commonly recognised by employers and trade societies ... in the district where the work is carried out'; but, with the evolution from district to national bargaining, this wording became increasingly ambiguous. The Resolution accordingly became a battleground between the contracting departments (wishing to minimize public expenditure) and the TUC (seeking to win recognition for national agreements); and its administration fell increasingly into disrepute, as contracting departments expanded or contracted the relevant 'district' to suit their needs and the Industrial Court (which was the final arbiter of the Resolution) defined 'recognized' as 'prevailing practice' not nationally negotiated settlements—a distinction which was crucial as the depression led to frequent agreements by local employers and unions to undercut national settlements. Junior officials within the Ministry, who wished to use the Resolution (after the fashion of the 1934 Cotton Act) to encourage 'good' employers, were angered by what they considered to be evasion of its original purpose and also by open administrative abuse (such as the War Office's contract with a Scottish baker whose 'keen' prices were known to depend on the

---

[104] This paragraph is based on the definitive study: B. Bercusson, *Fair Wages Resolutions* (1978).

illegal practice of night-baking). However, assured by Leggett that
TUC objections were merely tactical exercises to assuage political
pressure within the Labour movement, the Ministry did nothing
despite the fact that Phillips was chairman of the co-ordinating
committee (the Fair Wages Advisory Committee) and the minister
shared responsibility with the chancellor of the exchequer for
policy. Only when Bevin threatened in 1936 to propose a new
resolution in the House of Commons did it agree to set up a public
inquiry.

The outcome of this inquiry (the Ross Committee) to an extent
vindicated the Ministry's legislative inaction. First it was ad-
journed, so that the NCEO and TUC could negotiate a private
agreement, and then, during the war, a new resolution was agreed
which in fact made the situation worse rather than better. The
Ministry's condoning of administrative abuse, however, cannot be
so easily vindicated, and neither can its insistence that a promise
to observe the Resolution (which it was acknowledging elsewhere
to be a 'dead letter') should be the sole guarantee of good industrial
practice in a subsidized industry. Mindful of the problems of wage
regulation in the First World War, however, the Ministry shrank
from any other expedient. As Leggett insisted, for instance, during
the drafting of the 1937 British Overseas Airways Bill (which was
the legislative blueprint for post-war nationalization), there should
be no elaborate new negotiating machinery but merely a reliance
on free collective bargaining. It was, he argued,

desirable in the case of Imperial Airways, as of all other employers in the
country, to leave the existence of collective arrangements to be determined
by the facts. President Roosevelt has had some unfortunate experience in
regard to his legislation for imposing collective arrangements ... and that
experience is not encouraging for similar action in this country. I see no
reason for distinguishing between a company upon which in any case the
Government would be able to exercise considerable moral influence and
other employers.[105]

Rather than risk non-compliance, the Ministry was prepared to
rely on the mere hope that industrial goodwill and moral suasion
would safeguard public money and the public interest.

The Ministry's position as a legislator on industrial conditions
was equally low key, as its attitude towards proposed legislation on

---

[105] Lab 10/100. For the use of the Act as a precedent, see Lab 10/586.

hours of work and holidays with pay revealed. Throughout the 1920s, the TUC had campaigned unsuccessfully for the ratification of the Washington Hours Convention, by which the ILO had hoped to restrict the normal working week to 48 hours, and in the 1930s it had (rather surrealistically) started to demand a 40-hour week with the twin objectives of relieving unemployment and counteracting the dehumanization of modern industry. The campaign was mounted primarily at the ILO, where it was resisted not only by employers' representatives but also by the Ministry officials who, unlike the delegates of foreign governments, openly supported the employers on the grounds that so general a commitment ignored the particular circumstances of individual industries. In 1936, a compromise convention was eventually passed which recommended an industry-by-industry approach to a 40-hour week. The Ministry accordingly opened negotiations at home with 40 employers' associations, but, as nothing tangible resulted, it was accused by the TUC of cynical obstruction. This, however, the Ministry denied. By negotiating with individual employers' associations, it claimed, it was merely trying to circumvent the chronic procrastination of the NCEO; moreover, the TUC was guilty of a serious error in equating lack of legislation with lack of social progress. To ensure permanent progress, the Ministry argued, it was 'of supreme importance that, wherever possible, anything that was done should be done not by government intervention, but by means of collective agreement and regulated by voluntary association'.[106] Fascist states like Italy might rely on state action to curry favour with Labour but Britain reserved such action for fundamental needs (such as unemployment and sickness pay) and relied for progress elsewhere on the healthy independence of free collective bargaining. After the Second World War, the TUC—significantly—acknowledged the Ministry's case.

The Ministry's reaction to the demand for statutory holidays with pay was important for three reasons. First, as with fair wages policy, the Ministry resisted all demands for action until the threat of a back-bench revolt in parliament obliged it to appoint a public inquiry (the Amulree Committee). The Committee's unanimous

---

[106] TUC archives, box 355, J156/7, meeting with Oliver Stanley, 24 Jan. 1935. For more detailed discussion of hours legislation, see R. Lowe, 'Hours of labour: negotiating industrial legislation in Britain, 1919–39', *Economic History Review*, xxxv (1982), 254–71.

recommendation, in favour of statutory paid holidays, was thus a sharp reminder to the Ministry that its policy of non-intervention, however well intentioned, could lead to industrial practice falling behind standards common in foreign countries and expected at home by public opinion. Secondly, the implementation of the Committee's recommendations demonstrated the Ministry's determination to maintain industrial devolution even after legislation had become inevitable. A three-year moratorium was placed on statutory enforcement in order to encourage collective agreements; the independent Industrial Welfare Society was made responsible for deciding the practical details; and the Ministry largely restricted itself to a co-ordinating role with direct responsibility only for trade boards and unorganized workers (commitments which the Cabinet characteristically strove to evade). Finally, the Amulree Committee was an illustration of the Ministry's rejection of corporatism. The Ministry was happy to appoint representatives of the NCEO and TUC to such a committee but, as it made plain, this was only to stimulate industrial agreement and not to commit government to binding agreements which excluded other, especially parliamentary, influences. The Ministry did not, as some historians have suggested, seek a corporatist accommodation. Rather, it welcomed the decline of the NCEO and, despite its intimate links with Bevin and Citrine, remained resolutely opposed to the TUC's demand that its representatives (or even nominees) should sit on every government committee to the exclusion of other working-class representatives.[107]

Throughout the 1930s, therefore, the Ministry's policy remained subterranean, seeking genuine improvements in working conditions and practice through covert negotiations. Such a policy won the approval of many contemporaries, one of whom wrote:

At a time when Government Departments have in manifold ways encroached on the ordinary activities of private citizens it is encouraging to find a Department which so far from limiting the work of outside groups does everything possible to strengthen them and resists temptations to add

---

[107] See, for instance, K. Middlemas, *Politics in Industrial Society* (1979). The fullest summary of Ministry–TUC relations is in Lab 10/1 and Lab 10/525. Leggett opposed talking to the TUC on civil servants' hours on the grounds that, after the 1927 Trade Disputes Act, the TUC could not represent civil servants. He was, however, over-ruled by Wilson who felt it a 'technical mistake' not to see the TUC on an issue they felt to be 'of first class importance'. See Lab 10/56.

to its own powers. Bureaucracy triumphant cannot be applied in any sense to the Industrial Relations Department of the Ministry of Labour.[108]

The policy also enjoyed considerable success for, as the most authoritative study of inter-war industrial relations has concluded, 'the practice of conciliation and arbitration and the setting up of standing bodies for negotiation ... contributed to a real change of attitude between employers and unions and ... reduced the severity of strikes'.[109] However the doubt still remains, as it does for the 1920s, about whether all that might have been achieved, was achieved. With employers and trade unions so unequally matched, owing to the recession, free collective bargaining did not automatically guarantee (as government assumed) all the improvements that technological advances in production allowed. Moreover, as Butler and Mallon had warned, 'home rule for industry' could easily degenerate from a positive to a negative policy. Significantly, logical inconsistencies started to appear in the Ministry's defence of its policy. General laws (such as the imposition of a 40-hour week) were rejected on the grounds that they ignored the needs of particular industries; but simultaneously sectional improvements were rejected on general economic grounds (as in the case of civil servants' hours) or on the pretext that they might establish unwelcome precedents (as, before 1934, in the rejection of the statutory enforcement of agreements). Towards the end of the 1930s, Leggett even began to revive the old Treasury orthodoxy (so decisively rejected before the Geddes Committee) that, by raising expectations and weakening self-discipline, state intervention caused strikes.[110] The evolving relationship between Leggett and Bevin, indeed, does suggest that administrative as well as political sights were being set too low. As a trade union leader in the 1930s, Bevin had the highest regard for the way in which Leggett respected industrial autonomy and 'fondled' disputes; but later as minister, intent on constructing a 'new industrial code of conduct, inspection, enforcement and welfare', he quickly dispensed with Leggett's services.[111]

---

[108] Lockhead in Vernon and Mansergh, *Advisory Bodies.* Since four of the six civil servants who helped compile the book had served in the Ministry, its conclusions were perhaps not surprising.

[109] Knowles, *Strikes*, p. 65.

[110] See, for example, Leggett in Jackson, *Meeting of Minds*, p. 67.

[111] Lab 10/248.

Conclusion

Industrial relations were, therefore, the most critical of the Ministry's inter-war responsibilities and an area of policy in which both great influence devolved upon officials and, statistically at least, great success was enjoyed. Superficially, policy remained remarkably consistent. State intervention was minimized and free collective bargaining maximized in order to safeguard individual freedom and industrial flexibility; intervention was countenanced only to defend the 'national' interest, to secure minimum standards, and (when invited) to provide industry with a free conciliation and arbitration service. Beneath such principles, however, major differences of practice could and did exist. What was the 'national' interest and at what point should it be defended? What were the desirable minimum standards? What degree of overt or covert influence should be used to encourage good industrial practices? Very different answers were provided to each of those questions by Butler (in particular under Roberts as minister), Wilson (under Steel-Maitland) and Leggett (under Betterton and Brown). Benevolent paternalism turned gradually into benevolent neutrality, positive voluntaryism into stoical realism. These changes were not occasioned solely by official personality but by economic circumstance, fluctuations in the relative strength of employers and trade unions, Treasury control, and Cabinet direction. Policy reflected in turn the early radicalism of the Lloyd George Coalition, the paternalism of Baldwin, and the fatalism of the National Government.

To what purpose did the Ministry put such influence as it enjoyed? Its establishment raised hopes that the anti-Labour bias of government would be qualified and these hopes were not wholly disappointed. Inter-war governments were well-informed of working-class opinion (as political and industrial change demanded); the Ministry was more sympathetic to Labour than most departments (as the administration of the Fair Wages Resolution demonstrated); and it was able to dispel political ignorance (for example championing Bevin as a force for moderation after the General Strike, when even Baldwin considered him an evil influence).[112] Although conversant with trade union aspirations, how-

---

[112] Baldwin confused not only the reality of internal TUC politics but also historical allusion by referring to Bevin as a Napoleon to MacDonald's Kerensky. See Jones, *Whitehall Diary*, vol. 2, p. 38.

ever, the Ministry was never a slave to them. Rather it cultivated trade-unionism as a means of social control. Strong unions were welcomed as a means of simplifying communications between government and industry, of minimizing the institutional friction which caused unrest and, above all, of preserving order. The Ministry's policy was infused always by a desire to preserve the credibility of moderate leaders and to strengthen union executives against their more militant members. In the First World War, the Ministry opposed restrictive legislation because, 'in diminishing the power of official trade unionism for fighting purposes, emergency legislation at the same time succeeded in diminishing its power of assistance in case of trouble'. In the 1920s, Steel-Maitland opposed the Trade Disputes Act because it would hamper moderate leaders in their attempt to 'conduct a consistent and dignified policy compatible with the interests of other classes and the state'. In the 1930s, objections to the legalization of voluntary agreements were suspended in relation to the cotton industry because 'the fact that young men and women are not joining unions ... is creating a new problem. The effect is to give an impetus to minority movements and these do not make for stability.' Indeed, one of the Ministry's overriding concerns was how to strengthen trade-unionism. Legislation was tempting but, in the long term, it was no substitute for 'trade union discipline and control'. Legislation in fact was feared, not just because it infringed individual freedom and raised the spectre of non-compliance, but because, by relaxing union leaders, it threatened an estrangement between union executives, local leaders, and the rank and file which militants might exploit.[113]

Whilst seeking to manipulate the trade unions, the Ministry also conformed to Marxist theory by appearing openly to sympathize with employers. Butler's pioneering policy was in accordance with pre-war Liberalism (which had equated selective social expenditure with national efficiency) as well as the wartime views of Allan Smith and the FBI. In order to put more 'fight' into the employers, the Ministry helped create the NCEO (although it was well aware of

---

[113] Lab 2/254/13; Cab 24/182/CP 394(26); Cab 27/566/CT 34(2); Lab 10/281. As the Intelligence Department reasoned in 1919, 'organized industrial power is a thing that cannot be absorbed any more than physical force can be abolished, but can only be dealt with by being turned in the right direction and harnessed through the superposition of a corresponding responsibility'. See Cab 24/80/GT 7361.

the EEF's powers of passive resistance) and thereafter shared its views (both at home and at the ILO): minimizing state intervention, industry-by-industry negotiation, and voluntary agreements. In 1926, for instance, Lithgow wrote 'I gather that Sir Arthur [Steel-Maitland] deprecates the Government interfering in industrial disputes on the ground that parties come to depend on government assistance to help them out of their difficulties. This, of course, I entirely endorse.' In a phrase reminiscent of Leggett, the FBI, at the time of the 1934 Cotton Act, also insisted that 'compulsory powers in no way facilitate the finding of the correct solution to a problem ... rapidity of action is rather the characteristic of voluntary association'.[114] After the battle with Hilton in the early 1920s, moreover, Wilson and Leggett both fully embraced the employers' economic assumptions (which, as good civil servants, they recognized to be similar to those of the Treasury), and, in the 1930s, new appointees such as Tribe admitted that they felt more at ease with employers than with trade-unionists.

To what extent, therefore, did the Ministry's industrial relations policy actually substantiate Marxist theory? On the assumption that 'industrial relations' is merely a 'consecrated euphemism' for the class war, did officials act as the agents for class rule, promoting state intervention only when employers' hegemony was challenged?[115] Did voluntaryism signify not the neutrality of the state but its abstention in favour of the employers? Finally, was the policy of 'home rule for industry' adopted to depoliticize industrial relations by turning attention towards the particular problems of individual industries and away from a critique of the capitalist system as a whole? Butler's reconstruction programme during and immediately after the First World War might certainly be interpreted as an attempt to 'moralize' capitalism at a time when it was under serious pressure from organized Labour. Significantly, it was dropped in the early 1920s when depression strengthened the relative economic power of capital just as, in the 1930s, legislative experiment (designed to assist 'good' employers during a recession) was disowned as soon as the economy revived. 'Home rule for industry', especially after the abandonment of Butler's more grandiose

[114] Lithgow to Pearson, 1 Dec. 1926 (Lithgow papers, L/74); FBI, *Report of the Committee on the Organization of Industry* (1935). For Smith's wartime views, see Steel-Maitland papers, GD 193/570.
[115] R. Miliband, *The State in Capitalist Society* (1973), p. 73.

schemes, was also designed to keep politics out of industrial relations as Leggett's objections to the NIC made plain. Moreover, officials were alive to the significance of changes in policy, especially the abandonment of post-war reconstruction as working-class power waned. In 1922, for example, Leggett opposed the revival of the NIC because 'on the former occasion employers and workers were equally matched in industry and then the latter were in a position of power in the industrial field but of weakness elsewhere. Recent events have shown that, broadly, the workers' organizations are unable to withstand those of the employers.' Similarly, the expansion of trade boards was abandoned despite the Ministry's admission that 'the tendency has been for organization on the workers' side to become weaker while wages have been dropping ... This is itself a danger signal indicating precisely the sort of conditions which the Trade Board Acts are intended to deal with.'[116]

Despite its superficial plausibility, however, Marxist theory is an inadequate explanation of the Ministry's behaviour. First, there is the question of timing: Treasury retrenchment had started to erode Butler's reconstruction programme long before depression had effectively increased employers' bargaining strength. Secondly, as the strained relationship between the Ministry and the NCEO demonstrated, especially in the 1920s, employers regarded the Ministry as many things, but certainly not as an ally. Thirdly, free collective bargaining was demanded as much by the trade unions as by employers and, indeed, the TUC went to considerable lengths to prevent the first Labour Government from intervening in disputes. In its conciliation role, the Ministry had no coercive powers and its policy was based on the entirely justified assumption that trade union leaders would accept so-called 'economist' settlements and (even more importantly) that the rank and file would follow their lead. The counter-arguments might be advanced that employers and civil servants disagreed merely over the tactics to be used in the class war, not the strategy; and that trade union leaders were afflicted by a 'false' consciousness. But there is little hard evidence to support this. Employers' anger was very real and experienced conciliators, from Askwith in the First World War to Emmerson in the Second, all concluded that strikes were essentially industrial

[116] Lab 2/775/3; Lab 2/1038/TB 145/1924.

and not political.[117] There is a limit to which the actual, documented behaviour of the working class can be described as 'false', merely on pre-judged theoretical assumptions.

The most substantial criticism of the Ministry's industrial relations policy, therefore, lies not in its suppression of working-class aspirations but in its failure actively to promote constructive reform. Policy witnessed a constant retreat, as, for example, in the 1920s when the NIC recommendations on hours were abandoned in favour of the Washington Convention, which was then itself abandoned; when defence of the 'national' interest was projected before the Geddes Committee as the Ministry's major concern and then dropped; and, in the 1930s, when the promise was broken to extend the legalization of voluntary agreements should it prove successful in the cotton industry. As a result, in areas regarded as being so important by Butler and the wartime, liberal advocates of the Ministry (which included working conditions, income-equalization, the raising of minimum standards, and the encouragement of better relations on the shop-floor), the achievement was less than economic circumstances permitted.

Admittedly, in the promotion of any positive policy, the Ministry was confronted by a series of formidable dilemmas. State intervention was needed to avert the need for further state intervention; legislation could only be effective if the will to obey existed, but if such a will existed then voluntary agreement could be reached; forcing the pace of change might be counter-productive, but inactivity bred disillusion. Indeed, the whole field of industrial relations, in which settlements were achieved by force not reason, was unsympathetic to rational solutions. Were the Ministry ever seriously to tackle these dilemmas, however, it had to use its expertise to build up trust and to guide industry and politicians single-mindedly towards particular solutions. This it failed to do. The solutions it chose—'home rule for industry' and social control via moderate union leaders—were means to an end rather than ends in themselves: they assumed that devolution would automatically produce solutions in harmony with successive governments' perception of the national interest. Once that hope was disabused, devolution as a positive policy was surreptitiously abandoned and trust broken.

[117] Lord Askwith, *Industrial Problems and Disputes* (1920), p. 357; Emmerson in Lab 10/281. For the discouragement of the first Labour Government, see Cab 24/CP 36(24).

Given the lack of effective industrial consensus and political leadership, the retreat by Ministry officials into a 'second best solution' is perhaps understandable. By so acting, however, they inevitably abandoned the democratic ideal of 'ordered freedom'.

CHAPTER 5

THE RELIEF OF UNEMPLOYMENT

Although responsibility for industrial relations policy determined the general ethos of the inter-war Ministry, the bulk of its work was as a social services department. From its inception, the Ministry's establishment and budget were dominated by the former Employment Department of the Board of Trade;[1] and, although the original purpose of this department had been economic (the rationalization of the labour market), its responsibilities after the 1911 National Insurance Act became largely social (the administration of unemployment insurance). This bias was reinforced by the onset of mass unemployment after the war. As *The Times* of 3 January 1921 commented:

the government is endeavouring to deal with unemployment in two ways. One is the province of the Board of Trade and the other is that of the Ministry of Labour. The first is directed toward the revival of overseas trade and the stimulation of the industries which supply the home market. The second is more definitely concerned with measures for mitigating and relieving distress.

A year later, before the Geddes Committee, the Ministry confirmed this distinction by justifying its separation from the Board of Trade on the grounds that its services were related no longer to 'the Board ... but to the Poor Law side of the Ministry of Health and the factory side of the Home Office'.[2] Not until 1935, when the creation of the Unemployment Insurance Statutory Committee (UISC) and the Unemployment Assistance Board (UAB) relieved it of detailed responsibility for unemployment relief, did the Ministry assume the broader economic role that had been envisaged for it by, amongst others, the Webbs.

It was the Ministry's role as a social services department which, more than any other, ensured both its survival and its historical significance. In the early 1920s, it was 'the volume of necessary work' performed by the decentralized network of over a thousand employment exchanges and offices (paying out annually up to

[1] See Appendix 1, C and D.   [2] Lab 2/1822/CEB 461/2/1922.

£50m. in unemployment benefit) that finally convinced the Treasury that the Ministry should not be abolished. Thereafter, it was this work which placed the Ministry at the heart of the adjustment by government to democracy. Politically, it involved the Ministry in such major crises as the fall of the second Labour Government and the public outcry against the introduction of unemployment assistance in 1935. Administratively, it required Ministry officials to pioneer expedients, such as delegated legislation and administrative direction (which so excited Lord Hewart), and qualified them to help run the new statutory commissions.[3] Nothing, indeed, epitomizes better the changing role of inter-war government than the Ministry's evolving relationship with traditional relief agencies— the family, self-help institutions, private charity, industry, and local government—and, consequently, the Ministry's history as a social services department can shed considerable light on such contentious issues as the motivation behind, and bureaucracy's role in, the expansion of central government. Was, for example, the principal motivation a rational, humane response to newly perceived problems, mere political expediency, or social control? Did civil servants, in both the formulation and implementation of policy, act consciously as 'agents of class rule'? Or, alternatively, did bureaucratic vested interest take undue precedence over both political principle and the needs of clients?

The answers to such questions lie in the Ministry's response to the three problems which dominated inter-war unemployment relief. First, which of four possible agencies should assume ultimate financial and administrative responsibility? Should it be industry itself (in accordance with the policy of 'home rule for industry'); local government (whose boards of Poor Law guardians and, after 1929, public assistance committees had the local knowledge and established expertise to check and cater for the needs of individual claimants); central government (which had the financial resources to tackle unemployment as a national problem and the network of employment exchanges to keep the unemployed in contact with industry); or an 'independent' authority (enjoying the financial resources of central government, but freed of political pressure from claimants who, after 1918, had the vote and thus the power to influence policy at both a national and local level)? Secondly, what should be the relationship between the rate of relief, wages, and

[3] See above, pp. 12, 44-5.

need? If rates of relief were to be too high, they might undermine work incentives, discourage industrial mobility, and thus hamper the rate of economic growth on which national living standards depended; were they too low, they might lose the government votes, provoke unrest, and condemn both claimants and their dependants to starvation. Thirdly, should, or should not, the able-bodied poor be treated as a homogenous group? If not, on what principles and practical criteria should distinctions be made?

Contrary to received historical opinion, but in conformity with its commitment to voluntaryism in industrial relations, the Ministry quickly developed an agreed overall strategy to resolve these problems. Unemployment, it recognized, was a national problem and hence the responsibility of central government; but, in order to minimize dependence on the state and thereby to maintain the principle of self-help, local authorities and industry should be involved in the administration and, above all, the finance of relief. This meant, in practice, that the Ministry championed a two-tier system of relief. The majority of the able-bodied unemployed (the short-term unemployed) were to be covered by a national system of contributory insurance, administered through employment exchanges, whilst the minority of claimants (the long-term unemployed) were to receive from local authorities means-tested benefit supplemented by specialized services (such as industrial training) provided by central government. In order to prevent demoralization, all benefit was to be paid below the level of unskilled wages.

Departmental policy, however, was never implemented. It required hard political decisions which successive Cabinets, if not ministers of labour, were unwilling to take. It also offended powerful pressure groups. Furthermore, as with voluntaryism, agreement between officials on matters of broad principle masked important disagreements over detailed questions of implementation, each of which begged major questions about the nature of the government's response to the advent of democracy. The full significance of these conflicts can best be examined during the three distinct phases of inter-war relief policy: the breakup of the Poor Law between 1916 and 1931, the establishment of a new permanent system of relief between 1931 and 1934, and the pragmatic adjustment of that system after 1934.

The Break-up of the Poor Law, 1916–1931

The Ministry's inheritance from the Board of Trade of responsibility for unemployment insurance confronted it with a major political challenge that had defeated a generation of pre-war statesmen: the breakup of the Poor Law. Administered by specially elected boards of guardians, locally financed, and dominated (in the public mind at least) by the workhouse, the Poor Law had long been acknowledged as an inappropriate remedy for poverty in a complex industrial society. However, consensus over the need for its replacement was matched by conflict over the means. The pre-war Liberal Government, by introducing welfare measures such as old age pensions and contributory national insurance, had sought to erode the Poor Law by removing from it specific groups of claimants. The creation of the Ministries of Labour and of Health in 1916 and 1919 had further raised the hope that relief would be rationalized and national finance used to provide specialized services based on need rather than deterrence. By the onset of mass unemployment in 1920, however, no such rationalization had been effected and, in the ensuing emergency, contributory unemployment insurance was hastily transformed (for the able-bodied at least) into a *de facto* substitute for the Poor Law. This transformation was highly improvised, provoked acute political controversy, and became widely regarded as one of the most serious failures of democratic government.[4] Much criticism was duly levelled at the Ministry. However, when placed in the context of overall policy development and, in particular, of contemporary political constraints, such criticism can be shown to have been largely unfounded. Indeed, when compared to that of its detractors, the Ministry's policy can be shown to have been consistent, courageous, and constructive.

Although highly complex in detail, the evolution of unemploy-

---

[4] See, for example, *Final Report of the Royal Commission on Unemployment Insurance* (Cmd. 4185), PP (1931–2), xiii, 393, p. 164. For the most comprehensive summary of the legislative and administrative changes, see B. Swann and M. Turnbull (eds.), *Records of Interest to Social Scientists: Unemployment Insurance, 1911–1939* (1975), appendices 6–9. For the most cogent commentaries, see the various works of two participants, W. H. Beveridge and R. C. Davison, cited in the bibliography; two contemporary American surveys, E. M. Burns, *British Unemployment Programs, 1920–1938* (Washington, 1941) and E. W. Bakke, *Insurance or Dole?* (Yale, 1935); and Gilbert, *British Social Policy*.

ment insurance in the 1920s was in general relatively simple: such complexity as did exist arose largely from the fact that—by three principal expedients—successive governments sought to pervert the scheme from a task it could perform (the relief of short-term cyclical unemployment) to one it could not (the relief of long-term structural unemployment). Unemployment insurance had been initiated by central government in 1911 when the then Liberal Government had required 2¼m. workers (together with their employers and the taxpayer) to contribute weekly to an Unemployment Fund from which, on 'actuarial' conditions, unemployment benefit well below subsistence level could be withdrawn as of right. During the First World War, in anticipation of the heavy unemployment that was expected to accompany demobilization, government had attempted to extend the coverage of the Fund and hence its reserves; but it had been defeated by both sides of industry.[5] Consequently, by the Armistice, no general provision for unemployment relief was available outside the Poor Law and, as the Lloyd George Coalition understandably shrank from condemning ex-servicemen and new voters alike to the Poor Law, the first of the three major expedients which were eventually to undermine the scheme was employed. All demobilized combatants and civil warworkers were temporarily provided as of right with a non-contributory, subsistence-level 'out-of-work donation', administered without stigma through the employment exchange.

As a permanent solution to unemployment relief the Lloyd George Coalition passed a new Insurance Act in August 1920 increasing, under very similar terms to the 1911 Act, the number of insured workers to 11¾m. It was, however, never fully implemented. Its enactment coincided with the onset of mass unemployment and so relief had immediately to be provided not only for the short-term unemployed (who could afford weekly insurance contributions) but also for the long-term unemployed (who could not). For the latter resort was made to the second major expedient: the 'actuarial' qualifications for drawing benefit from the Fund were relaxed and the duration of benefit was extended. Consequently, two types of benefit came to be paid from the Fund—covenanted benefit

[5] N. Whiteside, 'Welfare legislation and the unions during the First World War', *Historical Journal*, 23 (1980), 857-74. Unlike a private scheme, no state insurance scheme can be strictly actuarial, but the 1911 Act required a precise relationship between contributions and benefit.

(to which the claimant had a contractual right by virtue of his weekly contribution) and uncovenanted benefit (which was paid, at the Ministry's discretion, to those who had exhausted their right to benefit). This latter liability seriously jeopardized both the finances and the administration of the insurance scheme. First, by so increasing the Fund's liabilities in relation to its revenue, it plunged it into debt. Secondly, by introducing an element of discretion into the payment of benefit, it threatened to sow the seeds of suspicion between exchange officials and claimants. Both these dangers were accentuated by subsequent developments. In 1921, for instance, the Fund was further depleted by the granting of dependants' allowances to all claimants; and, in 1924, the first Labour Government, in an attempt to discourage fraud, required all claimants (including the genuinely insured) to prove to exchange officials that they were 'genuinely seeking work'.

The incoming Baldwin Government in 1924 sought to end all such expedients and to place unemployment insurance on a permanent, non-controversial basis. Accordingly it appointed an independent committee of inquiry (the Blanesburgh Committee) and on its unanimous report the 1927 Insurance Act was based. Under this Act, both types of benefit were to be merged with the sole qualification to benefit becoming a claimant's status as a genuine worker in an insured trade (established by whether he had paid 30 insurance contributions in the previous two years). Claimants were still to be liable to a 'genuinely-seeking-work' test, but the means test (which had been an additional check on claimants to uncovenanted benefit imposed by all but the Labour Government) was to be dropped. Like the 1920 Act, however, this Act was never fully implemented. Even by its relatively generous provisions, an estimated 120,000 claimants would have been consigned to the Poor Law and the Baldwin Cabinet was unwilling to take so unpopular a decision. Consequently the third major expedient was employed. For one year, it was decided, any genuine worker (who had either paid 30 insurance contributions at any time or eight in the previous year) should be paid a 'transitional benefit' from the Fund. With the approach of a general election in 1929, this expedient was inevitably extended.

The election of the second Labour Government in 1929 removed all possibility that the Act might be implemented. Instead, rates of benefits were liberalized and the number of claimants increased by the abolition of various qualifications, in particular the notorious 'genuinely-seeking-work' test. Exchequer liability was increased by two further reforms. The state's contribution to the Unemployment Fund was increased to match that of the employers and the employed (the principle of 'equal thirds', recommended by Blanesburgh but rejected by the Baldwin Cabinet) and, in an attempt to make the Fund self-supporting, the Government undertook to pay the total cost of 'transitional benefit'. Coinciding with a sharp rise in unemployment, these reforms placed a huge strain on the exchequer. Between the financial years of 1928/9 and 1931/2, the state's annual insurance contributions increased by almost half (from £11.8m. to £16.8m.), borrowing for the Unemployment Fund more than tripled (from £11.4m. to £39.6m.), and the debt of the Fund itself increased from just under £25m. to £115m. Exchequer liability for 'transitional benefit' simultaneously rose from nothing to £32.3m.[6] Such escalating costs inevitably caught the attention of the May Committee on National Expenditure, which, in anticipation of an unparalleled budget deficit, recommended cuts in public expenditure of £97m., two-thirds of which were to be effected in unemployment insurance. At the height of the financial crisis in August 1931, unemployment insurance thus became what it had long threatened to become, the vital political symbol of a government's determination on the one hand to uphold fiscal probity or on the other to maintain working-class living standards. Inability to choose between these two options destroyed the second Labour Government.

The ignominious collapse of the Labour Government was taken by the Ministry's critics to epitomize the damage caused to democracy by the current administrative practices of unemployment insurance. Apart from their fundamental allegation that (by its laxity and the escalation of public expenditure) unemployment insurance had demoralized the work-force and deepened the depression, the critics rightly pointed to the disrepute into which government had been brought by the recurring deficits of the Unemployment Fund and the constant need to revise legislation. There were, for example, 15 new insurance acts between 1920 and 1926 alone, two actually reversing legislation that had yet to become operative. Furthermore, government had evaded legal commitments and condoned administrative contradictions. The insurance contract, for instance,

---

[6] *Final Report of the Royal Commission on Unemployment Insurance*, para. 668.

had been broken when the contributions of workers and employers had been used for a purpose (the relief of the uninsured) for which they had not been collected; and the 'genuinely-seeking-work' test directly contradicted the original purpose of the employment exchanges, which was to relieve the unemployed of the need to tramp in search of work. For all the substance of these charges, however, the critics' case had one fatal flaw. As an examination of the four principal sources of opposition to the Ministry—the TUC, the NCEO, informed public opinion, and the Treasury—will show, no practical alternative policy could be devised, let alone agreed upon. It is against this lack of a viable alternative, rather than against some ideal standard, that the relative achievements of the Ministry should be judged.

The most consistent critic of the Ministry was the TUC, which, under its traditional slogan of 'work or maintenance', demanded throughout the 1920s an unemployed worker's right to non-contributory, subsistence-level benefit. It urged on successive Labour Governments the right to benefit, duly securing the abolition of the means test in 1924 and the 'genuinely-seeking-work' test in 1930. When the Blanesburgh Committee unanimously reaffirmed the principle of contributory insurance in 1927, the TUC denounced Margaret Bondfield (the Labour representative); and, in 1930, it almost forced her to resign as minister of labour when, in an attempt to 'educate' its own supporters, the Labour Government appointed a Royal Commission on Unemployment Insurance whose terms of reference deliberately excluded discussion of non-contributory insurance.[7] Finally, by rejecting the proposed 10 per cent cuts in benefit in 1931, it demonstrated that, in the last resort, it was committed more to the maintenance of working-class living standards than of a Labour Government. For all its high-principled consistency, however, TUC policy in the given political and economic circumstances was totally unrealistic. Insistence on non-contributory insurance was, for example, increasingly at variance with the wishes of its own members who, after their wartime revolt, had started to favour unemployment insurance—if only because it was thought to guarantee an inalienable right to relief.[8] Anger at the

[7] PRO 30/69/5/42, Bondfield to MacDonald, 6 Jan. 1931. The secret drafting is recorded in MH 79/294 and the confrontation in T 172/1764.

[8] See, for instance, Bakke, *Insurance or Dole?*, pp. 120–1 and PEP, *Report on the British Social Services*, p. 30.

10 per cent cuts in 1931 ignored the fact that, owing to the fall in the cost of living, rises in benefit levels and the introduction of dependants' allowances, the real value of benefit had risen sharply over the previous 11 years—by 92 per cent for a single man and by as much as 240 per cent for a family of four.[9] Finally, as the Labour Government argued and the 1931 election showed, such massive increases in public expenditure as non-contributory insurance entailed were electorally disastrous. The TUC, nevertheless, refused to compromise, even with a Labour Government, as it had compromised on economic policy with employers after the General Strike: indeed the specific purpose of the 'new direction' in economic strategy had been to obviate the need for a 'new direction' in social policy.

The NCEO was not so obdurate as the TUC.[10] Its opposition to unemployment insurance was based on the orthodox economic belief that benefit retarded economic recovery by discouraging labour mobility and the downward flexibility of wages; insurance contributions (which it equated with a 'poll-tax on employment') were also resented as an additional industrial cost which reduced export competitiveness and investment capital. By the mid-1920s, however, the NCEO recognized that starvation had to be prevented and that alternative policies (such as 'insurance by industry') would be prohibitively expensive for the depressed labour-intensive staple industries which it particularly represented. Its solution was, therefore, to minimize employers' and maximise the taxpayers' contributions to an actuarially sound insurance scheme for the short-term unemployed, whilst the long-term unemployed were maintained by a means-tested local service (to which, after the rating reforms of 1927, industry would have to pay relatively little). Apart from the insistence on an actuarially sound scheme, this policy had much in common with that of the Ministry and helped it to persuade the Treasury that the state had to accept ultimate responsibility for unemployment. The NCEO, however, was reluctant to follow the logic of its policy and to offer the Ministry its active

---

[9] *First Report of the Royal Commission on Unemployment Insurance* (Cmd. 3872), PP (1930–1), xvii, 885, appendix 1, 66. The 1919 base figure was, admittedly, very low and benefit still remained below the subsistence level.

[10] NCEO, *Report on Unemployment Insurance* (1924), para. 13. For the most comprehensive summary of the NCEO's views, see Rodgers, 'Work and welfare', ch. 3–4.

support. A far easier option was to attack the alleged maladministration of the employment exchanges. It consequently adopted a hypocritical stance, best illustrated by the issue of job notification. The charge most commonly levelled at the exchanges was their wastage of taxpayers' money through the payment of fraudulent claims; and the NCEO acknowledged that the only check against such abuse was the exchanges' ability to offer each claimant a job. Yet throughout the inter-war period its members never notified the exchanges of more than one-fifth of their vacancies.[11]

Informed public opinion was equally hostile to the Ministry's administration of unemployment insurance. This hostility was based not only on orthodox economics but also on the moral objection (most authoritatively expressed by Beveridge) that, for both industry and the individual worker, the current practice of relief was both demoralizing and inequitable. For industry, it was demoralizing because, unlike the 1911 Act or 'insurance by industry' (the policy which Beveridge favoured after 1916), no positive attempt was made to encourage either employers to decasualize their work-force or industries to take responsibility for their unemployed. Consequently, it was inequitable, because ill-organized industries could discharge with impunity unwanted workers on to the Unemployment Fund to be financed (either temporarily or permanently) by the well organized. For the individual, current practice was equally demoralizing, since a claimant's effective right to permanent relief discouraged occupational and geographical mobility: relief for the long-term unemployed was not made conditional on specialized treatment, such as retraining. It was also inequitable because the long-term unemployed (who chanced to have worked in an insured industry) had an effective right to stigma-free relief that was denied a worker in an uninsured trade (who still had to resort to the Poor Law); and, in an insured industry, the treatment of the long-term unemployed was virtually identical to that of a regular worker who had consistently paid his contribution. In short, policy in the 1920s had none of the constructive purpose of the 1911 Act and displayed the classic symptom of bad policy: the expenditure of vast sums of public money to compound the very problem it was designed to resolve.

Such criticisms were undoubtedly pertinent but, as Beveridge him-

---

[11] In 1924, the right to a refund on retirement of any outstanding balance in a worker's account was withdrawn.

self later admitted, they were totally negative. Of the two stated remedies, the 1911 Act (with its 'actuarial' base) may have been an effective palliative for pre-war cyclical unemployment but it was no answer to the problem of long-term structural unemployment; and 'insurance by industry' was equally impractical after the onset of depression, since it was rejected by both the TUC and NCEO. Moreover, it should be remembered that it was not the perceived inequities of inter-war improvisations that actually provoked a shop-floor revolt but those of Beveridge's own pre-war legislation. Indeed Beveridge, as an academic, despaired in the late 1920s of finding a policy that was both morally sound and politically acceptable.[12] This was a luxury no practising politician or civil servant could afford.

The last major critic and thus constraint on the Ministry was the Treasury, whose discouragement of constructive long-term policy has already been noted. Rather than seek principled consistency, it varied its policy according to whichever option appeared at any given time to be the cheapest. Hence, at the time of the Geddes Committee it could argue:

It is difficult not to feel that the main justification urged by the Ministry of Labour for the [Insurance] Acts stands good and that looking to the danger of violence on the one hand and extravagant doles or still more extravagant relief works on the other, a universal State unemployment insurance scheme is the cheapest of the alternatives that present themselves.

In 1917 and the late 1920s, however, it anachronistically urged the 'disengagement' of the state from unemployment relief and the return of responsibility to local government or industry.[13] By 1931, the Treasury was particularly vehement in its denunciation of the Unemployment Fund because, through its failure to build up a contingency reserve, it had forced the Government to borrow not only for a 'non-productive' purpose (that is, for a measure which did not yield an income from which interest on the resulting debt could be paid) but also to meet current expenditure. It was thus guilty of unbalancing the budget, the cardinal sin of orthodox economic policy.[14]

---

[12] J. Harris, *William Beveridge* (Oxford, 1977), pp. 258-61, 353-7.

[13] See above, p. 50, T 163/12/G 538.

[14] Treasury evidence recorded in the *First Report of the Royal Commission on Unemployment Insurance*, para. 68.

What the indignation of Treasury officials conveniently ignored, however, was that, in four major ways, the Treasury itself bore a major responsibility for the chronic indebtedness of the Unemployment Fund. First, orthodox monetary and fiscal policy had failed to contain and had even intensified unemployment which the Fund was then expected to relieve. Secondly, in sharp contrast to its probity over the repayment of international debts, the Treasury had quickly appropriated industry's insurance contributions for a purpose for which it had not been collected—the relief of the non-insured—and had thereby depleted the Fund's resources. Thirdly, it had consistently fought to minimize the state's contributions, two particular rearguard actions (its reduction of industry's insurance contributions in 1925 and its refusal, as promised, in 1926 to compensate for such cuts by an increased state contribution) being responsible for all but £4m. of the Fund's accumulated debt of £28m. in 1928.[15] Finally, it had charged a rate of interest on the Fund's debt which even Snowden was moved to agree was 'Shylockian'.[16] Treasury officials, moreover, failed to take account of the countervailing economies which insurance effected. Seventy per cent of the Ministry's administrative expenses, for example, was paid by appropriations-in-aid from the Fund and, more importantly, industry (by paying two-thirds of the cost of able-bodied unemployment) relieved the exchequer of a major burden. This was a boon only fully appreciated in the Treasury after 1930—when central government had been obliged to accept sole responsibility for the financial relief of all the uninsured unemployed.

Throughout the 1920s, therefore, the Ministry faced—in the breakup of the Poor Law—a momentous political challenge, with its freedom of action severely constrained by hostile critics both within and without government. Its response was both practical and heroic. It was always desperate for consensus, one official confessing to Margaret Bondfield in 1926 (when urging her to work on the Blanesburgh Committee for a unanimous report):

We have had a dreadful time in recent years on account of the fact that our fundamental aims have been in dispute. One section of the community

---

[15] Cab 24/198/CP 312. Industry's contributions were cut to facilitate the extension of contributory pensions. Rather than provide, in compensation, an extra 2¼d. per contributor, the 1926 Economy Act cut the state's contribution by ¾d.
[16] T 172/1336.

has thought that we were not going far enough and the other have treated
us with little short of ridicule ... The Government, if faced with divergent
views, is bound to choose one ... Probably one political party would
espouse one view and the other another ... Thus the stability for which
we at the Ministry of Labour are pining and which the unemployed really
need, would not be secured.[17]

Consensus, however, was not to be bought at any price. From the
start, the Ministry accepted the conventional wisdom that the current system of insurance created marginal unemployment, demoralized the work-force, and retarded economic recovery; but, unlike
the Treasury, it also recognized that, in the absence of any credible
alternative, central government had to accept the ultimate responsibility for able-bodied unemployment. Consequently, as has been
seen, it came to champion a new two-tier system of relief. On the
one hand, there was (in contradiction to TUC policy) to be a
scheme of contributory insurance to maintain the short-term
unemployed on as generous terms as possible (not on the
'actuarial' basis introduced by the 1911 Act and demanded by the
NCEO). On the other hand, for the long-term unemployed there
was to be means-tested relief administered by local government,
made 'humane' and constructive by means of grants and expert
assistance (such as industrial training) from central government.[18]
Such a policy, it was believed, would minimize both the cost to the
exchequer and the danger to the economy. Contributory insurance,
as opposed to free hand-outs, would help to maintain the self-
respect and self-reliance of the ordinary worker; the demoralization
of the long-term unemployed would be forestalled by a mixture of
deterrence and specialized assistance; and the Ministry's exchanges
would not degenerate from 'respectable' manpower agencies into
mere relief bureaux. Departmental policy, consequently, would
satisfy equally the needs of the economy, the unemployed, and the
Ministry.

In contrast to its critics, therefore, the Ministry had by the
mid-1920's developed a policy which, on matters of principle, was
both constructive and consistent. The evolution of this policy, how-

[17] M. Bondfield, *A Life's Work* (1948), p. 270. The best single summary of the
views of individual officials is in Pin 6/46/2F 816/1932.
[18] The weakest link in the Ministry's logic, as the 1930s were to show, was the
assumption that any relief scheme, related to the Poor Law by the household means
test, could be regarded as 'humane' by the unemployed.

ever, had been punctuated by periods of uncertainty, and conflict continued to arise over questions of implementation. Consequently a final assessment of the Ministry's achievements must be suspended, until four critical areas of the Ministry's activities have been examined: policy-implementation, post-war planning, the initial reaction to mass unemployment, and the continuing search after 1924 for a 'sound' policy.

Undue concentration on the formulation of policy has too often in the past obscured the executive achievement of unemployment relief which, from the initial crisis of post-war demobilization to the onset of the world depression in 1930, was exceptional. In 1919, for instance, the Ministry emerged from the war quite powerless to relieve the anticipated unemployment. The industrial revolt against insurance in 1916, Cabinet vacillation, and a Treasury moratorium on all employment exchange expenditure until six days before the Armistice had denied it respectively the accumulated reserves, the agreed policy, and the administrative resources that were essential for unqualified success.[19] However, with the same efficiency that characterized its own administrative reorganization in 1919, the Ministry rapidly implemented a system of relief (the out-of-work donation) by which, over the next two years, £66m. was disbursed with (in the opinion of the independent Aberconway Committee of Inquiry) the minimum of fraud and delay. It was, as P. B. Johnson has concluded, a remarkable 'success story'.[20] This success story was repeated throughout the 1920s. Under the unprecedented pressure of mass unemployment, central government assumed for the first time direct responsibility for a nation-wide system of relief which guaranteed the majority of the unemployed the prompt payment of an income ensuring 'basic economic security'.[21] For its own peculiar reasons, the popular press sought to minimize the achievement, but on every serious charge of maladministration and inefficiency, a series of public and private inquiries absolved the

[19] *Evidence to the (Aberconway) Committee of Inquiry into the Scheme of Out-of-Work Donation* (Cmd. 407), PP (1919), xxx, 219, qq. 359–72.

[20] Cmd. 305, PP (1919), xxx, 201, paras, 12 and 14. Johnson, *Land Fit for Heroes*, p. 334.

[21] Burns, *British Unemployment Programs*, p. 324. See also E. W. Bakke, *The Unemployed Man* (1933) and the *Final Report of the Royal Commission on Unemployment Insurance*, para. 598.

Ministry.[22] The routine payment of unemployment benefit was an unqualified executive success.

Where the Ministry's implementation of policy might more justifiably be criticized is the exercise of discretion by its officials over who should receive benefit. In 1924, as has been seen, administrative discretion was greatly increased following the extension of the 'genuinely-seeking-work' clause to all claimants. This, according to the Labour Government, was a reasonable price to pay in order to safeguard from abuse by a minority more generous payments to the majority of the unemployed. However, as Alan Deacon has shown, the influence of this discretion grew gradually more pernicious.[23] Through a series of 'tightening-up' campaigns in the 1920s, an increasing number of claimants were surreptitiously excluded from benefit; officials started to assume a 'groundless and dangerous' confidence that they could instinctively assess a claimant's state of mind;[24] and the Ministry as a whole became obsessed with the eradication of abuse to the detriment of more constructive objectives, such as counselling claimants and canvassing for jobs. Between 1919 and 1925, for example, nine inquiries were mounted into malingering (each of which confirmed that under 2 per cent of all claimants were 'scroungers') whilst, until 1931, no inquiry was undertaken into what presumably should have been the concern of any responsible social service department—the fate of claimants disqualified from benefit.[25]

On five grounds, however, this apparent lack of imaginative humanity can be explained, if not wholly explained away. First there is the obvious point that, owing to Treasury retrenchment, the Ministry's staff were overworked, undertrained, and working in premises that were largely unsuitable. Such conditions constantly discouraged sympathetic administration. Secondly, although senior officers such as Bowers and J. F. G. Price were adamant that checks

---

[22] Deriving much of its revenue from advertising jobs, the press had an ill-concealed vested interest in the discrediting of exchanges. The only thing it did conceal was the evidence to substantiate its accusations, as many inquiries (starting with the Aberconway Committee) noted. See *Evidence*, para. 4. For an example of a private vindication of the exchanges, see J. J. Astor, *Unemployment Insurance in Great Britain* (1925),

[23] A. Deacon, *In Search of the Scrounger* (1976).

[24] Steel-Maitland papers, GD 193/94/2: John Hilton, 'Reflections on a tour of certain employment exchanges' (June 1929), para. 12.

[25] Bakke, *The Unemployed Man*, pp. 84-7.

against abuse were necessary, there is little evidence to suggest that successive 'tightening-up' campaigns were an administrative initiative.[26] Rather, they were a political necessity, dictated by the need of successive Cabinets to reconcile their generosity towards the unemployed (occasioned by elections) with parsimony (occasioned by the need to balance the budget). Officials exercising discretion, in other words, were scapegoats for ministers who, in seeking votes, had failed to exercise theirs. Thirdly, the 'tightening-up' campaigns were largely in accordance with public opinion, as expressed not only by the press but also by claimants themselves. Fourthly, in defiance of public opinion, the Ministry repeatedly stressed that it was not the majority but only a small minority of claimants who were malingerers.[27] Finally, it was a Ministry official (John Hilton) who, having toured the exchanges dressed as a tramp, wrote a most damning report on the 'genuinely-seeking-work' clause which helped finally to secure its abolition. By encouraging otherwise honest workers to lie, he concluded, it caused the 'real demoralization of the dole':

If they want to keep their benefit they have to choose between two evils, that of actually going from works to works where they know there is not the least chance of work and where they will be treated with a certain amount of wrath and contumely, or that of saying that they have been when in fact they have not. Of the two evils they choose the latter. It is not lying: it is a mere ritual required by the authorities.[28]

Like all healthy organizations, therefore, the Ministry contained amongst its staff individuals who were prepared to identify and remedy abuse; and the presence of such officials ensured that the Ministry's larger executive achievements were never seriously compromised.

The second traditional ground on which the Ministry has been criticized is its alleged failure in the early 1920s to anticipate and respond to mass unemployment. For example, the 1920 Unemploy-

---

[26] Deacon, *In Search of the Scrounger*, p. 37. In other contentious areas, such as the disqualification from benefit of married women and strikers, there is similarly little evidence that officials did anything but follow conservative public opinion. For the impact of benefit on levels of unemployment, see below, pp. 217-18.

[27] See, for example, Bakke, *The Unemployed Man*, pp. 88-9 and Lab 2/1804/CEB(G) 111/1928, ch. 2, where allegations of widespread scrounging are dismissed as a 'monstrous untruth'.

[28] Steel-Maitland papers, GD 193/94/2, para. 19.

ment Insurance Act, which was the Ministry's major contribution
to post-war planning, has been condemned as a typical example of
bureaucratic ineptitude: after a five-year delay, the terms of the
1911 Bill were largely re-enacted with a few alterations which reduced, rather than increased, the Unemployment Fund's ability to
cater for mass unemployment. Similarly, the Ministry's reaction to
the onset of mass unemployment is conventionally depicted as one
of unprincipled panic which demoralized claimants (whose rights
to relief were continually altered), angered the Treasury (which
sought reliable estimates for the budget), and infuriated local
authorities (who had to relieve claimants disqualified by the Ministry). Such traditional criticisms, however, are largely unjustified.

First, the 1920 Insurance Act was not an example of bureaucratic
ineptitude. The main charges levelled against it are that, rather
than preparing the Unemployment Fund for the strains of mass
unemployment, it threatened to decrease its revenue in two ways:
by permitting industries with low levels of unemployment to 'contract out' of the national scheme and by reducing the level of
unemployment at which it was to balance.[29] Such charges are anachronistic. Not only do they beg the question of how far anyone
in early 1920 could have anticipated the extent and persistence of
inter-war unemployment, but they also concentrate on events which
succeeded rather than preceded the Act. In the real world of 1920,
a major influence on planners was the memory of the trade union
revolt against the attempted extension of insurance in 1916: to
prevent further non-compliance, individual industries had to be
given the opportunity to 'contract out'. Likewise the Act had to
acknowledge the contemporary consensus that the financial provisions of the 1911 Act were excessively cautious for normal peacetime needs and should be relaxed. In any case, it was not the
inadequacy of post-war planners that caused the later chronic indebtedness of the Unemployment Fund but the subsequent political
decision to make insurance a substitute for (rather than a supplement to) the Poor Law. When in the 1930s, it was allowed to revert
to its original purpose, it reverted also to solvency.

Similarly, the Ministry's reaction to the onset of mass unemployment was not one of unprincipled panic. Rather, acting as a
'national authority for unemployment' in a manner which (had

[29] See, for example, Gilbert, *British Social Policy*, p. 74.

they noticed) would have gladdened the hearts of the Webbs, the Ministry—in conjunction with the Ministry of Health—forcefully warned the Cabinet in August 1920 that, although the unemployment rate was only 1.6 per cent, falling orders and accelerating redundancies foreshadowed a serious depression. The Government, it continued, was ill-prepared to meet such a crisis. Unemployment insurance was not an appropriate palliative for mass unemployment, and traditional relief measures, such as the labour test and corporation work, were both impractical and discredited; non-contributory doles, moreover, were indefensible in principle and expensive. 'The essence of dealing with the situation', the Ministry concluded, 'was preparation in advance,' and, as the department responsible 'for dealing with all phases of unemployment', it requested from the Cabinet authority to formulate and implement a new relief programme.[30]

Such prescience, however, did not achieve significant results. This was partly due to factors outside the Ministry's control. On the eve of one of the severest depressions in British history, for example, the Treasury's considered response to the warnings was that 'the attitude of panic in which the Ministry of Labour approaches unemployment questions is more likely to create unemployment rather than alleviate it'.[31] The Cabinet's response accordingly lacked urgency. Failure was also due, however, to the Ministry's own weaknesses of which two were paramount: the inadequacy of its economic policy (which will be discussed in the next chapter) and a debilitating internal disagreement over the principle of devolution.

Devolution had already occasioned a set battle within the Ministry during the drafting of the 1920 Insurance Act. True to their policy of 'home rule for industry', Butler and his allies had argued that it was not only necessary in practice but also right in principle to permit individual industries to establish their own insurance schemes and thereby 'contract out' of the national system. Government would be relieved of an unnecessary burden and, more importantly, sectional manpower policy and industrial relations would be improved by the mutual interest of both sides of industry in the success of 'their own' insurance schemes. Phillips and his colleagues from the Board of Trade, however, vehemently opposed 'contracting out'. Administratively, they argued, it was impossible

[30] Cab 24/110/CP 1747.   [31] T 161/46/S 2933.

to define the scope of individual industries, especially if they employed a large number of fringe or casual workers. Economically, sectional schemes would discourage occupational and geographical mobility and undermine employment exchanges as a source of national information upon which future policy could be based. Financially, the viability of the Unemployment Fund would be jeopardized were the state to be left with all the bad risks. Finally, if taxpayers' money were to be apportioned to sectional schemes, there was the critical constitutional question of public accountability. As Phillips concluded:

The problem is not really one of deciding whether an industry should be allowed to fend for itself ... but of deciding whether an industry should be allowed to set up a sort of *imperium in imperio* with compulsory powers conferred by the State, and a state contribution, but without presumably the measure of state control which would ordinarily be a concomitant of those privileges.[32]

The battle was finally won by the devolutionists, but their victory was largely pyrrhic. Under pressure from the Treasury, only an attenuated form of 'contracting out' was permitted by the 1920 Act and, as a result of mass unemployment, only two service industries (banking and insurance) took up the challenge.

The second battle over devolution revived the pre-war debate over the relationship between the Ministry and local government during the relief of unemployment and was far more debilitating. Officials such as Wolfe and Masterton-Smith, supported by Sir Montague Barlow, were confirmed centralists, arguing that the Ministry should assume full responsibility for the able-bodied unemployed. As they agreed with Beveridge during a secret meeting in October 1920, 'the finding of work for the unemployed is the essential thing,' and so it was vital 'to secure one responsible ministry for the control of both employment and assistance so that policy as to both can be considered ... under the same head'.[33] Local government was unable to provide work on a national scale and therefore it should assume (as the Webbs' compromise with the Labour Party in 1912 had anticipated) a subordinate role under a central public assistance commissioner (who might be the Ministry's parliamentary secretary). Its role should be limited to the

---

[32] Pin 7/13. For a fuller discussion of this issue, see my debate with N. Whiteside in *Historical Journal*, 25 (1982), 437–46.

[33] Lab 2/762/7.

relief of those non-able-bodied claimants whom the employment exchanges certified as non-insured. These views, however, were opposed by officials such as Cunningham who, under the political leadership of Horne and Macnamara, feared that, by accepting responsibility for all the able-bodied unemployed (including vagrants), the Ministry would be infected by the 'Poor Law taint'.

The devolution issue was further confused by narrow departmental interest. On the one hand, it was recognized that, were the Ministry to accept full responsibility for all able-bodied unemployment, the pretension of the employment exchanges to be serious manpower agencies would be jeopardized. Skilled workers would be further discouraged from attending, the temptation would grow to place men on the grounds of personal hardship rather than industrial qualifications, and (in directing applicants to relief works) exchanges would for the first time be obliged to require claimants to take work below union rates of pay. On the other hand, as one former Board of Trade official argued, were the Ministry not to take full responsibility, it 'might be decentralized out of existence'.[34] Throughout the early 1920s, official advice remained hopelessly divided.

Such irresolution on a matter of fundamental principle demonstrated the Ministry's inability authoritatively to respond to the actuality of mass unemployment, which it had so correctly identified in its 1920 memorandum. Faced by the immediate crisis, it resorted to a series of conflicting expedients and—in a desperate attempt to end uncovenanted benefit—even reverted to recommending a greater use of the Poor Law.[35] Then, faced by the continuing need to devise a permanent relief policy, it started to discount bold initiative. Three examples may illustrate the Ministry's declining zeal. First, dependants' allowances—potentially the most radical innovation of the period—were not enthusiastically endorsed (because they varied the social, unlike the industrial, wage to individual need) but grudgingly conceded (because, by providing selective assistance, they removed the need to increase general benefit levels and so saved money).[36] Secondly, when Sir Montague Barlow tried to fulfil his party's pledge of all-in insurance—a

[34] Lab 2/288/2. A summary of departmental policy on the Poor Law throughout 1919 and 1920 is in Lab 2/502/ED 27444/1919.
[35] Cab 27/114/CU 25, minutes for 16 Aug. 1921.
[36] Cab 24/128/CP 339, 11 Oct. 1921.

unified insurance scheme which would guarantee all contributors against their three 'devouring terrors' of sickness, unemployment, and old age—it was opposed within the Ministry on narrow administrative grounds.[37] Finally, when a committee of officials (the Anderson Committee) was appointed to examine relief policy in December 1923, Sir Horace Wilson (in conjunction with the permanent secretary of the Ministry of Health) seized the opportunity to put foward a new blueprint for reform. This memorandum was not entirely without merit, for it proposed the payment of benefit as of right to the able-bodied (or, as Wilson put it, 'effective industrial units') for 26 weeks a year.[38] However, it also recommended that benefit should be paid below subsistence level from a self-supporting insurance fund and that, after 26 weeks, the minister of labour should have a wide discretion to withdraw it and consign claimants to the Poor Law, which was to remain firmly based on the principle of deterrence. Such conditions illustrated just how far, under Wilson's leadership, the idealism of reconstruction had been eroded in social, as in industrial relations, policy. Departmental ambitions had retreated on three main fronts since 1920. No longer was the finding of work for the unemployed to be the 'essential thing'; the impracticality of a deterrent Poor Law was no longer acknowledged; and, despite the transparent incompatibility of ministerial discretion and an unsubsidized insurance fund over the previous three years, both were to be retained.

The final phase of the Ministry's relief strategy in the 1920s was the renewed search for a 'sound' policy after 1924. This phase was marked by increasing official conviction, as Wilson's rigid blueprint was gradually replaced by the more flexible two-tier system of relief. It was marked also by consistent and courageous political leadership from two ministers who had as their clear objectives the need both to balance the Unemployment Fund (by the phased withdrawal of payments to the uninsured and an increase in the relative size of the state's contribution) and to resist the temptation to

---

[37] Lab 2/1596/I & S 452/1922; Pin 1/1. Had unity been achieved, the approved societies in charge of health insurance would have assumed responsibility for unemployment insurance. This, *inter alia*, would have deprived employment exchanges of any firsthand knowledge of unemployment and thus weakened them as manpower agencies; on the other hand, approved societies would have had no means of checking malingering. For proof that the Anderson Committee was established on Barlow's initiative, see Baldwin papers, vol. 7, fols. 257–60.

[38] Pin 1/1, memorandum of 14 Jan. 1924.

surmount emergencies by increased borrowing. In his determination to secure a sound permanent policy, for instance, Steel-Maitland regularly warned Baldwin that Treasury opposition to the 1927 Insurance Bill was 'penny wise, pound foolish' and that the Government's refusal to increase its insurance contributions to the level of other participants would 'land the Exchequer in the end in far greater expenditure'. In October 1928, he also overrode the temporary caution of his officials to insist that his dissent be recorded from the key Cabinet decision to extend the Fund's borrowing powers rather than to implement fully the 1927 Act.[39] Likewise Bondfield, working in a political climate less favourable to the Treasury, overrode traditional objections and swiftly attained both the principle of equal-thirds and the transfer of financial responsibility for the non-insured to the exchequer. Courting bitter unpopularity within the Labour movement, she then sought a reduction in the Fund's borrowing requirement by the reduction of benefit in line with the cost of living and the tightening-up of the qualification to benefit. Her determination, and that of her advisers, to act with integrity was made explicit in her first major submission to Cabinet. As she declared:

Optimistic forecasts are valuable in their proper place, but they have been poor friends to the Unemployment Insurance schemes. It is clear to me that we must base the finance of the scheme not on any forecasts of the future, but on the realised experience of the past few years ... I am strongly opposed to any further increase of the borrowing power, whether by itself or as a supplement to other measures. The borrowing power is already high enough and we must put a stop to the indefensible plan of living on over-drafts.[40]

Both ministers were ultimately defeated. Steel-Maitland was overwhelmed by the irresistible combination of Cabinet pusillanimity (which led to the continual refusal to disqualify the non-insured), the inconsistency of Churchill as chancellor, and Treasury parsimony.[41] Similarly Bondfield found it impossible to prevent the

[39] Baldwin papers, vol. 7, fols. 397, 451–2, letters of 3 May and 3 Nov. 1927; Cab 24/198/CP 312; Cab 23/59/48 (28) 6.

[40] Cab 24/204/CP 169 (29).

[41] Having asserted in 1925 that any government which 'dared to do its duty' would end uncovenanted benefit, Churchill then vehemently opposed the 1927 Insurance Act on the grounds that there was 'really no great hurry' for reform. Baldwin papers, vol. 7, fol. 378 (Churchill to Steel-Maitland, 19 Sept. 1925) and Cab 24/187/CP 168 (27).

escalation of the Fund's borrowing requirement to £125m., owing
to a combination of back-bench pressure and the onset of the world
depression (which greatly increased cyclical unemployment, which
the Fund was still expected to relieve). Their efforts, however, did
at least demonstrate that—in direct contradiction to contemporary
criticism and received historical opinion—there existed within the
Ministry the political courage, as well as the administrative will, to
devise a practical alternative to the Poor Law. Just as in the implementation of relief there was little of the maladministration which
the popular press professed to expose, so in the formulation of
policy there was little hard evidence of the sentimental spendthrift
Ministry of the NCEO's imagination.

Throughout the 1920s, therefore, the Ministry's role in the effective breakup of the Poor Law was far from discreditable. Clearly
its officials lacked the coorporate imagination and commitment
essential for the swift, comprehensive replacement of the Poor Law.
They never radically forced the pace of change, nor, after 1920,
appeared willing to do so. Consequently, opportunities such as the
Anderson Committee were missed at which, in the tradition of
nineteenth-century zealots, the initiative might have been seized
and the whole insurance debate raised to a higher level. However,
given the political constraints within which the Ministry had to
work and the absence of viable alternative policies amongst its
critics, the executive achievement of unemployment relief was remarkable and, after 1924, the formulation of policy was consistently courageous. What the Ministry essentially lacked in the
1920s was political weight and this—much to its as well as everyone
else's surprise—it suddenly acquired in the 1930s.

The Final Solution, 1931–1934

The permanent replacement of the Poor Law was one of the few
political nettles grasped and all but resolved by the National
Government in its first full term of office. In the immediate term,
it was forced to adopt the temporary expedient of transitional
payments, but in 1934 it passed a major new Unemployment Act
which, because it established the basic machinery by which social
security has since been administered, has rightly been described as
'one of the most important pieces of legislation of this century'.[42]

[42] T. Lynes, 'Unemployment Assistance Tribunals' in M. Adler and A. Bradley,
Justice, Discretion and Poverty (1976), p. 5.

This act created a new three-tier system of relief supervised by two new 'independent' bodies, the UISC and UAB, and the local authorities. The responsibility of the UISC was to ensure the solvency of a reformed unemployment insurance scheme, by which the majority of the unemployed were to be relieved. The responsibility of the UAB was to devise and implement a national system of standardized means-tested benefit for approximately 500,000–700,000 uninsured claimants who, in contemporary terminology, were 'able-bodied persons within the field of industrial employment'. This left the Poor Law to cater only for approximately 30,000 unemployed persons who—like vagrants—were able-bodied but enjoyed only a tenuous connection with the labour market.[43]

Between 1931 and 1934, the Ministry played a major part both in the evolution of general policy and in the drafting, presentation, and implementation of the Unemployment Act. The Act itself was hardly an unqualified triumph for the Ministry, because departmental policy had long favoured a two- rather than a three-tier system of relief. The political revolt against the UAB's initial relief scales (and their subsequent suspension) was also a serious rebuff for those of its officials who had been seconded to the Board. The evolution of policy in general, however, was a triumph. In Cabinet, Betterton inflicted on Chamberlain a series of rare defeats; in Whitehall, the Ministry finally established itself over the head of the Ministry of Health as the predominant social services department; and, in the staffing of the UISC and UAB, Ministry officials monopolized the senior positions from which, in later years, they were able to exercise considerable personal influence over the development of policy. This burgeoning strength is best analyzed in two phases: the administration of transitional payments (from which, in the implementation of policy, the Ministry emerged triumphant over the Ministry of Health), and the drafting of the 1934 Unemployment Act (during which, in the formulation of policy, it challenged successfully both Chamberlain and the Treasury).

Transitional payments can be dealt with briefly because, although they covered over one million claimants at their peak in 1932, they were always regarded as a temporary expedient.[44] The two priori-

---

[43] These figures refer to 1937, when the UAB was first fully operational. See also Appendix 3, A.

[44] They also have to be dealt with briefly, as the preservation of the majority of the records appears also to have been transitional.

ties of the National Government on its assumption of office were economy and speed. Economy demanded the replacement of the existing system of transitional benefits because, by its relative generosity, it both attracted marginal claims and threatened the future of the insurance scheme: why, if they were thereby guaranteed no extra privileges to the uninsured, should employed workers continue to pay their insurance contributions?[45] Speed necessitated the use of existing administrative machinery. Consequently, it was decided that, after a means test administered by the public assistance committee of local government, benefit (funded by the exchequer) should be paid via the employment exchanges to all those who had exhausted their insurance rights. This system, in the tradition of the 1919 out-of-work donation scheme, was an ingenious improvisation which was both immediately practical and, on balance, advantageous to all participants. For central government, the exchequer had still to bear the full cost of relief without any direct control over its expenditure; but it was relieved of the need to devise a new national relief scale and there were, in fact, in-built guarantees of financial restraint.[46] For local government, there was the political stigma of administering a tenfold increase in means testing; but at least the greater evil of full financial responsibility for unemployment relief was averted. Finally, for the claimants themselves, there was the indignity of the means test and the loss of the right to appeal against any reduction in benefit; but at least they were not fully pauperized as, for instance, the May Committee had recommended. They remained physically separated from paupers (being paid, for example, at employment exchanges and not the Public Assistance Committee (PAC) offices) and were threatened by none of the paupers' traditional disabilities (such as payment in kind and institutional confinement).

During the first year of its administration, however, potential contradictions in policy gradually became apparent and the Government was persuaded by them seriously to plan a new system of relief. There were three main problems. First, owing to the varying practices of local authorities, major discrepancies de-

---

[45] Admitted by Bondfield in Cab 24/213/CP 235 (30), 9 July 1930.
[46] Standards of means testing had, for instance, to be identical with those of public assistance, in which local government did have a direct financial interest. Transitional payments were in fact very economical and saved the Government twice as much as had been expected. See Burns, *British Unemployment Programs*, p. 141.

veloped in the assessment and levels of benefit, which were widely considered to be incompatible with a nationally financed system of relief. Secondly, there was mounting political criticism that, by failing to discount certain types of income (such as war pensions), the means test was undermining respectability and thrift. Thirdly, in the assessment of benefit, a minority of Labour-held local authorities openly refused to obey the law. The Ministry developed its own peculiar answers to these problems and, in so doing, started to assert its authority over its joint administrator, the Ministry of Health. In the first place, it argued that variations in benefit were the very essence of the scheme: to ignore local differences in the cost of living and public expectations would, by sanctioning payments 'above what a man's fellows approve', bring the whole system into disrepute.[47] In the second place, the Ministry—despite the formal statutory requirement that the standard of means testing should be identical for the recipients of transitional benefit and public assistance—was sympathetic to more favourable treatment for the former and secured in November 1932 the Transitional Payment (Determination of Needs) Act which exempted certain sources of income from means testing. Finally, it admitted that in about 5 per cent of cases the rates of benefit were illegally high, but countered this by stressing that the vast majority of local authorities had acted with unexpected efficiency and that the real abuse lay in the 25 per cent of cases where payment was unjustifiably low.

These essentially pragmatic responses to issues, which the Cabinet had purposely left unresolved, occasioned major disputes within and without the Ministry. Within the Ministry, Eady (who had been promoted to take direct responsibility for transitional payments policy) became increasingly lenient in contrast to the more legalistic attitude of Phillips in Whitehall and of Adams in the provinces.[48] Without, the Ministry (which—from its experience of uncovenanted benefit in the 1920s—was alive to the political

[47] Bowers in Pin 7/198, 26 Aug. 1931. For the rest of the paragraph, see Pin 7/124, Dec. 1931–Feb. 1932. Ministry officials even colluded over the payment of illegally high benefit by the Public Assistance Committee at Merthyr Tydfil—in Jan. 1935 the scene of the initial protests against the UAB. See Pin 7/139, Price to Phillips, 13 Sept. 1934. I am indebted for this reference to Max Krafchik.

[48] Pin 7/124. Adams claimed that, as divisional officer, he was responsible for the supercession by commissioners of the errant Rotherham and Durham Public Assistance Committees, see Markham papers, 9/3, Adams to Markham, 7 Feb. 1935.

need for pragmatic flexibility) came into direct conflict with the
Ministry of Health which (despite its joint drafting of the 1920
memorandum on unemployment) still hankered after deterrence
and was greatly concerned by the permanent 'damage' being inflicted on public assistance by the laxity of transitional payments.
A simmering row finally erupted in the autumn of 1932 when the
Determination of Needs Act was being drafted. Ministry of Health
officials joined the Treasury in condemning the Act on the
grounds—virtually identical to those employed by the Treasury to
condemn the 1920 memorandum—that 'panic legislation of the
kind suggested would be little short of disastrous'.[49] In 1932, however, unlike 1920, the Cabinet decided that the Ministry of Labour
was right and the Act was duly passed.

This defeat clearly stung Neville Chamberlain, as chancellor of
the exchequer and a former minister of health, into a fundamental
reappraisal of unemployment relief during which he determined not
only to end all temporary expedients (which had so bedevilled
policy over the past 12 years) but also to reverse the cardinal
principle on which policy had been based since 1931: the assessment
of all discretionary benefit by local, not central, government. Until
October 1932, conventional wisdom both at Westminster and in
Whitehall had strongly favoured a system of relief for the non-
insured whereby need was assessed by local government and benefit
was largely financed by the national exchequer. Whenever a totally
centralized relief agency had been mooted (as, for example, before
the Royal Commission on Unemployment Insurance between 1930
and 1932) it had always been firmly rejected on the grounds of the
potential political embarrassment for central government, administrative duplication, and the undesirability (if not impracticality)
of national standards of relief. Chamberlain, himself, had been a
leading opponent of centralization.[50]

In October 1932, however, Chamberlain set conventional wisdom on its head by proposing a new statutory commission,
financed by the exchequer, to take control of all able-bodied relief
including the payment of a standardized, means-tested benefit. At
a stroke he cut through the indecision of outside experts, most of
whom, as their evidence to the Royal Commission on Unemployment Insurance illustrated, had come to favour centralization. His

[49] T 172/1769, 13 Oct. 1932.
[50] See, for example, Cab 24/223/CP 211 (28 Aug. 1931) and MH 57/10.

new commission was to cover unemployment assistance and insurance, to be executive not advisory, and to determine the principles of relief not just draft regulations in accordance with broad principles laid down by parliament.[51] He also—at least potentially— resolved two of the traditional objections to centralization. Ministerial embarrassment was to be avoided by the independence of the commission from parliamentary scrutiny: the responsible minister, therefore, would not have to answer parliamentary questions on individual cases of relief. Administrative duplication was also to be avoided by the commission's responsibility for all able-bodied relief (that is for those claimants who had exhausted their right to insurance benefit *and* for those who had never been insured). The sole unresolved problem was one which Chamberlain considered to be a largely straightforward task for rational bureaucracy: the devising of national standards for the assessment and payment of relief.

Chamberlain's proposals were enthusiastically welcomed within government, not only as the administrative means to resolve the seemingly intractable problem of able-bodied relief but also as a political device to prove that (after cuts in benefit and the extension of the means test in 1931) the National Government did, after all, have a constructive policy. His one consistent critic was the Minister of Labour (Betterton) who, for over a year, fought a dogged rearguard action on two Cabinet subcommittees (the Unemployment Insurance Committee, between October 1931 and April 1933, and the Unemployment Insurance Policy Committee, between May and October 1933). This action, which was highlighted by a major showdown in full Cabinet in April 1933, was based on three principal objections: the general need for, and practicability of, such a dramatic new initiative; the bureaucratic nature of the proposed commission; and (in a much repeated phrase) the treatment of unemployment relief 'not as an industrial, but as a Poor Law problem'.[52] As will be seen, the Ministry was overruled

---

[51] The Commission set up by the Labour Government to educate its supporters was generally held to have enlightened no one (private information from its secretary, Emmerson). Of the experts who appeared before it, Beveridge and the NCEO wanted a commission to cover unemployment assistance only; Beveridge wanted an administrative, G. D. H. Cole a quasi-legislative body; the NCEO wanted it to decide principles of relief, whilst the TUC wanted it only to draft regulations.

[52] See, for instance, Cab 23/75/25 (33), appendix, p. 8. This appendix is a vital verbatim record of the Cabinet meeting on 7 Apr. 1933 which was not incorporated into the full minutes.

on the first of these objections but successfully sustained the other two.

Chamberlain's volte-face had been provoked by his sudden conviction that immediate action was needed both to prevent the collapse of local government and to provide remedial help for the long-term unemployed. As minister of health in the 1920s, he had witnessed the 'damage' which the extension of the franchise had done to the integrity of Poor Law administration; and the difficulties of transitional payments (culminating in the suspension of the Rotherham PAC in September 1932) convinced him that similar damage was about to be suffered by the system of local government which he himself had reformed only three years before.[53] Simultaneously, as chancellor, he became convinced that no conceivable upturn in the economy could eradicate unemployment and that local government could neither finance nor co-ordinate the national programme of organized recreation that was necessary if life was to be made 'as tolerable as possible' for the long-term unemployed.[54] Centralization for him, therefore, suddenly became a distinctly attractive proposition. The Ministry of Labour demurred. On the one hand, its officials had been favourably impressed by the resilience of local government under the strains of transitional payments; on the other, they noted cynically that the Ministry's retraining programmes had always been a prime target of Treasury economies and that, even now, the Treasury was making no extra funds available. Existing machinery, they argued, would be perfectly adequate if only it were to be properly financed.

This defence by the Ministry of the status quo was disingenuous. Existing laws governing transitional payments and unemployment insurance expired respectively in April and June 1933 and the time

[53] E. Briggs and A. Deacon, 'The creation of the Unemployment Assistance Board', *Policy and Politics*, 2 (1973), 43–62. Throughout the municipal elections of Nov. 1932, Chamberlain was also being constantly alerted by Central Office to the fears expressed by local Conservative parties concerning the attractiveness to voters of 'socialist' policies towards the means test and to the difficulty of recruiting candidates, especially those willing to serve on public assistance committees.

[54] Neville Chamberlain papers, NC 18/1/801; Cab 27/501, memorandum 2. The Ministry's reply is in memorandum 3. Bowers (who was soon to join the London County Council had written in Jan. 1933: 'How far the Chancellor's diagnosis of the position is right must be a matter of opinion, but local government has shown an amazing capacity for overcoming difficulties of this kind. So long as I have known anything about local government the same cry has been heard, but history has always shown it to be ill-founded.' See Pin 6/80.

was therefore opportune for reform, were reform needed. That it was is evident from the Ministry's own papers.[55] In May 1932, for example, Eady admitted that the separation of the administrative and financial responsibility for transitional payments was 'fundamentally wrong ... No Authority representing a local electorate can reasonably be expected indefinitely to resist pressure from large numbers when it is spending money it does not have to find.' Similarly Betterton—unnerved by the hunger marches in October 1932—warned the Cabinet that the linchpin of existing policy, the means test, might have to be abandoned. Finally, the Ministry was fully aware of large numbers of local authorities which had either requested to be relieved of the responsibility for transitional payments or had agreed to administer them solely on the understanding that they would be temporary. Existing practice clearly provided no basis for long-term policy and local government was becoming ever less willing to co-operate with Whitehall. Chamberlain was right to seek rational, permanent reform.

If the Ministry's resistance to change was disingenuous, however, its suspicions concerning the recreational programme (which was Chamberlain's positive justification of the commission) were valid. Throughout 1932-3, the Ministry was forced into the distinctly unfamiliar position of having consistently to warn the Treasury (or at least Chamberlain) against financial rashness.[56] The proposed commission, it argued, would be deceptively expensive for several reasons. Central government would become responsible for all the able-bodied unemployed, not just for those from the insured industries. It would incur the administrative costs of relieving those extra claimants. National standards (because they would be catering for a wider range of economic and social circumstances) were bound to be more lax than local regulations. Finally, these laxer standards would 'attract' extra claims and might even casualize industries, such as agriculture, because employers would be tempted to discharge the unemployed on to the central fund rather than maintain them during periods of seasonal inactivity. With

[55] The three examples are: Pin 6/46/2F 816/1932, draft of 4 May 1932; Cab 27/501; Ast 7/24, notes on clause 35.

[56] Pin 6/46/2F 816/1932 (Bowers to Floud, May 1932) and, for example, Cab 27/552/UIC (33) 12, para. 3. Chamberlain remained close to his former Ministry of Health advisers throughout this period, in particular Sir Arthur Robinson. How far Treasury officials ever accepted his social, as opposed to his economic, objectives must remain open to doubt.

such extra expenses (estimated at between £5m. and £10m.), how was a 'constructive' policy to be financed? This mystery was never resolved and public misgivings about its financial implications were to be a key in the public outcry against the UAB in January 1935.

By April 1933, the Ministry had lost its battle to preserve the status quo and was fully engaged in its next battle over the nature of the proposed reforms. It agreed with the Treasury and Ministry of Health that, as far as parliamentary responsibility for individual cases of relief was concerned, 'the responsible minister should have the protection of a statutory commission';[57] but it was opposed to any further extension of bureaucracy, in particular the removal from parliament of all control over the commission and the denial to claimants of the right to appeal against official decisions. In the first instance, the Ministry (quoting Disraeli on the irresponsible Poor Law Commission of 1834-48) accused Chamberlain of a 'moral crime and a political blunder' in seeking to remove from parliamentary control a policy involving over half a million people and the expenditure of over £50m. a year.[58] Officials stressed the moral objections, whilst Betterton—with his keener political nose—argued that, if the parliamentary safety-valve were removed, there might well be a popular explosion. Unconstitutional behaviour by the Government would directly encourage unconstitutional behaviour by the unemployed. The Ministry soon won this particular battle and the UAB was subsequently responsible to parliament: Cabinet controlled its policy, the comptroller and auditor-general examined its expenditure, and parliament had the right to debate its actions during any adjournment debate or when its regulations, annual vote, or annual report were laid before the House.[59]

The dispute over the right to appeal was not won by the Ministry until July 1933. The Treasury opposed appeals to a tribunal outside the commission on the grounds of financial irresponsibility:

[57] Cab 27/552/CP 90 (33), appendix 1 (b).

[58] Cab 27/501, memorandum 4; Cab 27/552/CP 10 (33), which contains a summary of the battle positions in Jan. 1933, and Ast 7/24. For evidence of the attempt by Young and Chamberlain to muzzle the electorate and an incoming Labour government, see Cab 27/501, memorandum for 16 Dec. 1932 and Cab 23/75/25(33), appendix, pp. 11-12.

[59] Between 1935 and 1939, there were to be 11 debates on the UAB and over 800 parliamentary questions. The suspension of the UAB's initial scales in Feb. 1935 resulted from uproar during an estimates debate.

The Commission will be answerable for the proper expenditure of its funds and must be able to control expenditure in the field of individual awards and it is in this field where extravagance comes in. To give the right of appeal to an outside body on individual awards would in effect take away their discretion from the Commission.[60]

The Ministry countered this 'completely bureaucratic' attitude on the constitutional grounds that there should always be the opportunity to appeal against 'a decision by officials to an outside body'. Its stand, however, was not solely based on principle, because experience with unemployment insurance had already convinced it that an appeals system was expedient, practical, and cheap. Only with such a public safety-valve could parliamentary questions on individual cases in effect be evaded. Moreover, it was

wrong to suppose that such tribunals would destroy the control of the Commission. Indeed it is only by such a system that the Commission will be able to enforce general standards which are flexible enough to deal with special cases and not too extravagant for the normal standards which form the greater part.[61]

As the Ministry was well aware, the careful selection of tribunal members could ensure (to the government's advantage) a satisfactory compromise between the perceived irresponsibility of decentralized democracy (where control was effectively exercised from below not above) and the inflexibility of centralized bureaucracy (which might fail to respond to the 'irrationality' of public opinion).

In its third area of dispute with the Treasury and the Ministry of Health, the scope of relief, the Ministry's political sensitivity again served it well. Both Chamberlain and Hilton Young (the minister of health) sought to bedazzle the Cabinet by claiming that their proposals placed within the National Government's grasp the holy grail of twentieth-century social reformers—the abolition of the Poor Law. Whilst the non-able-bodied were to be cared for by the specialist committees of local authorities, all the able-bodied poor were to be catered for constructively by the new commission

---

[60] Cab 23/75/25(33), appendix, p. 6; T 175/69. The advisor was Sir Ernest Strohmenger, former accountant-general of the Ministry of Health and later a rather less than successful deputy chairman of the UAB.

[61] Cab 27/552/UIC(33) 4 and 12. The latter provides a summary of the battle positions in May 1933.

which, promised Young, would be 'a new body with new methods which would be looked at in a new light as a body of trustees for the assistance of the unemployed'.[62] The Ministry, however, remained sceptical. It noted that the commission was to employ the same officials, the same machinery, and the same deterrent powers as the Poor Law and that no extra money was being earmarked for its new 'constructive' role. Officials scorned the proposals. As Eady wrote in March 1933:

It is quite certain that it cannot be presented as a great act of policy. It may do something to clean up the Poor Law and to relieve local authorities of an unwelcome administrative burden but it certainly exposes the greater part of those who will come under it to worse conditions and less security than they enjoy at present ... It is founded on a complete misunderstanding of the nature and size of the problem ... It purports to repeal the Poor Law but continues the Poor Law tradition and extends it to cover four times as many people.

More succinctly, Betterton claimed in Cabinet that the proposal 'applied Poor Law methods, through a Poor Law Commission, in Poor Law language'. To the Ministry, in short, the proposed reforms were purely cosmetic.

The substance of this dispute revolved around three particular issues: departmental responsibility for the commission, the exact extent of its responsibilities, and the relationship between the commission and unemployment insurance. Chamberlain, in accordance with the Webbs, was prepared initially to cede responsibility for the able-bodied to the Ministry of Labour but, as its campaign of civil disobedience unfolded, he quickly transferred his allegiance to the Ministry of Health. The Cabinet disagreed. Having flirted with the possibility of merging the two departments into a ministry of social service, it decided in April 1933 that for administrative reasons it was preferable, and for psychological reasons essential, for the Ministry of Labour to take charge.[63]

Betterton accepted this decision only on condition that policy would not be 'retrograde' and this condition gave the Ministry a crucial advantage in the subsequent battle over the exact scope of

[62] Cab 23/75/25(33), appendix, pp. 14-15. The Ministry's response is in Lab 2/1474/ET 1750/1933 and Cab 23/75/25 (33), appendix, p. 8.

[63] Cab 23/75/26 (33). Rather than being tainted by the Poor Law, the Ministry was traditionally responsible for 'constructive' economic services such as the employment exchanges and industrial training.

the commission's responsibility: should it relieve all the able-bodied unemployed or solely those 'in the industrial field'? Chamberlain and Young argued that all the able-bodied should be relieved because no rational distinction could be made between those who had 'a reasonable prospect of getting employment' and those who had not. Were such a distinction indeed to be attempted, administrative duplication and friction were bound to result.[64] Such arguments had, of course, supported the Ministry's traditional policy of a two-tier system of relief, which Betterton himself had publicly endorsed. However, he now claimed that, both politically and substantively, circumstances had changed. Politically, it was inexpedient to introduce so radical a reform when up to $1\frac{1}{4}$m. workers—either to their intense anger or to their demoralization—might be condemned to relief alongside the 'ordinary poor'. Moreover, when the means test had been reintroduced in 1931, the National Government had pledged that no genuine worker would be subjected to any pauperizing conditions, such as 'test work', to which Chamberlain still adhered. Substantively, the distinction between those 'in the industrial field' and those outside was not based on mere privilege, as Chamberlain claimed, but upon the origin of need. 'Need arising from unemployment', Betterton argued, 'is in practice today treated differently from need arising from other causes but this does not involve any question of artificial privilege for unemployment over sickness or old age.'[65] Given its initial strategic advantage, the Ministry was able to win its case.

The final battle, over the relationship of the commission and unemployment insurance, was fought not so much between Betterton and Chamberlain but between Betterton and his officials.[66] Betterton wanted both unemployment insurance and assistance to be administered by one body. Two commissions, he argued, might result in expensive administrative duplication and would, more importantly, give the distinct impression that the non-insured were to be treated more harshly. His officials' reaction revealed their deep scepticism of the Government's—or at least the Treasury's—ultimate intentions. On the one hand, they argued, the commission's role concerning insurance would be advisory and popular (the

---

[64] Ibid.

[65] Cab 23/75/25 (33), appendix, p. 10; Cab 27/552/CP 90 (33), para. 2; Cab 27/552/UIC (33) 12, para. 2.

[66] This paragraph is based largely on Pin 6/60, part 1.

guarantee of the Unemployment Fund's solvency and thus the claimant's right to benefit) while its role concerning assistance would be executive and unpopular (as, under pressure for economy, it inevitably developed the 'hard outlook characteristic of Poor Law administration'). On the other hand, they expected consistent pressure from the Treasury to transfer claimants from assistance (wholly funded by the exchequer) to insurance (two-thirds of which was financed by industry), which would make it extremely 'difficult for the assistance body to handle the Insurance Fund patiently, carefully and on its merits'. Therefore, the continuing popularity and integrity of unemployment insurance—always the principal concern of departmental policy—demanded separate commissions. So too did departmental vested interest. Just as the opposition of senior officers to centralization was undoubtedly eased by the prospect of accelerated promotion (the creation of a commission to provide for 'the poor and Eady'), so their commitment to separate commissions was strengthened by their fears for the Ministry's future. As Bowers admitted:

If one body acts in respect of both insurance and assistance, it will be seen to put the major part of the Ministry's work 'in commission' so powerful will that single body be. On the other hand with two bodies the case would be quite different and the Ministry would not be prejudiced.

Betterton finally conceded.

By September 1933, therefore, when Betterton introduced the Unemployment Act in parliament, the Ministry had—in this area at least—established its ascendancy over both the Ministry of Health and the Treasury in Whitehall and even over Chamberlain in Cabinet. Chamberlain, by his political drive, had forced the Ministry's officials to draft an Act which, on their own admission, differed 'considerably from anything we have previously considered or from what we would have proposed on our own initiative'.[67] In their turn, however, they had forced Chamberlain to accept a commission the (UAB) which, in both its constitution and its scope, was substantially different from the one which he had originally planned. The Ministry was at last reaping the full reward from the administrative expertise and political realism which it had painstakingly acquired over the past 17 years. It might be argued that the Ministry's principal contribution to reform had been the initial

[67] Eady in Pin 6/86.

negativism of its officials and the political timidity of Betterton: the UAB as the final solution to the 'breakup of the Poor Law' had none of the administrative boldness or purity of Chamberlain's (or the Webbs') blueprint, for the able-bodied continued to be relieved in two different ways by two different bodies. Such an assessment, however, would be wrong. By its lone stand the Ministry (in the emotive phrase of a future member of the UAB) had prevented the Government, under local electoral pressure, from sliding from 'democracy to fascism';[68] and by forcing the Cabinet to acknowledge public antipathy (however irrational) towards the Poor Law, it prevented a public outcry even greater than the one which eventually erupted. Moreover, as the following section will show, the system of relief which eventually evolved had the essential flexibility to overcome its initial troubles and achieve a remarkable, if little appreciated, success.

Pragmatic Adjustment, 1934–1939

Once established in 1934, the UISC and the UAB successfully resolved the problem of inter-war unemployment relief. In contrast to the 1920s, unemployment insurance became a popular and uncontroversial means of providing relief for the majority of the unemployed. After the public outcry against—and suspension of— its initial relief scales, the UAB also won grudging respect for its executive efficiency and flexibility. Moreover, both commissions, by developing a specialist expertise, helped, through private promptings and public reports, to create a body of informed opinion which prepared the way for the establishment of the welfare state after the Second World War. The Ministry's contribution to this success was considerable and contradictory. Ministers remained responsible for policy, and officials within the Ministry supervised the commissions' activities, whilst the commissions themselves were largely run by officials seconded from the Ministry.[69]

[68] The phrase was coined by a future member of the UAB, Tom Jones, in his diary for 3 Feb. 1933.

[69] The secretaries of both commissions were Ministry officials—A. Reeder and Wilfrid Eady. On the UISC all the administrative work was done by Ministry staff, whereas on the UAB Ministry officials dominated the policy and legal departments, while redundant Treasury and Ministry of Health officials controlled establishments, finance, and the regional organization. As permanent assistant secretary, G. T. Reid (Eady's eventual successor as secretary) controlled regulations and, as assistant secretaries, H. D. Hancock and G. S. Owen, were responsible respectively for appeals and training.

Conflict inevitably arose within this tripartite contribution to policy.

Of the two commissions, the UISC was the more prestigious and the more overtly successful. Constitutionally, it was a purely advisory body with the power to enquire into, challenge, and publicize any government proposal which might affect the solvency of the Unemployment Fund; but, in practice, it soon established itself as a widely respected 'policy-making' body.[70] There were two main reasons for this success. Personally, the appointment as chairman of Beveridge assured the Committee a grasp of detail and a clarity of vision which commanded official and public respect. Politically, unemployment insurance—once permitted to revert to its original purpose—lost its notoriety. Compulsory insurance contributions were no longer regarded by the insured as an infringement of personal liberty, but as a guarantee of the right to non-means-tested benefit. The healthy surplus in the Unemployment Fund removed the need for unpopular decisions concerning conditions and level of benefit. The UISC itself, moreover, reduced political tension by employing one of the traditional detractors of insurance to muzzle the other three. Beveridge, in the determination of policy, quickly disposed of the ritual requests by the TUC and NCEO (who were represented on the Committee) for increased benefits and decreased contributions; and, in his cross-questioning of its officials, he also exposed the Treasury's short-sighted expedience.[71] All these developments vindicated the Ministry's traditional policy. Its officials had long sought to involve Beveridge more closely in policy-making. They had also argued consistently that political controversy would be minimized if both the Unemployment Fund were put on a sound financial basis and the negativism of their critics subjected publicly to expert scrutiny.

The very expertise of the UISC, however, endangered the Ministry itself by threatening to expose the limitations of its own pragmatism. Conflict was latent in many issues, but especially in the solution to the dilemma which was to force both the Ministry and the Government into a series of contortions throughout the 1930s—the problems of how, in a low-wage economy, to relieve need without undermining work incentive. Official policy was con-

[70] Stocks, *My Common-Place Book*, p. 169.
[71] See especially the meeting of the UISC on 20–1 June 1935 (Beveridge papers, VIII, 4 i–ii).

tradictory. On the one hand, it maintained that, in order to safeguard the work ethic and self-help, wages should exceed insurance
benefit which, in its turn, should exceed non-contributory unemployment insurance. On the other hand, it required unemployment assistance to relieve need, whilst insurance benefit was regarded solely as a contribution towards maintenance, and wages
bore no relation to need, merely to the 'value of work done'.
Clearly a large family with no other resources could, and sometimes
did, receive more in assistance than insurance benefit; and both
unemployment benefit and assistance (with their dependants' allowance) could, and did, exceed take-home pay. Beveridge's solution
to the first of these problems was to use the Unemployment Fund's
surplus to increase children's allowances for the insured unemployed and, to the second, either to raise the wage ceiling (through
the grant to all wage-earners of a family allowance) or to accept it
(by the imposition of a 41s. wage stop in insurance benefit). The
Ministry rejected all three solutions.[72] The first, it argued, would
further undermine the principle of 'less eligibility'. The second
would be too costly and was, in any case, opposed by the TUC,
which interpreted it as a device for holding down wages. The third
was impractical, inequitable, and politically embarrassing. Any
arbitrary amount, such as 41s., would exceed the wage of certain
claimants and so, whilst penalizing higher wage-earners, would not
universally ensure the work ethic. A specific figure would also imply
an 'official fair wage', which might occasion more controversy than
a few unpublicized breaches of the principle of 'less eligibility'. The
problem, in the opinion of the Ministry and the Government, was
therefore better disguised than faced.

Beveridge temporarily accepted the Government's veto with the
result that the (supposedly independent) reports of the UISC never
recommended the use of the Unemployment Fund's growing surplus in ways of which the Treasury disapproved. How far the
acquiescence could, or indeed should, have lasted is uncertain.
What is certain, however, is that—in the specific circumstances of
the late 1930s—the UISC was a success. It supervised the efficient
relief of the vast majority of the unemployed. It created a climate
conducive to reform by both focusing government attention

[72] Cab 27/575/UAR (34) 11. The Ministry opposed a wage stop which varied
with an individual's earnings on the ground that flat-rate contributions required
flat-rate benefit.

on essential issues and informing public opinion. Moreover, by reintroducing Beveridge to the realities of working-class life and thereby convincing him that wage cuts were no automatic solution to unemployment and that contributory insurance was highly prized by the majority of workers (who were not scroungers), it rescued him from the pessimism and economic orthodoxy into which he had sunk by the early 1930s.[73] In short, the UISC not only helped to solve the immediate problem of unemployment relief; it also played a crucial—if little appreciated—role in preparing the ground for both the drafting and the enthusiastic public reception of the 1942 Beveridge Report.

In contrast to the UISC, the UAB was a weak body which, faced by a harder task, initially aroused far more controversy. That the Board was weak, and intended to be so by the National Government, was evident from the head-hunting activities of Neville Chamberlain. In order to achieve the Board's 'constructive' recreational purpose, Chamberlain initially sought as chairman someone (like Beveridge) who had 'initiative, originality and drive' and on these criteria Betterton was easily dismissed as a candidate. Instead the virtues of Sir Wyndham (later Lord) Portal were extolled; but, once he had failed his proficiency test (as a special commissioner to South Wales), the choice reverted to Betterton on the grounds that he was 'safe'.[74] All the other members of the Board were equally safe. This was particularly true of Strohmenger (as deputy-chairman), Reynard (a director of public assistance from Glasgow, much disliked by Labour) and Hallsworth (an orthodox professor of economics). It was true also of the two other appointments, which were rather more imaginative: Tom Jones (deputy secretary to the Cabinet and a confidant of Baldwin, who characteristically knew him not when the cock crowed in January 1935) and Violet Markham (the chairman of the Central Committee on Women's Training and Employment, through which the Ministry discharged both its money and statutory obligation for women's training). Both were deeply committed to the welfare of the poor; but in the last resort they too, as old-fashioned liberals, worked within the 'safe' assumption that greater expenditure of money would retard

[73] Harris, *Beveridge*, pp. 359–60.
[74] Neville Chamberlain papers, NC 2/23A, entries for 16 Mar., 9 May 1934. Portal disgraced himself by making the 'crude' suggestion that government money should be used to reopen the Ebbw Vale steel works.

rather than stimulate economic recovery and would threaten demoralization.[75]

The Board thus lacked incisive leadership and such leadership was vital if it were immediately to surmount the four fundamental problems left unresolved by the tactical compromises of 1932-4. First, could executive efficiency be reconciled with democratic accountability? Given that unemployment relief had 'corrupted' both national and local politics in the 1920s, could it now be 'taken out of politics' by the devolution of individual casework to an 'independent' body? Would parliament (which remained directly responsible for the principles of policy) be able to resist public pressure resulting from unpopular decisions by the UAB? Secondly, in defiance of conventional wisdom prior to 1932, was it possible to devise a national relief standard that was both flexible and economic? Thirdly, given the vital connection between the formulation and implementation of policy, could the Ministry of Labour—to parliament's satisfaction—supervise the UAB without seriously duplicating its work? Finally, was the Board to be innovatory (as Conservative Party propaganda proclaimed) or 'safe' (as the choice of Board members suggested)?[76] If the former, how was it to respond to popular conservatism, especially over the issues of less-eligibility and self-help?

The Board's initial inability to resolve these conundrums was cruelly exposed when its new relief scales and regulations were introduced on 7 January 1935. They were greeted by a spontaneous outburst of anger which, by 28 January, had become so widespread that it invaded Westminster, where a debate on the Board's estimates was transformed into a bitter confrontation between parliament and the Government. This confrontation—most disconcertingly for the Government at the start of an election year—was led by Conservative back-benchers representing marginal industrial constituencies. The Cabinet panicked, in particular Stanley (Betterton's successor as minister of labour); and a 'standstill' was swiftly announced, whereby claimants could continue to be paid at the old

[75] See, for example, Baldwin papers, vol. 169, fol. 155, where Jones even accuses the Treasury of extravagance.

[76] See, for example, the 1934 Conservative Party pamphlet *A Great Social Reform*, which claimed the UAB to be 'the most comprehensive national system which has ever been instituted by any country for the care and maintenance of the able-bodied as a whole'.

transitional-payments rate wherever that was to their advantage. The standstill was a dereliction of good government. Not only was the UAB required to double its workload (by assessing each claimant twice, by the old public assistance committee and the new UAB regulations) but it was itself forced to sanction, for over two years, 'illegally' high rates of benefit, which it had been its express purpose to end. Not until 16 November 1936—a year after the election—was a new start made to end those illegalities; and not until 1 April 1937 did the UAB fulfil its primary progressive function of assuming from local government responsibility for all able-bodied persons 'within the industrial field'.

To what extent was the Ministry responsible for this débâcle? Was it the fault of successive ministers (Stanley and Brown), officials within the Ministry, or those seconded to the UAB? Or did responsibility lie primarily with the inherently weak Board and the contradictions within both Government policy and public expectation? Culpability can best be examined in three distinct phases: during the planning of the new regulations between July and December 1934, the crisis of January and February 1935 and the standstill.

The planning of the new regulations failed largely because of financial miscalculation, the insufficient use of discretion, and bureaucratic insensitivity; and at the root of each of these failures lay the advice of Ministry officials seconded to the Board. In the first place, benefit under the new regulations was undoubtedly less generous than transitional benefit—the annual cost of the two schemes being estimated at £38m. and £41m. respectively.[77] Such stringency had been the intention neither of the Board (which had expected the new scales to exceed the old by 5 per cent) nor the Chancellor of the Exchequer (who, under questioning from sceptical colleagues, consistently committed himself to a new increase in expenditure).[78] It was the result simply of miscalculations arising from officials' use of a biased control sample (as pointed out to the Board by the Ministry in October 1934), ignorance of the conventions governing wage-earners' liability for their relatives, and an attempt to adjust benefit to the varying level of rent (which local

[77] Most of this paragraph is based on Cab 27/576/UAR (34) 5, which is the Ministry's damning rejoinder in March 1935 to the UAB's accusations of treachery.
[78] Markham papers, 6/1, minutes of the 6th meeting of the UAB, 13 Sept. 1934; Cab 23/80/Cabinet 84 (34), para. 1, 30 Nov. 1934.

government had traditionally ignored). Given the short time in which the new regulations had had to be devised, the Board had of necessity to rely on the experience and expertise of its officials. These officials were clearly found wanting.

Ministry of Labour officials within the Board (who had administered transitional benefit since 1931) were perhaps, in this instance, no more culpable than their Ministry of Health counterparts (who had long supervised local government relief). However, in the other instances it was they—and in particular Eady, the Board's secretary—who were specifically at fault. In respect to discretion, Ministers had consistently argued that its liberal use by the Board was vital to the success of the new regulations. 'Important as these regulations are', Stanley for example warned the House of Commons on 17 December 1934, 'even more important will be the way they are going to be carried out. A great deal has necessarily to be left to the discretion of the Board.'[79] The Board itself was also alive to the need for flexibility, with the ex-Ministry of Labour triumvirate of Betterton, Eady, and Read warning local officials early in December 1934 that, in contrast to unemployment insurance, discretion was now an 'integral part' of assessment and its full use essential if the 'charge of bureaucratic control' was to be avoided.[80] In private, however, Eady sought on both administrative and political grounds strictly to limit its use. On the one hand he argued:

The Board would not be working through a highly skilled and experienced staff, in intimate touch with the thoughts of the Board, but through 250 Area officers of differing experience and trained under administrations of differing standards. The officers must be told from Headquarters exactly and in some detail how they are to apply the Regulations. Nothing else would be fair to the officers.

On the other hand, it would be both improper and impolitic to expect the principles on which the regulations were based to be compromised by discretion. As he warned:

[79] *Parl. Deb.*, 1934–5, 296, col. 858, 17 Dec. 1934.
[80] Ast 9/86. Eady's retraction is in the Markham papers, 6/1, minutes of the 9th meeting of the UAB, 10 Oct. 1934. In 1933, under Treasury influence, Eady had conversely argued: 'it was hoped that the regulations to be approved by Parliament would be in a form that allowed real discretion to the area officers ... The alternative was comprehensive regulations attempting to provide exactly for each type of household and each kind of "need" ... Though this meant simpler administration it meant much greater expenditure' (Ast 7/28).

The wise as well as the proper policy is to enforce the Regulations as their meaning intends them to be enforced and to rely upon the general justice and reason of the Regulations and their fair and open administration to rally public support to them even in the areas that will suffer. This is the old lesson of administration, learned again in recent times in Durham—where the Commissioners 'cut the dole' by about £350,000 p.a. and yet, after an initial period of hostile demonstration which was organized, have produced a situation of greater quiet than exists in any other large area which is under the means test.

Accordingly, local officials were encouraged to exercise discretion in a conservative, not a liberal, fashion.

Past experience also encouraged Eady (against the fleeting doubts of the Cabinet and the Board) to advise against the staggering of major cuts. 'The process becomes no easier', he insisted, 'if it is delayed. The delay becomes a matter of convention and opposition to enforcement becomes concentrated.'[81] Consequently, the main thrust of his policy (which was duly endorsed) was that claimants, where applicable, should suffer an abrupt cut in their benefit, with any proven hardship being relieved either by a gradual increase in discretionary payment or by the appeals tribunal (after a delay of some eight weeks). Such a policy, condemning claimants to sudden deprivation and an intolerable degree of uncertainty, revealed an appalling degree of bureaucratic insensitivity; and this was a sin further compounded both by Eady's resistance of wider publicity (advocated by Tom Jones, with his memories of the successful launching of health insurance in 1911) and by failure to establish before January 1935 the local advisory committees, which were intended to ensure a constructive rapport with the public.[82]

To blame the failures of planning solely on officials, and Eady in particular, would clearly be unfair. The guilty men, and women, were indeed many. The UAB itself, for instance, was chaired by Lord Rushcliffe who (having served, in his earlier guise as Sir Henry Betterton, at the Ministry of Labour in all Conservative govern-

---

[81] Markham papers, 6/1, minutes of the 9th meeting of the UAB.

[82] Eady rejected publicity on the grounds that 'in the mind of the government the Board are not creating a new first class social service of high political value whose benefits need to be rammed down the throats of the public' and that, rather than forestalling unrest in South Wales, it would have been 'an indulgence in political controversy'. See Tom Jones papers, C 15/6, Eady to Jones, 1 Nov. 1934 and Markham papers, 6/1, minutes of 23rd meeting of the UAB, 4-6 Feb. 1935.

ments since 1923) should have been alive to all potential pitfalls.
Violet Markham, concerned by the increasing austerity of the regulations, had also challenged her colleagues to answer the fundamental question: 'Is our approach ... only that of the old Poor
Law Board—the relief of destitution as cheaply as possible ... or
do we stand frankly for high taxation and a certain redistribution
of wealth by dealing generously with poverty?'[83] Nevertheless, the
Board endorsed its officials' advice. The Cabinet was equally guilty.
Not only had it selected a 'safe' Board to resolve contradictions
within its own policy (and demanded the drafting of a national
standard of relief in an impossibly short time), but is also officially
sanctioned the regulations. Finally, even the Labour movement
cannot escape its share of the blame, since the Labour press had
generally welcomed the regulations in December 1934 and no serious reservations were made by Labour MPs during the 21 hours
they were debated before a poorly attended House of Commons.[84]
Nothing, however, can disguise the fact that, finally presented with
the long-demanded opportunity to act where politicians had traditionally feared to act, officials failed.

During the second phase of the débâcle, the crisis of January and
February 1935, the failure was largely political, not administrative.
It was also the direct responsibility of the Ministry. Faced with the
long-awaited crisis for which (in the event) it was unprepared, the
Government capitulated and the main culprit was Stanley who,
precipitately conceding the fallibility of the new regulations and
accusing the Board of maladministration, failed—as was his clear
ministerial duty—to defend the Board. 'New men doing a new job',
he concluded in respect of the inadequate use of discretion, 'act
with a timidity that experienced men do not'; and, to add to the
Board's sense of betrayal, he then received a deputation from South
Wales (where the traditional refusal of Labour councils fully to
implement the means test made the Board's return to probity all
the harder) and praised it for 'the moderate way in which their case
had been put'.[85] Stanley's motive was partly personal: an attempt

---

[83] Tom Jones diary, Markham to Jones, 7 Aug. 1934.

[84] At one count, only six Labour MPs were present, perhaps because the principal complaint of their leading spokesman (Greenwood, when presumably sober)
was that the regulations reduced human need to arithmetic. How else a specific level
of benefit was to be determined was left unclear.

[85] *Parl. Deb.*, 1934–5, 297, col. 246, 29 Jan. 1935; Markham papers, 7/13.

to safeguard his reputation as a progressive politician (which he achieved). His attitude, however, reflected also genuine anger within the Ministry that its earlier trust in the Board had been betrayed and the continuing opposition of certain officials to the very principle of centralization—an opposition openly expressed by the parliamentary secretary (Hudson). On reflection, Chamberlain (admittedly no unbiased witness) concluded that it was the Ministry which had been largely responsible for the crisis: 'Stanley had no courage and Hudson was positively disloyal.'[86] Consequently, after a decent interval, both were removed from the Ministry.

It would, again, be over-simplistic to place all the blame for the crisis on these two ministers. Much of the public anger arose from a feeling of impotence—the belief that, once unemployment relief had been 'taken out of politics', there was no constitutional means of redress. This was a danger against which the Ministry had persistently warned and the result of a political sham for which Stanley bore no responsibility. The sham had already obliged the Ministry to act unconstitutionally (by referring the regulations back to the Board in October 1934 without, as was the constitutional requirement, explaining to parliament the reasons for the political interference). It had also brought it into ridicule when, as a result of parliament's ability only to approve or reject the regulations (but not to amend them), the House of Commons mounted a 30-minute debate on whether a misprint could be corrected. Was a 10*s.* allowance a misprint for 20*s.*, queried Stafford Cripps, and could it be amended?[87] The sham was then fully exposed by its two authors. Chamberlain, without reference to the Cabinet, agreed to float the idea of a standstill; and when, in protest against such blatant political interference, the Board threatened to resign, Betterton restored order by asserting that 'the Board are in effect officials of the Government and cannot act in the last resort contrary to the policy of the Government'.[88] In the crisis, the Board itself was also far from blameless. Long before the eruption of unrest it was expressing private fears about the 'too accurate assessment'

[86] Neville Chamberlain papers, NC 2/23A, diary entry for 3 May 1935. For Stanley's resilience and Hudson's bluntness, see *Parl. Deb.*, 1934–5, 297, cols. 2024 and 2059.

[87] *Parl. Deb.*, 1934–5, 297, cols. 918–9.

[88] Cab 23/81/8 (35) 8; Markham papers, 7/13, memorandum of a meeting 5 Feb. 1935.

of the investigation officers and, after her initial outburst of indignation, Violet Markham admitted:

The role of injured innocent hardly fits the Board. We blundered grossly in our statistics. In view of all I am seeing and hearing I am not surprised there was a row. And if *I* were Minister of Labour I should go very cannily with the Board! The blunt truth is that we made a horrid mess of the job and we cannot push off the responsibility for all that has happened on to Stanley's shoulders.[89]

Nevertheless, Stanley must bear the principal responsibility. By failing to defend the Board, he escalated parliamentary and popular unrest, and, by declining to communicate promptly and frankly with the Board, he generated within government suspicion and confusion. His lack of political courage seriously deepened the crisis.

To apportion responsibility for inordinate delay during the third phase of policy, the liquidation of the standstill, is rather more complex. Liquidation required agreement between the Government and the UAB on two main issues: the Board's new regulations (submitted to the Ministry of Labour in May 1935 but not approved by Cabinet until June 1936) and the terms of their gradual implementation (started in November 1936 but not completed until May 1938). In the first instance much of the responsibility lay with officials within the Ministry, in the second with the vacillation of the Cabinet (amply represented by Ernest Brown).

Agreement on the new regulations was impeded by the personal, administrative, and political behaviour of Ministry officials. Personally, their relationship with former colleagues on the Board was acrimonious, with no one more acerbic than J. S. Nicholson (the head of the Unemployment Insurance Department) who was directly responsible for daily contacts between the Ministry and the Board.[90] Consequently, little was done to circumvent the inherent dangers of administrative duplication and indeed the Ministry re-

---

[89] Markham papers, 6/1, minutes of 20th meeting of the UAB, 16 Jan. 1935; Tom Jones diary, Markham to Jones, 3 Nov. 1935. This did not prevent Markham, however, referring later to the 'criminal cowardice of Stanley' (Tom Jones diary, 5 June 1936).

[90] For references to the 'ill-mannered levity' and sustained hostility of officials, see Tom Jones papers, C 16, fol. 1 (Barnston to Jones 8 Feb. 1936) and diary, 17 Dec. 1937. For hard evidence of Nicholson's misdemeanours, see Ast 7/57, 116, 125 and 136.

stricted and frustrated its 'subordinate' department with a zeal
reminiscent of the Treasury—Phillips's demand, for example, in
January 1935 that (in order to ensure the proper use of discretion)
the Ministry should be given prior notice of all the Board's instructions to its local officials mirrored exactly the excesses of Treasury
control of which he had so bitterly complained himself in 1923
when the authority of Bowers, as accountant-general, had been
extended.[91] Behind this behaviour—as with Treasury control—
there was also a political motive. Faithful to the traditional departmental policy of a two-tier system of relief, officials remained
highly sceptical of the practicality of a national relief standard and
wished to see reponsibility for relief either restored to local authorities or devolved to local committees, which had 'a real share in
administration'. This was made quite explicit in the first extant
departmental response to the new UAB regulations in June 1935;
and, a year later, on the eve of the Cabinet's acceptance of the
regulations, Rushcliffe could still write pessimistically that he had
'more than a suspicion that Brown and the official Ministry of
Labour share the view—as certainly did Stanley—that national
uniformity was impractical' and that 'we should have varying scales
which reflect local opinion and local previous practice'. Such a
policy, as he noted, would reduce the Board to 'little more than
agents for the Government, whose duty it was to administer *in
accordance with* the advice they got from the [local] committees'.[92]

Official scepticism, however, could only delay and not destroy
the Board's regulations, because in the last resort (which, in this
instance, was the need to draft a manifesto for the 1935 election)
a majority in the Cabinet was unprepared to accept the loss of
face—and the possible return to local authority 'profligacy'—that
the collapse of the UAB might entail. Political expediency dictated
that nothing unpopular should be attempted before the election in
November; but detailed negotiations started soon thereafter and,

[91] Ast 7/57; see above, p. 58. Warren Fisher's request that Eady should be regarded as the Minister's senior adviser was rejected on the grounds that a separate
department (Nicholson's) was needed independently to draft answers to parliamentary questions concerning the standstill legislation.

[92] E. Brown in Markham papers, 6/5, item 4; Ast 7/114, memorandum of 1 July
1935; Tom Jones diary, Rushcliffe to Jones, 11 Apr. 1936. For the return to favour
of local authorities see, for example, Neville Chamberlain papers NC 2/23A, entry
for 13 Feb. 1935. Their foremost supporter was Davison who kept in close contact
with former colleagues at the Ministry.

by the following January, new regulations had been agreed at a departmental level. Several members of the Board, seeking (as required by the 1934 Act) uniform national standards based exclusively on need, were perturbed by concessions made to satisfy Brown's perception of what was politically expedient. Their concern, however, was nothing compared to the anger which accompanied the resolution of how the standstill was to be liquidated. This brought the whole Board to the brink of resignation in April 1936.[93] The Board now acknowledged that any cuts in benefit should be gradual, in accordance with the advice of local committees, and delayed until after any appeal had been heard; but (rightly suspicious of the Government's good faith) it insisted that there should be a specific time-limit and that, in order to maintain the momentum of liquidation, all 'new' claimants should be paid immediately under the new regulations. Brown, on behalf of the Cabinet, demurred. In order to keep his options open—as the UAB suspected—he deprecated any firm commitment, such as a time-limit, and argued that 'discrimination against new claimants' would provoke unrest both at Westminster and in the country.[94] How could he justify either to parliament or to deputations the unequal treatment of claimants in similar circumstances? Cabinet colleagues finally persuaded him to accept a definite time-limit (12 months, later extended to 18) and that no new claimant should receive more than 10s. above his UAB assessment. Such compromises, however, were blatantly based on political expediency, not principle, and made a total mockery of the original justification of the 1934 Act, that it would take unemployment relief 'out of politics'.

On both an administrative and political level, therefore, the Ministry emerged from the standstill with little obvious credit. In defence of the officials, it might be argued that they acted initially in accordance with long-held departmental views (which still commanded wide political support) and that, when serious negotiations started, they did attempt to salvage some principles from Brown's expediency. In Brown's defence, it could also be argued that he was acting on Cabinet instructions and that, with Chamberlain firmly behind him, he resisted an attempt in June 1936 by the

---

[93] For a summary of the negotiations, see Cab 27/575 and 576; Markham papers, 6/5. For talk of and Jones's attempt at resignation, see Markham papers, 7/13 and 9/2.

[94] UAB memorandum 134, 24 Feb. 1936.

Secretary of State for Scotland to force further concessions from the UAB.[95] Furthermore, the UAB itself was far from blameless. Its supply of incomplete and incorrect information justified to some extent the Ministry's administrative duplication. The Board itself was also known to be weak and divided and negotiations were hardly expedited by the lack of detailed knowledge amongst its chief negotiators (a failing admittedly shared by Brown, but then he—unlike Rushcliffe—was not paid more than the prime minister to master such details). Despite the extenuating circumstances, however, the Ministry must bear its share of the responsibility for one of the least heroic episodes in British social policy.

Given the lack of heroism and the initial failure of the UAB to resolve its four major challenges, how then can the first years of the Board's administration be said to reflect on either the Ministry or its former officials seconded to the Board? There are two answers.

First, as with the 1919 out-of-work donation scheme and the implementation of unemployment insurance in the 1920s, there was—despite the political confusion—a major executive achievement. With its responsibility for the household means test, the UAB could never be wholly popular; and, with the low pay and status of its staff, it was also unable to achieve that degree of sensitivity for which social workers—despite their own obvious failings—might have wished.[96] Nevertheless, as was widely recognized at the time, the assessment and payment of relief soon reached a high degree of efficiency. Initially, two of the Board's most bitter critics were former Ministry officials, who had resigned partly in protest against increased centralization. By 1937, however, Hilton was claiming that 'no social service on so large a scale has ever been created in this country within so short a time—or so admirably and efficiently created' and, in 1938, Davison admitted that:

To the credit of the Board ... they had made a resolute attack upon their problems. They had lived down the ill effect of their unhappy start and had, in three years, established a national assistance service which was respected and even popular, no odium whatever attached to their allow-

[95] Cab 27/575/UAR (34) 13–16; Ast 7/136.

[96] Social workers, rather than claimants, criticized the Board. See J. Harris, 'Did British workers want the welfare state. G. D. H. Cole's survey of 1942', in J. Winter (ed.), *The Working Class in Modern British History* (Cambridge, 1983), pp. 200–14.

ances. Last but not least they were served by a staff who showed every sign of being competent and eager for its great tasks.

These conclusions were largely endorsed by individual social scientists, broad expert opinion, and the one major survey of contemporary public opinion. One commentator, moreover, left no doubt as to where the credit lay. The Board's ultimate success, she concluded, was the consequence of the 'flexibility' of its administration, and that 'was attributable in large measure to the imagination and vitalizing energy of Mr. C. W. G. Eady'.[97]

The second source of credit for the Ministry and its former officials was that, for all their appearance of unprincipled expediency, the negotiations of 1934-6 did at last provide an effective remedy for the long-festering sore of able-bodied relief. The implementation of the Board's initial regulations may have provoked a storm of protest similar to that in 1916 (when the Board of Trade had attempted to extend its pre-war legislation), but the protest was short-lived and the revised regulations aroused little animosity when they were introduced in 1936. The main difference between 1916 and 1936, it might be argued, was the changed temper of organized Labour. As one previously militant Clydesider confessed in parliament, for example, in 1936:

If I were to consult merely my own limited political interests I should say let rip, let the agitation go ahead and the whole thing boil up and boil over. But I have to recognize that there are human issues immediately pressing in millions of homes in this country and I am not prepared to allow my own narrow political interests to be placed in front ... of the needs of those people.[98]

Such an argument, however, obscures the very real achievement of the Government and the Ministry. In the short term, the needs of claimants were met by a willingness to compromise in the light of proven public grievances; and, in the longer term, the UAB's developing expertise prepared the ground for more fundamental reform. The UAB, in other words, just like the UISC, provided an effective solution to the specific problems of the late 1930s.

[97] See *Public Administration*, 15 (1937), 3-9; R. C. Davison, *British Unemployment Policy: The Modern Phase since 1930* (1938), p. 88; Burns, *British Unemployment Programs*, pp. 321 and 233; PEP, *Report on the British Social Services*, p. 28; Nuffield College social reconstruction survey, Cab 87/82. Eady's admirer was Burns.

[98] *Parl. Deb.*, 1934-5, 297, col. 202.

A final balanced assessment of both the Ministry and its seconded officials in the later 1930s can be based on their policy towards two further issues: administrative devolution and the demoralization of the unemployed. Administrative devolution was championed by contemporaries as the solution to the key problem of how to reconcile executive efficiency with democratic accountability; and, in unemployment relief, it worked—in principle—on several different levels. Power was supposedly devolved from central government to the 'independent' UISC and UAB (to forestall political corruption); from the UAB to 'independent' local advisory committees and appeals tribunals (to contain the power of officials); and from the Board to its local officials (to minimize red tape). However, as the Ministry's critics have rightly noted, on none of these levels were political promises in fact transformed into administrative reality. The independence of the UISC and UAB (as has been seen) was a 'convenient fiction' behind which the Government could evade overt responsibility for unpopular decisions.[99] Similarly, the independence of local advisory committees and appeals tribunals was spurious. During the 1920s, government had learnt that effective central control depended not on restrictions placed on the exercise of discretion but on the careful selection of those who exercised it; and this lesson was not forgotten. As Phillips advised the UAB, for instance, during the drafting of the constitution of its local advisory committees:

The crucial question is whether it is possible to devise machinery which will satisfy Parliament that sufficient effective weight is being given to local opinion without placing the matter in the hands of local politicians whose main objective it would be to push the scale as high up as possible.[100]

Finally, the discretion of local officials was also largely illusory. In the assessment of individual cases, they were unable to use their independent judgement but had to conform to internal case law which to the Government's advantage but the claimants' disadvantage was secret.[101] Clearly what the Ministry and its seconded officials wanted—and what they in fact achieved—was not a full devolution of power (as political rhetoric suggested) but 'controlled

---

[99] J. D. Millett, *The Unemployment Assistance Board* (New York, 1940), p. 275.

[100] Briggs and Deacon, 'The creation of the Unemployment Assistance Board', 52; Ast 7/118.

[101] J. Fulbrook, *Administrative Justice and the Unemployed* (1978), p. xv.

discretion', 'controlled localism', and even a controlled parliament.[102]

To describe the Ministry's achievement as a cynical subversion of democracy—as have some critics—is, however, misguided. Rather it was a necessary and successful adjustment of parliamentary government to very real political and administrative problems. First, if the implementation of policy (which, by affecting individual voters, was an intensely political activity) was to be subject to parliament, but not to undue delay and gerrymandering, then the opportunity for parliament to amend—but not to debate—delegated legislation had to be curtailed. Secondly, if local variations in the cost of living and expectations were to be acknowledged, without the exchequer being abused, then localism had to be controlled. Finally, if bureaucratic inflexibility in the payment of benefit was to be avoided, without claimants being at the mercy of official whim, then discretion had to be limited. Other expedients had been tried in the 1920s and they had failed. New answers were now required and these the Ministry provided. Moreover, the real test of policy was not the precise degree of devolution attained but the extent to which the system (shorn of immediate democratic accountability) remained sensitive to public opinion. The UAB, as well as the UISC, passed this test. As Tony Lynes has argued, for instance, in relation to a specific case of controlled discretion in 1936, it was 'no doubt regrettable' that the UAB itself called together the chairmen of its 'independent' appeals tribunals and 'even reprehensible' that the 'conferences were used as a means of influencing the chairman's conduct'; but, 'at that particular moment in history', it was both inevitable and desirable that this should happen.[103] There simply was no other practical way by which, in response to public opinion, benefit could be simultaneously coordinated and liberalized.

The Ministry cannot, therefore, be unduly criticized over its attitude towards administrative devolution; nor can it be criticized, despite the assertions of contemporary experts, for its failure to tackle constructively the potential demoralization of the unemployed—an issue which pre-war Board of Trade officials (and,

[102] 'Controlled discretion' was a phrase coined by Millett in *The Unemployment Assistance Board*, p. 213; 'controlled localism' by Strohmenger in UAB memorandum 44, 6 Nov. 1935.
[103] Lynes in Adler and Bradley, *Justice, Discretion and Poverty*, pp. 22-3.

rather less convincingly, Chamberlain) prided themselves on having addressed. The responsibilities of the UISC were innately 'constructive'—the encouragement of self-help and respectability—whilst the UAB's freedom of action was unduly constricted by the Special Areas Commissions (which, as will be described in the next chapter, Chamberlain belatedly created in 1934) and voluntary organizations (which it did not want to discourage). The most significant obstacle, however, to 'constructive' action—and one which occasioned a battle between the Ministry and the UAB—was the very issue which had divided the Webbs and the Labour Party before 1914: the question of compulsion. Individual members of the UAB, and increasingly its officials, agreed with the 'experts' that, in the last resort, compulsory training was essential if the demoralization of the young was to be averted. As Violet Markham, for example, argued:

Compulsion is a word at which the average Englishman takes fright. It conjures up images of the complete system of the Gestapo, and the Concentration Camp. But a democracy, if the facts are placed before it fairly, can surely accept of its own free will certain minor modifications to what can be called the technical liberty of the individual if such modifications are for the general good.[104]

The Ministry, however, rejected all such pleas on the ground that 'such an infringement of individual liberty was in fact unacceptable in a democracy'. In this, as in so many other instances, Ministry officials were faced with a direct choice between the 'irrationality' of the public and the 'rationality' of the expert; and, persuaded that 'an antagonistic attitude on the part of the public may often turn the right thing to do into the wrong thing to do', they wisely chose the former. It was on just such fine judgements between what was administratively desirable and politically practical that the burgeoning authority of the Ministry in the later 1930s was based.

The Ministry as a Social Services Department

The relief of unemployment, unlike industrial relations policy, involved the Ministry throughout the inter-war period in acute political and administrative controversy. Politically, as was demon-

---

[104] Markham papers, 7/8. See also the strictures of Burns in *British Unemployment Programs*, p. 295. The aphorism is in Munro, *The Fountains in Trafalgar Square*, p. 13.

strated by its role in the fall of the second Labour Government, it was constantly in the eye of the storm over how to reconcile the short-term social needs of a democratic electorate with the perceived long-term needs of the economy. Administratively, it played a principal role in the historic transfer of able-bodied relief from central to local government, which not only posed an enormous executive challenge but also begged fundamental questions about the nature of increased state intervention. Was it possible to reconcile democratic accountability with executive efficiency, public irrationality with official rationality, and the needs of the taxpayer with those of the claimant?

During the resolution of these questions, the basic principles underlying social policy were redefined by administrative momentum, if not by explicit political design. Despite the primacy of less eligibility, for example, the right to full maintenance was gradually established (first, by implication, with the improved levels of insurance benefit, and then, by statute, with unemployment assistance). The long-standing contradiction between classical economic theory (which regarded the individual as the basic economic unit) and social services practice (which so regarded the family) was resolved by unemployment insurance in favour of the former.[105] Furthermore, with the addition of dependants' allowances to insurance benefit after 1921, the social wage—unlike the industrial wage—was made responsive to family need. Such developments resulted in British social policy—like German legislation at the turn of the century—being widely admired and exhaustively investigated by foreign observers. They also helped to justify Beveridge's claim in 1942 that the standard of social services in Britain was 'not surpassed and hardly equalled' by any other country in the world.[106]

The Ministry's history sheds considerable light on this silent revolution in social policy. Politically, it refutes the assertion that the expansion of social services was purely the result either of expediency or of a desire for social control. There were, admittedly, elements of both motives in all political decisions, from the concession of uncovenanted benefit in the early 1920s to the withdrawal

---

[105] M. A. Crowther, 'Family responsibility and state responsibility in Britain before the welfare state', *Historical Journal*, 25 (1982), 133. The reimposition of the household means test in the 1930s did of course, for a minority, temporarily arrest this development.

[106] Cmd. 6404, PP (1942–3), vi, 119, para. 3.

of unemployment relief from local government and the standstill. In Ernest Brown, political expediency was uncannily personified. However, both Steel-Maitland and Bondfield courageously (if vainly) defended the integrity of unemployment insurance and Betterton successfully averted Chamberlain's attempt to regiment relief. The events of 1933-5, over which Betterton presided, indeed provide an excellent case-study of the motivation behind reform. The creation of the UAB, and, in particular, the extension of administrative discretion at this time can be interpreted as having an essentially undemocratic purpose. One recent analysis, for example, has argued:

> The events of the mid thirties are a particularly good example of the role of discretion in reducing the visibility of government policy. The problems of the transitional payment system made it inevitable that the Government would introduce a centralized system for the administration of unemployment assistance necessarily involving considerable reductions in allowances. At the same time it wanted to avoid opportunities for political criticism of its actions, hence the establishment of an independent board. ... The reductions, to take place on the introduction of the new scheme, were disguised by official statements pointing to the discretion to increase allowances.[107]

Such an interpretation, however, is merely 'a particularly good example' of the misuse of history by a social scientist. By taking events out of their historical context, it conveniently ignores the long-term imperfections of earlier systems of relief which necessitated greater centralization; the evidence from Cabinet records that the 'considerable reductions in allowances' were intended to be matched by corresponding increases; and the fact that (at the insistence of the Minister of Labour) the exercise of discretion remained sensitive to public opinion through appeals tribunals, local advisory committees, and parliament. Above all, it also fails to appreciate the essential dynamism of policy-making and, in particular, the essential political role of the Ministry, which was to counterbalance more reactionary forces (such as the Treasury and the Ministry of Health). Successive ministers of labour may have had neither the political imagination nor weight actively to promote the silent revolution in social policy, but at least they ensured

---

[107] T. Prosser, 'The politics of discretion', in M. Adler and S. Asquith (eds.), *Discretion and Welfare* (1981), p. 160.

that, at a time of little constructive consensus, such a revolution could occur.

Administratively, the Ministry also failed positively to promote radical change. There were instances of unorthodoxy, as when Wolfe suggested a major exchange building programme to stimulate demand and Eady, stung by financial obscurantism, defended unemployment relief on the grounds that:

It is in fact no more a waste of money than the distribution of a similar amount of interest on War Loan. Indeed unemployment pay is put to more immediate use, for it is spent at once upon foodstuffs and other products of industry while some of the War Loan interest may be locked up.[108]

On the whole, however, radical change was neither sought nor welcomed by officials. As illustrated by their evidence to the Anderson Committee in 1924 and their initial response to Chamberlain's decision to replace transitional payments, they were content to defend the status quo. To safeguard the integrity of unemployment insurance, it is true, officials did zealously promote their own two-tier system of relief, but departmental policy was always based on the 'sound' orthodox economic principles of restricting public expenditure, guarding against the demoralization of the workforce, and resisting any major redistribution of income.

Two positive conclusions can be drawn from this moderate conservatism. First, although the outlook of officials and the small print of legislation may have coincided with the interests of employers, officials were not 'agents of class rule'. No attempt was made, except ironically under the second Labour Government, to enforce the work ethic by means of compulsory training; and the so-called 'moral' restrictions, which characterized the payment of uncovenanted benefit, were largely absent from unemployment assistance—because the means test had subsumed their real purpose, which had been to maintain the schemes' solvency. Indeed, it was not the restrictions but the relative generosity of unemployment benefit which concerned most contemporary experts, such as Beveridge in the 1920s and Burns in the 1930s. Burns, for instance, concluded that 'too one-sided' a balance had been struck between the interests of the claimants and of the taxpayer. 'The pendulum', she wrote, 'has swung far towards investing the government with

[108] Lab 12/69/OP 169; Pin 7/136/984.

vast responsibilities for the economic welfare of the individual, unaccompanied by a parallel development of the economic demands which the government may make upon the worker.'[109] Employers, especially in the 1920s, undoubtedly agreed.

The second conclusion to be drawn from the conservatism of officials is that they were the most reluctant of bureaucrats, whose self-interest did not unduly influence policy. There were, as have been identified, times when the interest of both the department and specific individuals impinged upon particular decisions; and there were fundamental disagreements between officials, in specific instances, about their relationship with local government and industry. However, self-interest was never the predominant factor in any decision and, typically, traditional agencies of relief were zealously defended, not attacked. Local authorities and voluntary organization were, for example—with varying degrees of success—protected from the encroachment of centralization; and both contributory insurance and the household means test were designed (however misguidedly) to encourage working-class self-help. In a perverted way, such a policy might be interpreted as being in the interest of civil servants: it assured a quiet life. Such an interpretation, however, would be wrong, for policy was conceived to provide positive protection for individual freedom and choice.[110]

Where Ministry officials are seemingly more open to criticism is in the implementation, rather than the formulation, of policy. In the 1920s, regular official inquiries into malingering, without any parallel investigation into the fate of disqualified claimants, gave the impression that the Ministry was primarily concerned with the well-being not of its clients but of its own administrative machine. In employment exchanges, the desire of investigation officers for a minimum of trouble also undoubtedly resulted in a certain impersonal brusqueness and a failure to explain to claimants their basic rights. Such failures, however, were less the consequence of maladministration by the Ministry than of Treasury parsimony and of the double standards of both politicians and employers. They were

[109] Burns, *British Unemployment Programs*, p. 333.
[110] The Ministry's occasional consideration of compulsory job notification to exchanges has sometimes been cited as evidence of latent bureaucracy. However, the suggestion was always rejected and indeed private exchanges were recognized as a specialised service, which government could not match and whose abolition would 'create hardship and public inconvenience'. See Cab 24/251/CP 287 (34).

also unduly exaggerated, at the time, by the press and public prejudice. Exchanges could but attract claimants' hostility as a percipient Mass Observation correspondent noted. They were the agency which, to safeguard the taxpayers' interest, required the unemployed (after a given period) to look for work outside their normal trade; they were also unable to fulfil the role which the public expected them to fulfil—the provision of jobs. Thus, they fell foul of a 'social tradition of hostility', as a result of which claimants, however satisfactory their own experiences, were prepared to believe the most damaging hearsay evidence concerning exchanges. Historians should not be so gullible. Not only is it 'optimistic and naïve' to expect any administrative machine to work perfectly, but such hard evidence as exists supports Burns's conclusion that 'officials ... have in the main subordinated mechanical administrative convenience to considerations affecting the welfare of the unemployed'.[111] Indeed, from the payment of out-of-work donation in 1919 to the work of the UISC and UAB in the late 1930s, one of the outstanding features of inter-war social policy was the sheer executive efficiency of unemployment relief.

Unemployment relief was an area of policy in which officials were faced with hard executive decisions within tight cultural and political constraints and—as in industrial relations policy—they were forced to adopt a certain stoical realism. 'In the relief of poverty', concluded Davison pessimistically, 'the golden rule is that there is no golden rule.' However, the pragmatic adjustments for which the Ministry was responsible did have their own internal logic. As another contemporary observer concluded more optimistically:

An evolution of measures which from one point of view appear to be expediency-ridden, planless attempts at panic legislation becomes from another point of view a quite different story. It becomes the record of a nation faced with industrial and human facts attempting to meet an obligation, based not upon theories but upon the inexorable pressure of necessities born of those facts. The result is a system which has conserved for years the industrial and social fibre of men who in the normal course of their industrial history would have been subject to the fear of loss of

[111] Bakke, *The Unemployed Man*, pp. 109-10; Mass Observation archive, FR 433 (1940); Burns, *British Unemployment Programs*, p. 311 and 324.

security and the demoralization following upon the realization of that loss.[112]

The inter-war Ministry found itself at a critical point in the evolution of society from a 'night-watchman' to a welfare state. In the former, a supervisory Local Government Board had been adequate and, in the latter, a specialist Ministry of Social Security was to be required. In the transition period, when there was the opportunity for government both to represent and regiment public opinion, the Ministry attracted and efficiently discharged the state's evolving responsibilities. In the formulation and implementation of economic policy it was to play a similar role.

[112] Davison, *British Unemployment Policy*, p. 73; Bakke, *Insurance or Dole?*, p. 237.

CHAPTER 6

THE CREATION OF EMPLOYMENT

The Ministry's least developed role throughout the inter-war period was that of an economic department. This had not been the intention of its early advocates who had envisaged the Ministry further developing the economic services provided by the pre-war Board of Trade. Nor was it the apparent purpose of inter-war governments which, except for the period between 1929 and 1931, bestowed formal responsibility upon the Ministry for 'employment' policy: it was, for example, the Ministry and not the two more obvious economic ministries (the Treasury and the Board of Trade) which collated the first official, full-scale rejection of 'Keynesian' economics, the 1929 white paper entitled *Memoranda on Certain Proposals Relating to Unemployment*.[1] In practice, however, neither the Ministry's political powers nor its administrative resources matched those suggested by its advocates or its formal responsibilities and, with some reason, Bevin could complain in 1944 that:

In the period between the wars, the Department ... was in the position of being held largely responsible for unemployment without being able to do anything ... to increase the volume of employment. This was naturally reflected in its organization within which the main emphasis was laid upon the alleviation of unemployment and not on the initiation of measures to stimulate employment.[2]

As an economic department, the Ministry might have adopted one of three positive roles. First, it might have realized the Webbs' plan for a 'national authority for unemployment' with the statistical expertise to predict downturns in the economy and the executive

---

[1] Cmd. 3331, PP (1928-9), xvi, 873. See also the memorandum of the former Ministry official, Sir Harold Butler, which convinced Mosley in 1930 of the need to restructure Whitehall: 'the employment problem ... is regarded as primarily the affair of the Ministry of Labour ... That Ministry possesses a great deal of valuable information about industry ... and is thoroughly versed in the intricacies of industrial organization and wage agreements, but it is not equipped to deal with the wider problems of industrial reconstruction' (PRO 30/69/1/457).

[2] Cab 87/74/MG (43) 7.

power to implement contra-cyclical public works. Secondly, as advocated by wartime Liberals, it might have developed as a 'ministry of labour and industry' committed to the promotion of industrial efficiency.[3] Finally, when the opportunity occurred (as, for example, it did in 1929 and 1930 with the Liberal Party's pamphlet, *We Can Conquer Unemployment*, and the Mosley memorandum), it might have established itself, in rivalry to the Treasury, as a centre of 'alternative' economic advice. None of these roles, however, was fully realized. Successive Cabinets denied the Ministry the requisite political authority and, until its assumption of parliamentary responsibility for regional policy in 1934, it enjoyed very few positive powers at all.

The Ministry's first political defeat was as a 'national authority for unemployment'. In 1920, as has been seen, it tried to adopt such a role by forewarning the Cabinet of the impending slump;[4] but overall responsibility for unemployment policy was entrusted to a Cabinet committee, of which the Ministry was even denied the chairmanship, and a new semi-official body (the Unemployment Grants Committee) was created to supervise public works. Then in 1924, when the Labour Party first entered office, its expectations were duly raised; but the Party's pre-war plans were quickly jettisoned and, ironically, it was Webb himself who was precipitately transferred from the Ministry to the Board of Trade on the grounds that he was to be 'chairman of the group of Ministers dealing with unemployment and that would hardly be possible if he were Head of the least important and most recently created Department'.[5] The Ministry's attempt to become a 'ministry of labour and industry' was equally unsuccessful. In 1920, for instance, it invited the industrialists and trade-unionists to attend a Committee on Increased Production to help revitalize industry; and, throughout the 1920s, individual officials consistently championed the rationalization of industry as the only effective remedy for unemployment. In 1920, however, the minister—Sir Robert Horne—was swiftly promoted to the Board of Trade and the Committee was allowed to languish until revived in 1924 as the prestigious but independent Balfour Committee on Industry and Trade.[6] Similarly, departmental plans

---

[3] *The Athenaeum*, no. 4613, 1917. For earlier plans for the Ministry, see above, p. 17.
[4] See above, pp. 148-9.
[5] Beatrice Webb diary, 18 Jan. 1924.   [6] Lab 10/2.

for rationalization were not allowed to mature until after 1929 when the relevant officials had been seconded, under Sir Horace Wilson, to the Lord Privy Seal's Office (the effective 'ministry of employment' during the second Labour Government). In 1931, Wilson was himself appointed the Government's chief industrial adviser but again only after his permanent transfer to the Board of Trade.

The Ministry's lack of political authority was matched by a dearth of administrative resources. Its pretentions as a 'national authority for unemployment', for example, were further undermined by a shortage of manpower, as a result of which (on its own admission) there remained in the early 1920s:

an urgent need in the Department for a Principal who will have time to consider the problem of unemployment, to master its facts and figures, and if necessary to produce an unemployment code which could be brought into operation when unemployment is severe as the Indian Famine Code is brought into operation in times of famine.[7]

Similarly, its ambition to be a 'ministry of labour and industry' was checked by the Home Office's retention of the 'factory inspectorate' and the reduction below 30 of the Ministry's own conciliation staff (who, as during the war, might have acquired not only industrial intelligence but also technical expertise). It was the Ministry's potential as a centre of 'alternative' advice, however, which— as was no doubt intended—administrative retrenchment most seriously damaged. Before the war, the Board of Trade had mounted its successful attack on orthodoxy in social policy on the strength of its statistical expertise; and during the war the Haldane Committee had insisted that 'the proper basis of policy' was 'the continuous acquisition of knowledge and the prosecution of research'.[8] On the pretext that a reduction of public expenditure was a prerequisite for economic recovery, however, the Treasury in the early 1920s launched an attack on the Ministry's Statistics and Intelligence Departments and especially against those of its officers who were 'thinkers and ... apply information and statistics to problems and indicate policy'.[9] Consequently, although John Hilton (as head of the Statistics Department) emulated nineteenth-century

---

[7] Lab 2/1708/CEB 590/1923.
[8] Cd. 9230, PP (1918), xii, I, para. 56 (a).   [9] T 162/6/E 372.

zealots by debating economic issues at the Royal Statistical Society and had ·sufficient ability to be canvassed as secretary of the Economic Advisory Council in 1930, he lacked the adequate administrative support to mount any sustained challenge to economic orthodoxy.[10] So too, as relatively unorthodox heads of the Employment and Training Department after 1929, did Eady and Wolfe.

The Ministry's formal weakness as an economic department, however, did not preclude it from developing—as in industrial relations and social policy—its own distinctive economic view. This view was indeed heavily influenced by the Ministry's other responsibilities; and herein lay both its strength and its weakness. Its strength derived from the fact that officials, from their administration of unemployment insurance, had both a detailed statistical knowledge of unemployment and a commitment to help the unemployed. It was not just, as Eady remarked in 1933, that 'we have all the facts at our disposal' but that 'we at the Ministry have a special responsibility to Government in that we alone of Departments have a living contact with very large numbers of working people'.[11] From their responsibility for industrial relations, officials had also a good understanding of—and a vested interest in resolving—the technological and structural problems that underlay both disputes and unemployment. The weakness of departmental policy was its restricted horizons. Denied political leadership and research facilities, officials became immersed in the detail of unemployment relief and (even more significantly) became committed to an 'industry by industry' approach to economic problems which, by its nature, was antipathetic to any new macro-economic initiative. Allied to a traditional bureaucratic reluctance to trespass on the preserve of other departments—and especially on the Treasury's responsibility for monetary policy—this meant that the Ministry was never in a position to pose a fundamental challenge to economic orthodoxy.

If the Ministry was unable fundamentally to challenge orthodoxy, however, its officials were prepared to use their energy and

[10] Prem 1/126.

[11] Lab 2/1474/ET 1750/1933. The Ministry's responsibility for conciliation also made it agnostic in regard to a fundamental tenet of orthodox economics, that unemployment was caused by high wages. In individual disputes officials did urge wage cuts, but they realized that a general reduction in money wages was impractical.

relative openness of mind to question it and to force the Treasury not only to defend its policy openly but also, within the confines of orthodoxy, to act. Their heresy assumed three main forms. First, in 1925, they became convinced (from their examination of unemployment insurance statistics) of the permanent, structural nature of much unemployment which a simple return to the Gold Standard could not cure. They sought, therefore, 'some novel and difficult relations between Government and capital expenditure' to expedite industrial rationalization.[12] Secondly, they realized that in the short term there was a surplus population in the 'derelict' areas and so devised and implemented, with characteristic efficiency, a system of allowances, training schemes and (in the reception areas) public works to encourage labour mobility. Finally, in the 1930s and in conjunction with transference policy, they induced the movement of industry into the depressed areas partly through rearmament contracts but, more importantly, through the provision of facilities and financial concessions to new industries. To the orthodox critics of such measures, the Ministry responded that the market was no longer working efficiently; in the location of industry, for instance, businessmen did not enjoy perfect knowledge and the private did not automatically accord with the public good.[13] Such expenditure as it proposed was consequently not wasteful but constructive. Industrial transference assisted the natural working of the labour market, by rationalizing a spontaneous flow of labour, and 'special areas' policy was economically sound since it aimed to diversify the structure of regional economies and thereby provide for their greater resilience in future depressions. By arguments such as these, the Ministry was able—for all its formal weakness—to start to exert a distinctive influence on government policy. Just as in social policy, in the early 1930s, it had successfully challenged in Cabinet the Ministry of Health and the Treasury and emerged as the foremost social services department, so in economic policy, with the development of regional policy in the 1930s, it had started

[12] Lab 2/1215/ED 48401/1926. Such contrasts throughout this chapter between the Ministry's 'heresies' and Treasury orthodoxy are open to the criticism that they underestimate the full subtlety of Treasury reasoning. This criticism is justified, for Treasury policy is deliberately judged here by what its officials did rather than by what they said. The two were by no means synonymous.

[13] Wolfe's evidence to the (Barlow) Royal Commission on the Distribution of the Industrial Population, *Evidence* (1938), 10th and 11th day, qq. 2779, 2651.

to encroach upon the traditional preserve of the Board of Trade and once again to question successfully Treasury orthodoxy.

The Ministry's increasing assertiveness raises two broad questions. The first, rather incongruously, is whether its creation actually weakened, rather than strengthened, the government's response to mass unemployment. To resolve such an exceptional problem, a radical change in policy was undoubtedly required; and to formulate such a policy, there was needed an ability to choose between the relative merits of rival academic theories, to translate abstract ideas into practical political programmes, and to sell those programmes to a highly conservative public. All this, moreover, had to be achieved when the bias towards orthodoxy in Whitehall had been reinforced by increased Treasury control. In such circumstances, would not the survival of the pre-war Board of Trade as a comprehensive 'ministry of labour and industry' have been—as Llewellyn Smith had predicted—an invaluable aid to good government?[14] It had proven administrative and statistical expertise as well as the resilience to withstand retrenchment. Moreover, with its dual responsibility for economic and social policy, it could have contributed to policy-making the dynamic tension which the more specialist inter-war ministries were unable to sustain. As it was, the Board's dismemberment consigned 'employment policy' to a departmental limbo and a series of expedients had to be improvised, such as the Committee of Civil Research (1924-9), the Lord Privy Seal's Office (1929-31) and the Economic Advisory Council (1930-40), in an attempt to satisfy the most basic requirement that 'national problems were actually being faced and thought out in advance on a basis of fact'.[15] They were by no means wholly successful. Was, therefore, the necessary restructuring and rationalization of British industry delayed by the prior need to restructure and rationalize Whitehall?

The second question is whether the Ministry's policy offered an appropriate solution or partial solution to inter-war unemployment. The Ministry (on the few occasions that its contributions have been noticed) has been subject to bitter criticism both by

[14] See above, p. 18. For the relative weakness of the rump that was the inter-war Board of Trade, see R. Roberts, 'The Board of Trade, 1925-39' (unpublished D.Phil. thesis, Oxford University, 1985).

[15] Cab 24/172/CP 195 (25). MacDonald's capacity to identify was, unfortunately, in inverse proportions to his capacity to solve problems.

those who favour and those who oppose an active role for government in economic policy. On the one hand, Lord Kahn reserved his particular contempt for the Ministry's contribution to the 1929 white paper; Mosley identified Wilson as a 'very conservative' influence within the Lord Privy Seal's Office and a leading opponent of his 1930 memorandum; and Eady has similarly been singled out as the most sceptical official involved in the drafting of the 1944 *Employment Policy* white paper.[16] On the other hand, contemporary economists and industrialists together with present-day monetarists have accused the Ministry of creating much of the unemployment it was supposed to relieve. High insurance benefits, for instance, were held in the inter-war period to have prevented the necessary downward flexibility of wages and inflated industrial costs (thereby decreasing international competitiveness) whereas today they are deemed to have reduced labour mobility and discouraged investment (by increasing real wages and thereby reducing profits).[17] Are not such arguments, however, mutually exclusive? Might not 'Keynesians' equally praise the Ministry for having helped to maintain the industrial and social wage and hence effective demand, in a depression? Similarly, might not the monetarists praise it for having helped to prevent a British 'new deal'? Indeed, was not industrial transference policy—with its object of expediting the search for work—exactly the antidote needed by monetarists to offset the ill effects of relatively high insurance benefits required by Keynesians to maintain demand? Given the present confusion amongst economists and economic historians over the 'correct' solution to inter-war unemployment, the time is opportune for an undogmatic reassessment of the Ministry's policy.

These questions can best be answered by a detailed examination of the Ministry's evolving policy in two distinct phases, before and after 1931. That year did not mark any significant change in the Ministry's attitude but it did witness a fundamental change in the

[16] Lord Kahn, 'Unemployment as seen by the Keynesians', in G.D.N. Worswick (ed.), *The Concept and Measurement of Involuntary Unemployment* (1976), p. 24; O. Mosley, *My Life* (1968), p. 237; A. Booth, 'The "Keynesian revolution" in economic policy-making', *Economic History Review*, xxxvi (1983), 103, and G.C. Peden, 'Sir Richard Hopkins and the "Keynesian revolution" in employment policy', ibid., 290.

[17] See, *inter alia*, D. K. Benjamin and L. A. Kochin, 'Searching for an explanation of unemployment', *Journal of Political Economy*, 87 (1979), 441-78 and M. Beanstock, F. Capie, and B. Griffiths, 'The economic recovery in the United Kingdom in the 1930s' (1983, unpublished).

atmosphere within which it worked. After 1931, industrialists were more insistent that their interests should be taken as seriously as those of financiers; politicians fully recognized the permanency of mass unemployment; and government enjoyed greater room for manoeuvre following the abandonment of the Gold Standard. The changed atmosphere is best symbolized by a subtle linguistic change. Between 1921 and 1931 the Cabinet committee responsible for economic policy was conventionally entitled the 'Unemployment Committee'. After 1931 it was renamed the 'Employment Committee'.

Reducing Unemployment, 1919–1931

The course of unemployment in the 1920s, during which Britain alone of the major industrial countries experienced sustained depression, is well known. A post-war boom, during which there was minimal unemployment, broke in 1920 and unemployment immediately soared to 17 per cent of the insured work-force (12 per cent of the estimated total work-force).[18] There was then a weak cyclical upturn during which unemployment never fell below 9.7 per cent (7.4 per cent) before, in 1930, Britain became involved in the world crash. By 1931, over one-fifth of the insured work-force (16.4 per cent of the total work-force) was unemployed.

The orthodox response of government to mass unemployment, to which the Ministry was officially a party, was that it should do no more than provide the conditions under which private enterprise could restore the economy to equilibrium at full employment. Apart from the balancing of the budget (in order to retain the confidence of businessmen at home and bankers abroad), this meant that government had two specific objectives: a return to the Gold Standard at pre-war parity (which was achieved in 1925) and the provision of low interest rates. The purpose of the former was to restore stability to the international currency market and thereby provide the conditions for a revival of world trade and, in particular, of British exports upon which much employment traditionally depended. The purpose of the latter was to lower the cost

---

[18] The statistics in this paragraph are largely taken from C. H. Feinstein, *Statistical Tables of National Income, Expenditure and Output of the U.K., 1855–1965* (1976). Unemployment insurance covered the 60 per cent of the total work-force which was most at risk and therefore its statistics underestimated the total number and overestimated the percentage of the unemployed.

of investment and thereby encourage the rationalization of British industry. Before 1925, high wages were regarded as the principal cause of Britain's international uncompetitiveness but thereafter even the Treasury began to realize that 'high costs of production were ... also due to the defects of equipment and organization for which the employers must be regarded as responsible'.[19] Low rates of interest were the necessary precondition for high rates of investment.

In theory, orthodox policy might have appeared eminently reasonable but, in practice, it was contradictory. The rapid reduction of British prices before 1925 (to enable the restoration of pre-war parity) and the maintenance thereafter of an overvalued currency required a relatively high bank rate which, in a period of deflation when money profits were declining, was an active disincentive to investment. Moreover, it soon became apparent that (for a variety of reasons) the Gold Standard alone could not revive British exports and that, in certain circumstances, it actually depressed them. Policy, however, remained unchanged, thereby suggesting that, in the Treasury especially, there were not just economic reasons for the support orthodoxy. This was indeed the case. Both the Gold Standard and the balanced budget were supported because they were seen to be automatic mechanisms by which the 'natural profligacy of politicians in a democratic political setting' might be contained: politicians could not resort to budget deficits or devaluation to overcome short-term emergencies.[20] Pre-war parity (as indeed free trade) was championed for similar 'moral' reasons. 'Depreciation', the Treasury insisted, 'is a drug, addiction to which must in the end underline the economic prosperity of any country that indulges in it.'[21] Pre-war parity was restored, therefore, not just to safeguard the interests of the City of London (as has so often been alleged) but to make industrialists face the harsh realities of the market and, above all, recognize the paramount need for industrial reorganization and re-equipment.

Economic orthodoxy was pre-eminent in the 1920s but four

[19] Cab 24/202/CP 53 (29), para. 25.

[20] R. Middleton, 'The Treasury in the 1930s: political and administrative constraints to acceptance of the "new economics"', *Oxford Economic Papers*, 34 (1982), 63.

[21] Cab 24/202/CP 53 (29), para. 23. The restoration of pre-war parity also reduced the price of imported raw materials and food and thus both industrial costs and the cost of living.

alternative strategies were, at various times, proposed. The first, embraced by the trade union movement at its most radical in 1919, was derived from Hobson's theory of underconsumption. Unemployment, it was argued, was caused in general by a lack of 'effective demand' and in particular by low working-class incomes. A threefold package (the establishment of a national 'minimum', a redistribution of income, and a general wage increase) was therefore demanded in order to improve 'the purchasing power of the workers' and thereby bring 'consumption up to something like equilibrium with production'.[22] The second, advanced by more moderate factions within the Labour Party until 1927, was a revival of the pre-war concept of a national authority for unemployment with a well-prepared programme of public works to 'regularize the National aggregate demand for Labour' over the trade cycle.[23] The third proposal, favoured by the FBI and enshrined in the Safeguarding of Industry Acts of 1921 and 1925 (but rejected by the electorate in 1923), was protection. Finally, there were the 'new deals' proposed by the Liberal Party in its 1929 pamphlet *We Can Conquer Unemployment* and by Mosley from within the Labour Cabinet in 1930. Both demanded in the short term an extensive programme of loan-financed public works to reduce unemployment to 'normal' proportions, whilst Mosley also sought in the long term to remedy Britain's underlying economic weakness by such means as a National Investment Bank (through which government could 'assume direct and effective control' of industrial rationalization).[24]

Given the persistence of mass unemployment and such an array of policy options, what could—and indeed what should—the Ministry have done? How soon did it fully appreciate the nature of mass unemployment? Did it at any point seek to expose the prejudice, as opposed to the reason, behind the support for orthodox policy? What—if any—of the alternative policies should it have championed? Its record can most effectively be examined in the context of its three potential roles as a centre of 'alternative' advice, a 'national authority for unemployment', and a 'ministry of labour and industry'.

[22] Trade union memorandum on the causes of and remedies for labour unrest, in Cmd. 501, PP (1919), xxiv, 21, appendix I, viii.

[23] For a summary of the bills, in which the most ambitious clause was inevitably clause 4, see Lab 2/976/ED 25493/1922.

[24] For the original memorandum and its later refinements, see Cab 24/209/CP 31 (30) and 211/CP 134 (30), appendix A.

The most favourable time for truly radical action was immediately after the First World War. In February 1919, amidst growing industrial unrest, the Cabinet was presented with a famous choice between four competing financial policies: the Treasury's orthodox Gold Standard policy; the FBI's policy of decontrol and subsidies to industry; the social (Better Britain) policy of high public expenditure; and an imperial policy of protection and emigration. It chose the 'Better Britain' policy, which was recognized to be 'quite incompatible with ... orthodox financial policy' and accordingly, a month later, Britain went off the Gold Standard.[25] The triumph of radicalism, however, was short-lived. Inflation was soon rampant and as early as August 1919 the Treasury was able to use it as the reason to start to reimpose orthodoxy.

Given its wartime weakness and post-war preoccupation with unemployment relief and industrial unrest, the Ministry can scarcely be blamed for the failure to devise a financial policy compatible with the objectives of reconstruction. Such a failure was clearly the responsibility of other bodies, in particular the Ministry of Reconstruction and the Cabinet's Demobilization Committee. What is equally clear, however, is that—despite its close contacts with the trade unions—the Ministry had neither the political will nor the administrative means to act as a centre for 'alternative' advice, particularly in support of the underconsumptionist policies. In 1919, economic policy was the responsibility of the temporary Civil Demobilization and Resettlement Department; and such radicalism as was favoured by its controller-general (Sir Stephenson Kent, the coal-owner) and indeed by Horne as minister reflected not Hobson's theories but the FBI's policy of industrial decontrol and subsidy.[26] Underconsumptionist arguments did admittedly surface in 1921, when Hilton tried to defend social reform, and particularly trade boards. The depression, he argued, was caused by a lack of home demand and so any reduction in the social or industrial wage (such as the Treasury wanted) would not only be unjust but would actually increase unemployment. But by then the political opportunity for radicalism had passed and, in any case, he was soon defeated by Sir Horace Wilson, who was thus able quickly to justify the confidence the Treasury had recently placed in him by promoting him to permanent secretary.[27]

[25] Cab 24/75/GT 6880.
[26] See, in particular, Lab 2/272/DR 523.   [27] See above, pp. 103-4.

Wilson's triumph over Hilton, combined with the simultaneous contraction of the Statistics Department, marked the end of any serious chance that the Ministry might develop a radical economic strategy. However, in the late 1920s—prompted by the Liberal Industrial Inquiry, TUC misgivings expressed at the Mond–Turner talks, and the approaching election—the Ministry at both a political and administrative level did start to question orthodoxy. In February 1929, for example, Steel-Maitland (having consulted several bankers, industrialists, and economists) openly challenged the Treasury in Cabinet.

Have we [he asked] left undone anything that might wisely have been done in relief of unemployment, without doing violence to the settled policy of the country?

Has that policy dominated our actions unduly and prevented us from adopting ameliorative measures which would have reduced the numbers unemployed and, if so, is it expedient to continue to acquiesce in that domination?[28]

His memorandum admittedly displayed all the characteristic weaknesses of the Ministry at this time. It was verbose. It was largely conventional (blaming, for instance, much unemployment on the 'criminal lunacy of the coal strike'). It was apologetic and also self-deprecatory: the whole issue, it was acknowledged, raised a 'cardinal principle of finance and financial policy on which, of course, my Department offers no opinion'. Finally, the Ministry's limited resources were freely admitted: 'I have tried in spare moments', Steel-Maitland apologized, 'to fit the pieces of the puzzle together, but in the pressure of work it has been impossible to do so satisfactorily.' Despite these weaknesses, the memorandum nevertheless posed a challenge to the Treasury, which no other department was able to match. 'After 8 years of financial orthodoxy and 8 years of unabating unemployment,' it demanded, 'ought we not to ask for a reasoned proof, for some foundation of belief, that the financial policy by which we guide our steps is right?' Several pointed questions were then asked. Had the full deflationary consequences of the Gold Standard been anticipated? Was a high bank rate inevitable? Did 'the strict orthodoxy theory

[28] Cab 24/201/CP 37 (29), on which the whole of this paragraph is based. Steel-Maitland's correspondents included a director of the Bank of England (E. R. Peacock, an old golfing colleague), the head of the National Provincial Bank (Sir Harry Goschen), and Hubert Henderson.

of credit' preclude all 'psychological' injections of demand into the economy and might not hire-purchase restrictions be relaxed (as in the USA) to boost demand?

At an administrative level, there was a similar questioning of orthodoxy during the public debate over *We Can Conquer Unemployment*. Officials remained highly sceptical of the pamphlet's underlying economic assumptions, but they at least recognized that it demanded something a 'good deal more convincing than the Treasury's usual efforts at "expert denials"'. As Hilton, for example, argued:

I still regard it as not conclusively proved that capital can be raised by a state loan without *pro tanto* diminishing the amount of capital that would otherwise have gone to employment-creating investment. But it seems to me that Henderson and Keynes have advanced arguments in favour of that view which have not been disposed of, or even faced, by the Treasury.[29]

The consequences of this political and administrative questioning, however, were not radical. The Cabinet asked the civil service to draft the white paper, *Memoranda on Certain Proposals Relating to Unemployment*; and, since it had been Steel-Maitland who had first requested a reasoned defence of economic orthodoxy, it was he who somewhat ironically was obliged to collate a document which has since come to be regarded as the classic rejection of Keynesianism.[30]

Before the Ministry's own contribution to the white paper can be properly assessed, some reference must first be made to its earlier attitude towards public works; and this involves an examination of the Ministry in its second potential role as a 'national authority for unemployment'. This role, as has been seen, the Ministry actively sought in 1920 and indeed, in the panic of the 1921–2 depression, it embraced all the palliatives traditionally associated with such a concept.[31] Whenever the time came to act, however, its confidence in the intrinsic merits of public works suddenly evaporated. Employment, it faithfully agreed with the Treasury, depended essentially on 'normal orders given in the normal way at the convenient

[29] Lab 2/1361/ED 9885/1929.

[30] See Cab 24/203/CP 113 (29) and Cab 23/60/17 (29) 7 for Steel-Maitland's demand for and the Cabinet's agreement to publication.

[31] See, in particular, Lab 2/493/ED 106/71 and 502/ED 27444/1919.

season by the ordinary purchaser'. In theory, public works could but be ineffective, since they would either weaken the eventual recovery by 'stealing' work from the future or (in a contradiction which it did not exploit) were unable at any time to create additional employment.[32] In practice, they might even be counter-productive, because they could actually increase unemployment in the short term (by undermining business confidence) and in the long term (by 'crowding out' more efficient private investment).

The Ministry and the Treasury did, however, have a significantly different institutional interest in public works and this eventually caused their policies to diverge. The Treasury was preoccupied by the need to reduce the National Debt and to convert the War Loan to a lower rate of interest, and therefore vigorously opposed any expenditure on public works which might consume the planned surplus in the balanced budget (designed to pay off the debt) or drive up interest rates. The Ministry, on the other hand, as the formal 'employment' ministry, whose officials had a 'living contact' with the unemployed, had a vested interest both in being able to announce publicly that something was being done and in having some practical means to counteract demoralization. Despite all its economic reservations, therefore, the Ministry—at times almost single-handed—did support limited programmes of public works, as can be seen from its support of the Unemployment Grants Committee (UGC).

The UGC, whose purpose was to assist local authorities to carry out schemes of 'useful' work, was a portent of the administrative devices that were to be used in the 1930s to take contentious issues 'out of politics': a semi-independent body, free from immediate parliamentary scrutiny, with a 'safe' membership, limited financial resources, and (it was hoped by the Treasury) a susceptibility to administrative manipulation. Given these initial handicaps, it is hardly surprising that its impact on aggregate unemployment was extremely limited. Between 1921 and 1929, it has been estimated, the work it sanctioned employed less than 0.3 per cent of the work-force or 4 per cent of the unemployed.[33] Even this limited

[32] Lab 2/976/ED 16093/1927. The contradiction is noted in K. J. Hancock, 'The reduction of unemployment as a problem of public policy, 1920–29', *Economic History Review*, xv (1962), 337.

[33] Ibid., p. 335. This estimate ignores the impact of the multiplier but, in compensation, assumes all planned work was completed whereas, in fact, less than

success, however, was more than the Treasury could tolerate and it sought its closure in 1921 (when the original £3m. grant had been spent) and again in 1926 (when all work of economic and social value, let alone of revenue-producing potential, appeared exhausted). The Ministry led the successful battle for its survival and in 1927 even revitalized it by devising a new justification for public works: the simultaneous solution of the social needs of the depressed areas and the economic requirements of more prosperous regions by the transfer and employment of the former's 'surplus' labour on UGC-financed public works designed to improve the infrastructure of the latter.[34] Such indeed was the energy shown by the Ministry at this time that the second Labour Government rewarded it at last with formal control over the UGC and thus an active administrative role in its greatly expanded public works programme.

The Ministry's response to *We Can Conquer Unemployment* was fully in accordance with departmental policy. In contrast to other departments, it welcomed a programme of public works in excess of normal government contracts. What it vigorously opposed was the sheer scale of the Liberal proposals. Officials had three main objections. First, they claimed, the maximum number of people available for such a programme was 250,000 and not 600,000. The Liberals had mistakenly conceived the unemployed as a permanent standing army of fully fit and mobile workers; in fact three-quarters of the 1.1m. unemployed were unavailable for public work either on social grounds (women, for example, and the old) or on economic criteria (the skilled, for instance, and the frictionally unemployed). Secondly, they argued, if employment proceeded on the scale proposed, it would have adverse affects on normal industry. Generous allowances would have to be paid to many workers (especially the married) to encourage—rather than to compel—them to leave home and this would not only make relief work uneconomic but would also attract men from low-paid employment such as agriculture. Finally, there was the problem of those

one-third was. Howson's more recent figures, for the more favourable period 1921–31, suggest at best the employment of an annual average of 45,000–54,000. See R. Floud and D. McCloskey (eds.), *The Economic History of Britain since 1700* (vol. 2, Cambridge, 1981), p. 280.

[34] For the battle between the Ministry and the Treasury, see T 161/549/S 6393/1–3.

who were made redundant at the end of the programme. 'Any suggestion that the whole programme is merely a "bridge" from idleness to normal employment within two years', it was concluded, 'disregards all the real economic and personal factors in the problem.'[35]

The Ministry's objections were, to an extent, disingenuous. The final reduction of available labour supply to 250,000 was based on rather imprecise arithmetic; and, whereas in defence of its own transference policy a year earlier it had been optimistic about economic expansion, in opposition to the Liberals it was decidedly pessimistic. In 1928, for example, it had insisted that there was 'no artificial limit to production or for the capacity of industry to absorb workpeople and to take on new growth like a living organism'; but in 1929 it was protesting, in noticeably similar phraseology:

There are theoretically no limits to the rate at which industry can expand and absorb labour but transference is not a matter of theory; it consists of moving men and women away from their homes and familiar surroundings ... It consists, too, in finding work for labourers in prosperous industries, which are doing all in their power to reduce the numbers of their unskilled personnel.[36]

The Ministry also disregarded the fact that size was the essence of the Liberal proposals and that, in its proposals for deficit finance (albeit inadequately conceived and presented), there was a novel means of breaking through traditional opposition to public works.[37]

On balance, however, the Ministry was surely correct to join the chorus of official disapproval against the Liberal proposals. Contemporary experience suggested, and econometric analysis has since confirmed, that so rapid an acceleration of public expenditure as proposed by the Liberals would almost certainly have failed. There would unquestionably have been problems in labour supply (as

[35] Cab 24/203/CP 104 (29), part II, ch. 2, para. 27. This was the draft of the Ministry's contribution to *Memoranda on Certain Proposals Relating to Unemployment* (Cmd. 3331), on which this and the two succeeding paragraphs are based. In 1930, when Lloyd George submitted revised proposals, the Ministry added that production bottle-necks would increase industrial costs at the very time they were supposed to be decreased (T 172/1734).

[36] Cab 24/198/CP 324 (28); *Memoranda on Certain Proposals*, p. 12.

[37] See D. I. MacKay *et al.*, 'The discussion of public works programmes', *International Review of Social History*, 11 (1966), pt. I, 16.

rearmament later showed). Few local authorities had well-prepared plans for new work and (as the experience of 1929-31 was to prove) even fewer were eager to act as a result of debts incurred earlier. Compulsory powers, restricting either local authority independence or individual freedom, were also unpopular and, rather than being boosted by increased demand, business confidence (and thus investment) would almost certainly have been undermined by an unbalanced budget. Econometric analysis, moreover, has shown the Liberal proposals to be theoretically unsound: they could neither have attained their stated objective (owing to the low government-expenditure multiplier) nor effected a long-term cure (owing to balance of payments and structural constraints).[38] Had the Government been prepared to take a calculated risk to reduce unemployment, therefore, the Ministry's own proposals to employ a 'hard core' of unemployed capital on a hard-core unemployed labour force of some 250,000 was undoubtedly the sounder proposition. Employment on so reduced a scale would have had a greater chance of being 'economic'; other industries would not have been adversely affected; and there was the reasonable hope that the majority of workers could be absorbed into normal industry on the expiry of their contracts. The programme would thus have been what the Ministry had always ideally wanted public works to be: 'a means to an end and not an end in themselves.'[39]

The Ministry's own programme was, of course, not implemented and so all it can be credited with from its rejection of the Liberal proposals was the exposure of some of their more unrealistic assumptions. In the late 1920s, however, the Ministry did achieve more positive success in a second area of policy traditionally associated with a 'national authority for unemployment': the rationalization of the labour market. Following the 1926 coal strike, yet another semi-autonomous body, the Industrial Transference Board, was set up to publicize the plight of an estimated 200,000 'surplus' miners and through its agency the Ministry was able to expedite

---

[38] T. Thomas, 'Aggregate demand in the United Kingdom, 1918-45', in Floud and McCloskey, *The Economic History of Britain* (vol. 2), pp. 337-8. Conventionally, it is estimated that every £1m. would employ directly 5,000 men and that the multiplier was between 1.5 and 2. On the given projects at this time, however, the employment of 4,000 men with the multiplier at unity in the short run is perhaps more realistic.

[39] *Memoranda on Certain Proposals*, p. 11. For the recognition of 'hard-core' unemployed capital, see Lab 2/1361/ED 9885/1929.

the transfer of the unemployed from the depressed regions.[40] Employment exchanges started to canvass hard for vacancies in prosperous regions which they then notified to 'distressed' regions, where the unemployed had been 'hardened' for work in transfer instruction centres. Free travel and a list of lodgings were provided and, once a transferee was securely employed, arrangements made for the transfer of his 'household'. A 'few risks' were even taken in transferring workers in expectation, rather than on assurance, of a job on the premiss that personal initiative could often locate vacancies faster than the exchanges.[41] By such means, which a far from uncritical commentator has described as 'generously conceived and well-devised', 100,103 individuals and 6,630 households were transferred between August 1928 and December 1930; and the Ministry's reputation for 'efficient and humane administration' was further enhanced.[42]

Industrial transference is, in theory, a controversial antidote to structural unemployment. Apart from the limited scale of any practicable scheme and the public hostility normally associated with it, transference can be damaging to a depressed area both in social terms (with the exodus of its most active inhabitants) and on economic criteria (owing to the reverse regional multiplier and the dispersal of an experienced work-force which might be an area's only hope of attracting new industries). Even in national terms, it

[40] Horace Wilson named the Board which the Permanent Secretary of the Ministry of Health proposed to Chamberlain who, against the wishes of the Treasury, urged it on the Cabinet as an alternative to maintaining surplus miners in 'comparative comfort in their area' (Cab 27/358/CTU; Chamberlain papers, NC 2/22, Dec. 1927; Baldwin papers, vol. 7, fol. 462). The three Board members were Sir Warren Fisher (suggested by Baldwin and vigorously opposed by Churchill), Sir David Shackleton (suggested by Chamberlain), and the businessman, Sir John Cadman (selected by senior civil servants). As secretary, Eady first publicly demonstrated his 'real quality' (Fisher to Baldwin, 28 June 1928, Baldwin papers, vol. 12, fol. 410).

[41] Cab 27/400/TC (29) 2. A. D. K. Owen, 'The social consequences of industrial transference', *Sociological Review*, 29 (1937), 350.

[42] Ibid., table 2 and p. 338, where Owen also notes that the estimated 'failure' rate for adult transferees over the whole inter-war period was 27 per cent. The Miners' Federation of Great Britain praised the 'magnificent work' of the Ministry and the 'sympathetic and broad-minded' nature of its officials. Bowers also reminded the Treasury that success was 'largely due to the enthusiasm and ungrudging spirit with which the staff ... have taken up the work. In the early days especially the staff have contributed out of their own pockets to meet expenses ... in cases of emergency' (PRO 30/69/5/163; T 161/1063/S 3229/2).

can be disadvantageous. The social infrastructure made redundant in the depressed area has to be reproduced in the more prosperous regions and, in the latter, geographical over-concentration can bring diseconomies of scale. Consequently, as the Ministry itself argued during the drafting of the 1944 *Employment Policy* white paper, when the Cabinet's Economic Secretariat was promoting transference as the *sole* provision for structural unemployment, 'a substantial degree of geographical mobility of labour ... is not only extremely difficult to produce but is probably not desirable in itself'.[43] In the practical conditions of the late 1920s, however, such reservations were hardly relevant. There was already a spontaneous flow of the more ambitious from the depressed regions and all the Ministry sought to do was to make it more rational and humane. Training and transference provided a positive antidote to the demoralization of the young and could, at the margin, create jobs.[44] Moreover, through the Industrial Transference Board (one of whose members was the head of the civil service, Sir Warren Fisher) the Treasury was finally persuaded that unemployment was not a temporary, cyclical phenomenon. For this latter service alone, transference was—despite the disappointment of the Ministry's initial, exaggerated hope that it might 'cure' unemployment—a considerable success.

In the final area of its potential responsibility, that of a 'ministry of labour and industry', the Ministry was again able to demonstrate its initiative but—in the short term at least—it was defeated by its lack of formal power. Like other proponents of rationalization, it was confronted by three interrelated problems: industry's low productivity, poor organization, and bad structure. Each problem, the Ministry quickly surmised, could not speedily be remedied by market forces—or what Steel-Maitland termed 'old reactionary individualism'—but how (if at all) should government act?[45] Should it

[43] Lab 8/733. Public resistance included the reticence of many potential transferees, the frequent hostility of workers in the reception areas, and the indifference of employers. Baldwin's appeal to 166,000 employers in July 1928 obtained only 4,000 vacancies.

[44] Hilton was one who believed that transferring the right person to the right place at the right time could create a job and therefore some 'economic magic' (Steel-Maitland papers, GD 193/94/2, para. 57).

[45] Cab 24/197/CP 255 (28). Steel-Maitland, like many rationalizers, recognized that state intervention might be portrayed as the start of a slippery slope towards nationalization but argued that, by increasing capitalism's efficiency, its effect would be the exact reverse (Steel-Maitland papers, GD 193/323).

be by private persuasion, public exhortation, legislative concession, or statutory direction?

The first problem which the Ministry tackled was low productivity. In March 1920 it established under the chairmanship of Sir Stephenson Kent a Committee on Increased Production at which it hoped leading members of the NCEO and TUC would meet bi-weekly to discuss essentially 'technical' problems. Then in 1925, Wilson presented Baldwin with a list of trade-unionists with whom he might discuss, industry by industry, increased productivity. Finally, in 1926, an industrial delegation was sent to the USA to study production methods there. In each of these initiatives the Ministry's prime concern was the improvement of industrial relations, but there was also an implicit economic objective.[46] Industrialists, it was hoped, could be privately encouraged to recognize the underlying technical reasons for Britain's uncompetitiveness and trade-unionists persuaded that increased productivity would not decrease employment or their members' share of industry's profit. The Ministry, however, was defeated by industrial apathy. Employers and trade-unionists soon failed to attend the Committee on Increased Production and, although (as one of the Labour delegates) Ernest Bevin learnt much from his American tour, the employers' representatives felt unable to complete the full programme. The Ministry quickly realized that it could achieve little on its own initiative and so joined with the Board of Trade to demand a thorough public inquiry to publicize the true 'conditions and prospects' of British industry. In 1924 the Balfour Committee on Industry and Trade was eventually appointed and it was significant, in the light of the vacuum left by the dismemberment of the pre-war Board of Trade, that it was Wilson, Hilton, and Llewellyn Smith who jointly drafted the first schedule of its work. One of the Committee's joint secretaries was also a Ministry official, W. L. Buxton.[47]

The Ministry's experiences in the 1920s convinced it also that

---

[46] Lab 3/1/CP 190; Baldwin papers, vol. 28, fol. 4; Lab 2/1213/8. The concern with industrial relations was explicit in the delegation's terms of reference and also in Wilson's response on the Committee on Increased Production to some disparaging remarks from the President of the Shipbuilders' Federation about workers' productivity (*The Times*, 29 Nov. 1920): 'from the point of view of industrial relations, I think it is important that the Ministry of Labour should make some effort to get to the bottom of what appears to be a very serious state of affairs.'

[47] Lab 10/2.

economic recovery could not be achieved were company structure, especially in the staple industries, to remain unaltered. What was needed, it was concluded by 1928, was a horizontal 'amalgamation of the better businesses into comparatively few units which can a) completely modernize their plant and b) join in a united policy *vis-à-vis* the Continental and American makers'.[48] The problem was how to achieve this goal. Both Steel-Maitland and his officials ruled out legislative concessions in the form of protection (although Barlow in 1923 and, more reluctantly, Bondfield in 1930 came to regard it as inevitable). They argued forcefully that industry and no less the banks should act first to concentrate production (by reducing capacity and scrapping uneconomic plant) and to write off depreciated assets. Were protection to be granted first, it was quite rightly surmised in the light of later experience, industry would be 'feather-bedded' and home producers placed at the mercy of inefficient suppliers. But how could industry and the banks be goaded into independent action?

In Cabinet, Steel-Maitland dutifully accepted the conventional constraints on state intervention in industry but, in private, he grew ever more determined to act decisively. Demonstrating the influence upon him of Keynesian economics, he sought to employ the 'idle balances' (which, he considered, Keynes had rightly identified) not to finance public works but to 'recondition' the staple industries.[49] Just before the 1929 election, he undertook with his officials a thorough review of the traditional objections to state intervention. The government had insufficient finance—but was it not paying for unemployment relief? Rationalization was the responsibility of the banks—but were the banks acting? Government lacked the necessary technical expertise to intervene wisely—but did not many experts think otherwise? Finally, once the precedent had been set,

[48] Steel-Maitland papers, GD 193/323: draft Cabinet memorandum, 8 Dec. 1928. His views, as summarized in this paragraph, were also expressed in a letter to Baldwin on 29 Oct. 1925 (Baldwin papers, vol. 27, fol. 226) and a Cabinet memorandum of 23 July 1928 (Cab 24/197/CP 255 (28)). His main correspondents were Sir William McClintock, Montagu Norman, and E. R. Peacock (Steel-Maitland papers, GD 193/322 and 323).

[49] Steel-Maitland to E. R. Peacock and Sir H. Goschen, 22 Mar. 1929 (Steel-Maitland papers, GD 193/500) wherein the Treasury view is described as 'absurd'. Steel-Maitland's views are noted as exceptional in the best brief history of the rationalization movement, L. Hannah, *The Rise of the Corporate Economy* (1976), p. 54. However, to call Steel-Maitland a 'senior Conservative economic minister', as does Hannah, is rather an overstatement.

the exchequer would be committed to limitless expense—but could not satisfactory safeguards be devised and should not each new case be treated on its merits?[50] Such a reappraisal of policy convinced him by 1930 that governments should directly provide finance for industrial rationalization; but by then, of course, he was in opposition and, when such a proposal was made within the Cabinet by Mosley, it was his successor (Bondfield) who, ironically on the advice of his former permanent secretary (Sir Horace Wilson), supported the Treasury in rejecting it.

Wilson's views had not always been antagonistic to those of Steel-Maitland. He had been amongst the first public figures to appreciate the structural nature of post-war unemployment and, as early as 1926, he had commissioned Eady to make a thorough study of the unemployment insurance statistics to establish exactly what were the new trends in regional and sectoral employment.[51] It was on the subsequent report that the Ministry's industrial policy in the late 1920s was almost exclusively based. This report conclusively established that there was a permanent surplus of labour attached to the staple industries which could not be reduced by rationalization (by which industry would shed more labour), price reductions (to which foreign governments would respond with tariffs, were home markets threatened), or the establishment of 'new' industries (which were relatively capital-intensive). 'We cannot expect the pre-war equilibrium to be restored,' Eady had concluded; 'we must look consciously to a new industrial balance.' The report was equally pessimistic about the ability of the market to achieve

[50] Steel-Maitland papers, GD 193/323. The final conversion is recorded in GD 193/119/1, whilst Bondfield's acquiescence in the Treasury rejection of Mosley's memorandum (based largely on Wilson's memorandum preserved in BT 56/37/CIA 1770) is implied in Cab 27/413/UPC (30). In a letter to MacDonald in July 1930 (PRO 30/69/1/418) Bondfield did, however, summarize Ministry policy well: 'I believe firmly that only rationalization can ... get rid of unemployment. It means for us essentially the getting rid of individualism in industry, co-operation, amalgamation, ruthless scrapping of out of date plant and out of date directors and it can only be done if the banks come out boldly ... and refuse to go on with frozen advances and insist on competent management.... I don't like it much but I must add that a little intelligent protection ... would probably be both psychologically and practically useful.'

[51] See above, p. 64. The Eady memorandum which was submitted in Nov. 1926 and revised in July 1927 is preserved in Lab 2/1215/ED 48401/1926. The comments on the file by J. F. G. Price, who remained faithful to emigration as the main cure for unemployment, illustrate the less acceptable face of the Ministry's economic 'thinking'.

this balance: in the long run, industry might alone be able to establish equilibrium, but in the short term it had shown itself to be too individualistic, haphazard, and short-sighted. 'Some systematic guidance' was required which 'government and only government' could provide. Accordingly the report ended with a call for 'Government action either direct or through the Bank, embarrassing though such action is bound to be'. It was here that Steel-Maitland's and Wilson's views diverged and the Ministry's formal weakness was exposed. Whilst Steel-Maitland despaired of the banks' ability to act, Wilson was convinced that the City (via the Securities Management Trust and the Bankers Industrial Development Corporation) was capable of providing all the necessary finance and advice for rationalization and that (on economic and constitutional grounds) government should limit itself to advise industrialists 'as to the kind of scheme which is likely to be acceptable to the City'.[52] Wilson's views accorded closely with traditional departmental ethos and, in particular, with the voluntaryist instincts of the Industrial Relations Department; but by 1930 it was noticeable that (as a result of the problems of rationalization in the cotton industry) the attitude of even this department was beginning to waver, with the arch-individualist Leggett temporarily abandoning his faith in voluntaryism. In opposition to Wilson's views, he protested that, in an increasingly competitive world, industry could not continue in its old 'haphazard' ways and that government in 'representing the people generally has a very special interest in the conservation of national financial resources'.[53]

The Ministry, however, lacked the resources to develop fully any alternative strategy. Eady had had to apologize for the sketchy nature of his report (which was a consequence of overwork and the lack of inter-departmental co-operation, without which 'a comprehensive treatment of the subject' was impossible); and, although financial policy was central to his recommendations, he reverted to the traditional disclaimer that it was really 'outside the province' of the Ministry. Likewise in 1930, when the Ministry was asked to monitor the effect of rationalization on unemployment, it had to admit that the information it could obtain from its exchanges was 'anything but satisfactory' and that its administrative staff had not the technical knowledge adequately to interpret it. In economic policy, unlike in social policy, the Ministry in the last resort lacked

[52] Cab 24/211/CP 134 (30).   [53] Lab 2/1377/ET 5286/1930.

the comprehensive statistical knowledge, the vital contacts, and the executive experience to sustain any new initiative.[54]

Despite this final exposure of its formal weakness, however, it would clearly be wrong to conclude that the Ministry was a passive participant in economic policy in the 1920s or that its departmental view was, as has been suggested, 'dogmatic and naïve'.[55] It had quickly perceived that post-war unemployment was not a temporary, cyclical phenomenon; it had challenged the Treasury on public works and the Gold Standard and had tried to devise a more positive economic role for government; and it had also shown considerable executive skill in promoting industrial transference. The need for such initiatives may have been common currency by the late 1920s, but the Ministry had acted before most commentators (and especially professional economists) had formed their views. The initiatives may also have fallen largely within the assumption of classical economics, but at least they were more practical (both administratively and politically) than most alternative suggestions and helped to project the Treasury into a more rational defence and refinement of orthodox policy. By 1926, the Treasury had accepted bad management as well as high wages as a cause of Britain's uncompetitiveness; by 1928, it had finally acknowledged the permanence of unemployment; and in the Treasury's own contribution to *Memoranda on Certain Proposals Relating to Unemployment*, it was conceded that 'the maintenance of Government credit and the cheapening of government borrowings may not be of paramount importance against the social advantages of reducing unemployment'.[56] Given the Ministry's own administrative and political circumstances, it would be unreasonable to have expected it, as an economic department, to have achieved more, especially when, at one of the times most favourable to radical policy (1929–31), it was—owing to the predominance of the Lord Privy Seal's Office and the unemployment insurance crisis—at its weakest.

Increasing Employment, 1932–1939

The 1930s were, economically, a paradoxical decade. Between 1931 and 1937, industrial production rose by more than 50 per cent

[54] Ibid.; Lab 2/2050/ET 692/1936.

[55] Hancock, 'The reduction of unemployment', 338. Hancock at the same time notes that the Treasury's reasoned defence of its views in 1931 have given historians the incorrect impression that it was always so logical in the 1920s.

[56] *Memoranda on Certain Proposals*, p. 53.

giving a distinct impression of economic recovery; but only in 1937 did unemployment fall below 10 per cent and the natural rate of unemployment (which had been estimated at 6 per cent in the 1920s) was revised upward by the Treasury to 11 per cent and by other government bodies to between 15.5 per cent and 17.7 per cent.[57] On the positive side, the economy was sufficiently buoyant to absorb an additional 2½m. workers between 1931 and 1938 but, on the negative side, the new phenomenon of long-term unemployment became firmly established. In January 1939, almost 300,000 people (15 per cent of the insured unemployed) had been out of work for over a year.

Government unemployment policy in the 1930s has been described as logical, consistent, and—on its own terms—successful.[58] Unlike the USA (where public works under the New Deal failed to stimulate self-sustained recovery) and in Germany (where 'full' employment was restored only by resort to dictatorship), industrial expansion and the containment of unemployment were achieved with little violation to the conventions of either the market economy or parliamentary government. As in the 1920s, the Government's overriding objective was simply to create the conditions under which private enterprise could return the economy to full employment; and, after the abandonment of the Gold Standard in September 1931, this entailed essentially the balancing of the budget (to prevent inflation and maintain business confidence) and the provision of low interest rates (to encourage investment). To help individual industries, tariffs were also introduced in 1932, bilateral trade agreements (supported by a managed exchange rate) negotiated, and voluntary rationalization (which in exceptional cases might be underwritten by the state) encouraged by Sir Horace Wilson and his colleagues at the Board of Trade. Given that the conscious objective of policy was to create permanent jobs and not to provide palliatives, public works were actively discouraged. Herein, however, lay the Government's most serious inconsistency. After 1935, a 'surrogate' form of public works was implemented in

[57] T 161/717/S 40500. The Economic Advisory Council predicted an average level of unemployment of 15.5-16 per cent between 1935 and 1945, whilst Beveridge at the UISC was working to an estimate of 17.7 per cent. Later figures for long-term unemployment are from Lab 8/250.

[58] F. M. Miller, 'The unemployment policy of the National Government, 1931-36', *Historical Journal*, 19 (1976), 453-76. See also S. Howson and D. Winch, *The Economic Advisory Council, 1930-1939* (Cambridge, 1977).

the shape of the rearmament programme. If loans could be raised to finance such expenditure, Government critics demanded especially during the temporary recession of 1938, why could they not be raised to finance traditional forms of public works?[59]

The 1938 outcry was the climax to a constant undertow of criticism to which the Government was subjected throughout the 1930s from Conservative back-benchers (representing marginal constituencies), the advocates of a planned economy (within the Labour Party and PEP), and the proponents of deficit finance (given greater confidence by Keynes's membership of the Economic Advisory Council and his publication of the *General Theory* in 1936). In 1933 and again in 1935, for example, there was intense pressure to reintroduce public works following the inauguration of the New Deal in America and then the presentation by Lloyd George of another 'employment package' prior to the general election. In 1934 and again in 1936, the plight of the depressed areas was also dramatically highlighted by a series of articles in *The Times*, the Jarrow hunger march, and the Prince of Wales's visits to Scotland and South Wales. Under such strong parliamentary and public pressure, even Neville Chamberlain (who successively as chancellor of the exchequer and prime minister dominated economic policy) was forced to acknowledge the political need to provide more direct assistance to the unemployed: hence the economic 'stunts' of the Queen Mary and the Special Areas Act of 1934. Simultaneously, under pressure within the Economic Advisory Council, Treasury officials were obliged to rethink and reformulate their basic ideas. No dramatic breakthrough in official policy actually occurred, as has sometimes been suggested.[60] Official faith in a balanced budget and an unmanaged economy remained unshaken. Within the confines of orthodoxy, however, there were undoubtedly increased opportunities for political and administrative experiment.

As in the 1920s, the Ministry was foremost in exploiting these opportunities. After the disbandment of the Lord Privy Seal's Office in 1931, it again came to be regarded as the informal 'ministry of employment' and as such attracted much of the obloquy

---

[59] Middleton, 'The Treasury in the 1930s', 70.

[60] The myth is effectively destroyed in G. C. Peden, 'Keynes, the Treasury and unemployment in the later nineteen-thirties', *Oxford Economic Papers*, 32 (1980), 1–18. Chamberlain, of course, continued openly to champion balanced budgets.

for the apparent sterility of government policy. It also attracted, however, parliamentary and administrative responsibility for one of Chamberlain's 'stunts', the English Special Areas Commission, from which it was able to gain first-hand experience of industrial problems. Furthermore, it was carried along on a rising tide of public expectation, with one MP in 1935, for example, reminding Stanley, the leading representative of 'middle opinion' within the Cabinet:

The Minister to be worthy of his name must be a Minister of Labour. The Ministry must be, not a Ministry of Relief ... but a Ministry of Employment. The ... Department was originally built up for the particular purpose of finding work ... Employment exchanges were originally started not to hand over money like a bank ... but for the purpose of being centres of employment, for recognizing that it was not healthy or good for people to be idle.[61]

In consequence, the Ministry was able to make an increasingly significant contribution to economic policy. Its most substantial contribution was the development of regional policy in the late 1930s, but earlier it had both challenged public prejudice against unemployment insurance and successfully modified the Government's attitude towards public works.

In the early 1930s, the Ministry was particularly concerned about unemployment insurance on two counts: did it create unemployment and could not the money paid out in benefit be spent more constructively? In the first place, in defiance of the NCEO and conventional economic wisdom (represented, in particular, by its former official Henry Clay), it concluded that insurance had little effect on the level of unemployment. At the margin, it admitted it might impede labour mobility 'in the sense that there is not the same immediate pressure upon a man to look for alternative ways of earning his living'.[62] It might also delay the downward flexibility of wages by providing an effective minimum wage for the low paid and by strengthening trade unions' bargaining power (in particular by relieving them of their traditional friendly society role and thereby of the need seriously to consider the consequences of

---

[61] *Parl. Deb.*, 1935, 297, col. 1799. For Chamberlain's admission of his resort to 'stunts', see above, p. 6.

[62] Eady's evidence to the Royal Commission on Unemployment Insurance, *Evidence*, 4th day, q. 1124. For the most sympathetic account of pre-Keynesian thinking on unemployment, see M. Casson, *The Economics of Unemployment* (Oxford, 1983).

pricing their members out of the market). But, argued Phillips (with his unrivalled experience of the practical problems of implementing insurance policy), the unemployed always eventually preferred work to idleness; and, argued Leggett (steeped in the realities of industrial relations), unions were not prepared to strike for substantial periods against wage reductions, owing to their loss of members in the 1920s and the difficulty of attracting new members—in no small part because the state now provided them with welfare services. Where employers had the will, therefore, wage levels could be—and indeed had been—lowered. Moreover, officials insisted, if workers did not act 'rationally' (on economists' assumptions), it was for reasons far more substantial than insurance, such as the local loyalties of the unemployed in the depressed regions and Labour's enhanced political—as opposed to industrial—strength. It was above all the advent of political democracy which, by increasing the status of individual workers, had introduced 'rigidities ... into the economic system, mainly in the direction of giving each individual greater protection against destitution and placing a greater onus on employers to have a convincing case for reductions of wages'.[63] Insurance, present-day monetarists should note, was but a symbol of this fundamental and irreversible political change.

The more substantial contemporary criticism of insurance was the instinctive belief that the money disbursed in benefit could be spent in a more constructive way. Four suggestions were examined by the Ministry in the 1930s and each was eventually rejected on the grounds that it was administratively impractical, threatened the Fund's obligation to guarantee future levels of benefit, or (like the nineteenth-century Speenhamland system to which frequent allusion was made) set uneconomic precedents which might delay per-

---

[63] The views of Phillips, Leggett, and other officials were collated for the Royal Commission on Unemployment Insurance but the memorandum was never submitted (Lab 2/1586/Stats 212/1931). Leggett equally dismissed the contention that insurance strengthened trade unions by publicizing standard union rates and removing the destitution that had formerly forced the unemployed to blackleg. Another criticism dismissed was that business confidence was undermined by the regular publication of unemployment statistics (biased by their coverage of the most vulnerable 60 per cent of the work-force) to the exclusion of more favourable statistics such as those for industrial production. The TUC certainly claimed that, by fighting cuts in benefit levels, they were helping to maintain wage levels. But this was largely propaganda. National wage rates were frequently undercut by local agreements.

manent recovery.[64] The first proposal thus dismissed was the use of the Unemployment Fund as a source of income, freed from the constraints of annual budgets, which might permit the Ministry to experiment in areas such as industrial training. The second, emanating from Bevin, was that the Fund should assist rationalization by providing redundancy pay: but, asked officials, would not the redundant be eventually re-employed and, if so, were not existing measures (such as benefits, training, and transference allowances) more appropriate? The third suggestion was that benefit should be used to subsidize wages, not in private industry (as recommended at the Mond–Turner talks and by such an eminent economist as Pigou) but to enable local authorities, who had exhausted their credit, to undertake 'really necessary' work. Such an idea attracted Betterton in 1933, but he was quickly disabused by senior officials who argued (in strict accordance with the Treasury) that 'really necessary work' was virtually impossible to identify and had, in any case, been completed in the 1920s. Finally, the suggestion was revived that, in defiance of pre-war plans for decasualization, the insurance scheme should be used temporarily to spread work over the greatest possible number of people. This too, however, was rejected on the grounds that the whole basis of determining wage levels would be jeopardized to little real purpose. Hard administrative experience determined, therefore, that the Unemployment Fund (especially after the unfortunate experiment with uncovenanted benefit) should be used solely to discharge its contractual obligations. 'Active' cures for unemployment should seek alternative sources of finance.

The traditional cure for unemployment had, of course, been public works, but in the 1930s, after the experience of the second Labour Government and of the American New Deal, they were rejected even more categorically by the Treasury. The Ministry accepted this ban, although Betterton, like MacDonald as prime minister, wavered in the depth of the 1932–3 depression. By 1933, however, even Eady (under the influence of Hubert Henderson)

[64] See respectively Lab 2/1248/ED 36802/1927; 1377/ET 5286/1930; Pin 7/136/ 984 and Lab 2/1167/ET 1354/11/1933. Bevin's suggestion that a central fund, other than the Unemployment Fund, should be established to finance redundancy pay was also dismissed on the grounds that it would increase industrial costs whereas the objective of rationalization was to reduce them.

had been convinced. As he responded instantly to Keynes's articles on the 'means to prosperity':

Nothing has been so damaging to the proper study of our competitive position over recent years as the amount of distraction that has been introduced by successive annual schemes of public works expenditure, and it is quite deplorable, as well as dangerous, that just at the present moment Mr Keynes has been encouraged by *The Times* to state the case for a loan policy on public works at its most extreme and its most fallacious.[65]

Throughout the rest of the 1930s, the Ministry continued to reject public works as an effective solution to unemployment.

Public works, nevertheless, were an issue on which the Ministry was able to demonstrate its growing independence and significantly to influence government policy. In the first place it had, since 1928, never advocated public works as a *solution* for unemployment; it had supported them solely as a *means* of stimulating recovery through the employment of a limited amount of unused capital on sound economic projects in order to provide both 'needed facilities' and a psychological boost to the market. By 1935, the Cabinet and the Treasury had accepted this position with, for example, the Cabinet admitting that 'at certain stages in the process of recovery, and particularly when men and money are cheap, the undertaking of public works may provide a useful stimulus by creating a fresh confidence in the public mind as well as adding something to the flow of capital expenditure'.[66] The Treasury could argue, of course, that its own basic position had not changed. In the late 1920s, interest rates had been high; now that they were low and private investment had failed to respond, it was theoretically consistent temporarily to increase public investment. Moreover, when the time came to act, it could—and did—protest that there were no suitable

[65] Lab 2/1474/ET 1750/1933. Eady, however, still favoured the government's acquisition of compulsory powers to restructure industry and local authorities, thereby embracing 'a policy of reconstruction ... which would ride rough-shod over a number of prejudices and fears'. The most comprehensive statements of the Ministry's unemployment policy in 1934 and 1939 are PRO 30/69/1/359 (12) and Lab 8/250.

[66] Cab 24/254/CP 46 (35) and Peden, 'Keynes, the Treasury and unemployment'. A covert link between Ministry policy in the late 1920s and the shift in government policy in 1935 was Sir Horace Wilson who, having reiterated all the orthodox arguments against public work in 1932, sought to 'encourage capital investment in business-like directions that will a) improve national equipment b) provide needed facilities of a revenue-earning character c) apply a stimulus to employment' (Prem 1/126).

schemes, apart from rearmament. However, the change in the public policy, if not private practice, of the Government was a clear vindication of the Ministry's earlier position and belated recognition of the real political pressures to which it had been trying constructively to respond.

A second shift in Treasury policy, the acceptance in 1937 of a counter-cyclical programme of public works varying capital expenditure by up to £50m. over two years, was an even more explicit victory for the Ministry. Exaggerated claims have been made for this development (including the conversion of the Treasury to Keynesianism) and similar claims for the Ministry should be avoided. The new policy was, after all, merely the realization—on a limited financial scale—of a principal aim of the pre-war plans of the Labour Party for a national authority for unemployment. Owing to the outbreak of war, it was also never implemented. However, for two reasons, the Inter-departmental Committee on Public Capital Expenditure, on which the new policy was agreed, was an unquestioned triumph for the Ministry.[67] First, its increasing status as an economic department was recognized by the fact that, in the frequent absence of the Treasury official (F. W. Phillips), it was the Ministry's representative (Humbert Wolfe) who took the chair. Secondly, and more importantly, Wolfe used his authority to challenge the Treasury's more fatalistic assumptions (such as the inevitable loss of confidence should public works be increased in a depression) and to close certain loopholes by which the Treasury, as in the past, might have evaded policy commitments by administrative action (or inaction).

Wolfe's major achievement was the redrafting of the Committee's conclusions.[68] Whereas, for instance, the Treasury had wished merely to list the 'formidable' practical difficulties in implementing counter-cyclical public works, Wolfe insisted on the more positive wording: 'these objections, which are formidable, do not in our view indicate that nothing can be done.' Whereas the Trea-

---

[67] See Cab 27/640 for the papers of the Committee, which was set up at the instigation of the Economic Advisory Council. It should also be cynically noted that, as with the acceptance of Keynesianism in 1948, it was the danger of inflation (caused by the coincidence of recovery and rearmament) and not unemployment that encouraged the Treasury to consider counter-cyclical public works.

[68] Ibid., PCE (37) 7. Howson and Winch, *The Economic Advisory Council*, p. 141, significantly select all Wolfe's amendments as evidence of changes in the Treasury's views.

sury had also wished to state it was mere 'common sense' to post-
pone capital expenditure in the boom of 1937, Wolfe stressed the
'double purpose' of postponement both in reducing inflationary
pressure (especially on the cost of rearmament) and in reserving
public works for a future depression when they would be of 'real
value'. Finally, he succeeded in adding an explicit commitment to
the immediate preparation of programmes of capital expenditure
and to the 'continuous watch' over their progress. Such amendments might appear trivial but in fact they were not. Their purpose
was to forestall the threat that Treasury officials would employ
counter-cyclical public works to reduce public expenditure in a
boom, only to suffer a collective bout of amnesia when the time
came to increase expenditure in a recession; and that they succeeded (in part at least) was demonstrated by the Ministry of
Health's immediate requirement that local authorities should prepare forthwith five-year programmes of capital expenditure and
purchase land compulsorily to ensure that they could be swiftly
implemented. Wolfe's victory, therefore, was not just semantic but
substantial.

The Ministry's major achievement as an economic department in
the 1930s, however, was unquestionably the evolution of regional
policy. Again, neither the contribution of the Ministry to nor
the immediate impact of policy should be exaggerated. Parliamentary pressure, other interested departments (such as the Scottish
Office) and the newly appointed Special Areas Commissioners—in
particular the first English commissioners, Sir Malcolm Stewart
(1934-6) and Sir George Gillett (1936-9)—each played a significant part in the evolution of policy. Moreover, little reduction in
either the relative or absolute levels of unemployment in the
depressed regions was ever achieved. Regional policy, nevertheless, permitted the Ministry once again successfully to challenge
the Treasury and, more significantly, to pioneer most of the ideas
that were to shape post-war policy. As Sir George Gillett asked in
1937:

If, as is not improbable, the State comes in the years ahead to assume an
increasing responsibility for the location of industry, whether on strategic
or economic or social grounds, will not historians point to Sir Malcolm
Stewart's third report and the Special Areas (Amendment) Act, 1937, as
marking the first definite step in this direction?

Unconscious of such a challenge, historians have largely concurred.[69]

Regional policy in the 1930s was initially dominated by two
earlier measures: industrial transference and training. Between 1932
and 1938, the Government transferred a further 183,025 workers
and 28,319 households—about 30 per cent of the estimated transfer
of labour at this time.[70] To facilitate this flow, there was an array
of training institutions, the most important of which were the
Government Training Centres (providing six-month courses to provide men with sufficient skill to 'hold their own' in industry) and
the Instructional Centres (providing three-month courses to increase the physical fitness of unskilled labourers).[71] These institutions, especially the former which enjoyed a high reputation and
were able to place in employment 90 per cent of those who completed their courses, might have given the Ministry a positive economic role: through the provision of new skills, they could have
helped directly the restructuring of industry and the removal of
bottlenecks during rearmament. The Ministry, however, deliberately declined the opportunity, placing the whole emphasis of training on the social needs of the unemployed and not the economic
needs of industry. As a major statement of policy in 1936, for
instance, maintained:

The Government Training Centre programme has always been regarded as
part of the industrial transference policy. The scheme has been based ...
on the theory that, while normally it is not the function of the State but of
industry to train its workers, the Government is justified in bearing the
expense of a training scheme so as to ensure a guaranteed job ... to men

---

[69] Cab 24/272/CP 274, para. 59; G. McCrone, *Regional Policy in Britain* (1969),
p. 99. The assumption here is that, whatever the perceived economic consequences
of post-war intervention (under the Board of Trade), government—if only for political reasons—had no option but to experiment with regional policy.

[70] Lab 8/218. The total cost was estimated in 1937 as £200,000 p.a.

[71] See Appendix 3, C. In 1939, the following estimates were made (Markham
papers, 7/29):

	Admitted	Drop-outs	Placed	Unplaced
Government Training Centres, 1925-39	120,130	31,492	79,468	9,170
Transfer Centres, 1929-32	22,358	5,464	15,746	1,188
Instructional Centres, 1931-9	126,728	25,233	21,442	76,576

There were also centres for juveniles (which were compulsory between 1934 and
1936) and for women.

living in areas ... where concentrated unemployment presents a serious social problem.[72]

The Instructional Centres, which were able to place in employment only 29 per cent of those who finished their courses, were even more explicitly a social measure designed to prevent the demoralization of the unemployed.

There were four main reasons for the Ministry's failure to realize the economic potential of training. First, consistent with the Government's basic faith in the market economy, the Ministry believed that training could be most efficiently provided by the employer. Secondly, and for the same reasons, Treasury funding of training remained on a temporary basis, although a permanent political commitment had been made at least to the Government Training Centres in 1928. Such *ad hoc* arrangements obviously affected the provision of facilities and the morale of staff.[73] Thirdly, there was considerable opposition not only from craft unions (who feared the consequences for skilled employment and trade union membership) but from the potential consumers themselves (only 8.2 per cent of those offered training in the six months to April 1936, for example, being willing to enrol).[74] Finally, there was a practical, administrative constraint. The Ministry remained convinced that, were the greater demoralization of genuine workers not to be risked, the provision of an appropriate job at the end of any training programme was essential. It felt bound, therefore, to limit the number of skilled trainees for fear of flooding the labour market and thereby losing the goodwill of both sides of industry. It also felt unjustified in compelling the unskilled to attend courses in order to maintain their employability, given the extent of unemployment. Their inter-war experience certainly convinced officials that the Ministry's courses were as efficient as most apprenticeships and could, therefore, accelerate occupational mobility; but, even in the face of Bevin's later vigorous assertions to the contrary, they remained highly sceptical of any government's abil-

[72] Joint submission of the Ministry and UAB to Ernest Brown, 23 June 1936 (UAB memorandum 148).

[73] T 162/834/E 8848/2.

[74] In 1944, the Ministry recalled that trade unions had kept to the barest minimum the number of disabled trainees immediately after the war and that later, in the depressed areas, unions 'at best turned a blind eye' (Lab 8/733 and Cab 87/63 (3)). The debate between Bevin and his officials is in Cab 87/13.

ity to predict skill-shortages or to compel workers (in their own and the national interest) to retrain.

In contrast to training, the new policies which were gradually introduced after 1934 specifically to reduce unemployment in four 'special' areas (Durham, West Cumberland, South Wales, and south-west Scotland) were increasingly economic. Before 1934, there had been considerable discussion of the means by which such areas as these might be revitalized, including the provision of financial inducements to 'new' industries, but little had resulted.[75] *The Times*'s articles of February 1934, however, injected a new sense of political urgency into the National Government. Four special investigators were hastily dispatched to the regions to study their problems yet again; and when they failed to suggest anything new (except of course Portal, who thereby forfeited the chairmanship of the UAB), Chamberlain determined to establish two Special Areas Commissions (one for England and Wales, and one for Scotland) with an initial grant of £2m. to pioneer new measures. 'The problem in these Special Areas', Chamberlain wrote to his sisters, 'can only be dealt with by breaking through ordinary rules and routine. They must be considered as experimental plots or research laboratories in which ideas can be quickly put into operation and tried out without reference to Departments.'[76] Explicit public commitments were consequently made that 'all the necessary and proper safeguards which are usually brought into operation when considering the expenditure of public money' would be waived and that the 'experiments ... could, if they proved successful, be applied later to depressed areas in other parts of the country'.

Thereafter, the reports of the Commissioners and parliamentary pressure forced Chamberlain to experiment whether he wanted to or not (and he invariably did not). In 1936 the Bank of England was persuaded to commit £1m. to the Special Areas Reconstruction Association to provide loans to small industries. Under pressure

[75] As early as 1929, Sir Horace Wilson had sought to attract new industries into Lancashire but had rejected direct financial inducements because of the 'indefensible anomalies' that would arise in the non-depressed regions (see Cab 27/390/DU 41 (29) and 468/PE (31) 20). The Ministry had simultaneously suggested tax concessions.

[76] Neville Chamberlain papers, NC 18/1, 27 Oct. 1934; *Parl. Deb.*, 1934, 293, cols. 1995–6; T 161/669/S 39853/1. For the cynical betrayal of these promises by Chamberlain and the Treasury, see A. Booth, 'An administrative experiment in unemployment policy in the 1930s', *Public Administration*, 56 (1978), 145–9.

from Chamberlain, Lord Nuffield established a £2m. fund to assist larger industries. Then, after a sharp political battle, the Special Areas (Amendment) Act was passed in 1937 which for the first time enabled government, through the Commissioners, to give direct financial aid to profit-making concerns. Guaranteed loans could be provided; factories built and leased at low rents; and rents, rates, and tax concessions made even outside the special areas. In 1937, the Cabinet agreed that the Act and Commissions should lapse after two years, with the responsibility for any outstanding commitments devolving to the UAB or other government departments. The 1938 recession, however, intervened. The Ministry immediately combined with the Scottish Office to argue successfully that it was politically expedient to retain the Commissioners and economically necessary to augment existing legislation.[77] On the outbreak of war, accordingly, the Commissioners were still in office and a Loans Facilities Bill had been drafted by which government might assist new undertakings in any area of high unemployment where there was undue dependence on one industry.

The Ministry's political and administrative status was immensely enhanced by this sequence of events. Politically, three examples will suffice. First, through the discharge of its parliamentary responsibility for the English Commission, the Ministry gradually established its capacity for positive economic action. 'If any existing Government Department is to take over these functions,' concluded Gillett in 1937 when the disposal of his responsibilities was being discussed, 'it should be the Ministry of Labour rather than the Board of Trade.'[78] Secondly, in the drafting of the 1937 Act and its defence of the Commissioners in 1938, the Ministry confronted and defeated the two men who were pre-eminent in economic policy throughout the 1930s, Sir Horace Wilson and Chamberlain.[79] Wilson poured scorn on the feasibility of attracting private industry to the depressed regions and was adamant that

[77] See the minutes and memoranda of the Cabinet Committee on the Depressed Areas, of which Chamberlain remained chairman from 1934 to 1939, Cab 27/578; and R. H. Campbell, 'The Scottish Office and the special areas in the 1930s', *Historical Journal*, 22 (1979), 167-83. Campbell does, however, exaggerate the Scottish Office's virility in relation to the Ministry which (on the Office's own admission) was even more emphatic in scorning Treasury blackmail in 1938 (SRO, DD 10/178).

[78] Cab 27/578/DA (34) 14, appendix 2.

[79] See Cab 27/577/CP 197 (35) 2 for a clear statement of Wilson's views in 1935. For Chamberlain's in 1938, see Cab 27/578/DA (34) 15.

public money should not be spent in inducements; yet this was exactly the principle and the practice that the 1937 Act endorsed. Chamberlain, too, was committed to the early demise of his own administrative experiment (or expedient), and yet he was finally compelled in 1938 to acknowledge that such a step was impolitic. Thirdly, the Ministry was once again able to defy surreptitious Treasury control. After the extension of legislation in 1938, the Chancellor wrote hastily to Ernest Brown stating that the decision had been taken for political reasons and that 'on merit' the case for expansion was 'not strong'. Further financial commitments should be limited, therefore, by administrative action.[80] Brown, after some initial wavering, refused to act unless an 'unequivocal' (and, as he well knew, politically impractical) public announcement was made of the reversal of government policy. This defiance provoked a further outburst from the Chancellor, in which the Treasury's contempt for the constitutional position of semi-autonomous bodies such as the UAB and Special Areas Commissions was clearly exposed:

The Commissioner by statute works under your general control and surely you have a right to indicate to him the general lines on which you wish his policy to be conducted without incurring any charge of issuing secret instructions. If you wanted the Commissioner to spend more money rather than less, I am sure you would see no difficulty. The Commissioner ought to realize that he is part of the Government machinery and should be willing to fall in line with general government policy.

The Ministry remained unmoved.

This political defiance of the Treasury was a reflection of the Ministry's growing administrative strength. Regional policy was uniquely the responsibility of officials who worked, or had worked, for the Ministry. The secretaries and most of the senior officials in the English Commission were seconded from the Ministry, as were the assistant Commissioners and financial directors of the Scottish Commission. When, moreover, they and the Ministry's full-time officials combined to confront the Treasury in 1939, they found themselves opposed by the ex-Ministry triumvirate of Wilson, J. A. Barlow, and Tribe. The Treasury's attitude at that time, of course, did not reflect well on this triumvirate (although Tribe, as a former

[80] See above, pp. 61–2; Ast 7/311; Lab 23/180; Lab 8/67.

secretary of the English Commission, was particularly embarrassed by the need to subject personal belief to the interests of his new department).[81] Nor indeed did the constant administrative delays, to which (despite all promises to the contrary) the Commissioners were subjected, reflect well on the Ministry as their sponsoring department. Nevertheless, the Ministry's reputation for innovative administration remained unimpaired. Even at their most critical, the Commissioners were eager to praise their own staff, with Stewart, in his first outspoken report (characteristically welcomed by the Ministry for its impressive 'candour' and condemned by Chamberlain for its 'many crudities and confusions') noting 'their keen interest in and devotion to work'.[82] Attributing delays implicitly to political vacillation, he added: 'the smooth and efficient working of democratic government in this country are [*sic*] largely due to the good work of our civil service.'

What, however, was the real significance of the Ministry's increasing status? Did it signify any real change in economic policy and what—if any—benefit did it bring the special areas? Unquestionably, official opinion within the Ministry was revolutionized. In 1934, the Ministry—as in social policy before the creation of the UAB—had denied the need for radical change, asserting that the proper limit of government action was the encouragement of voluntary development corporations and industrial mobility.[83] It opposed the appointment of special investigators; and, once they had been appointed, Betterton (hardened by the experience of broken promises in the 1920s) struck from Chamberlain's draft instructions the statement that they had been appointed 'with a view to the ultimate formulation of a scheme of regeneration and reconstruction'. Officials similarly strove to disassociate the Ministry from the whole venture. 'We must not overlap with the Board of Trade on their recreative activities,' Wolfe argued; 'our business is with labour not with industry.' By 1939, however, as Wolfe's own evidence to the Barlow Commission demonstrated, the Ministry's

[81] Tribe's discomfort at the Treasury has been confirmed privately.

[82] Cmd. 4957, PP (1934–5), x, 149; Cab 27/578/DA (34) 6. The good work clearly did not extend to good syntax nor, presumably, the praise to the Treasury. In 1937 a weekly Special Areas Emergency Committee was established to minimize the delays inherent in the requirement that the Commission's proposals should be sent to interested departments (for advice), the Ministry (as the department with parliamentary responsibility) and the Treasury (for financial vetting). See Lab 23/151.

[83] For the Ministry's initial negativism, see Lab 18/28.

attitude had totally changed. Regular contacts with the problems of the special areas had committed officials to their resolution and pragmatic experiments had conclusively proved the inadequacy of traditional remedies (such as land settlement, transference, and improvements to the social services).[84] 'The only real solution to the problem', asserted Tribe in 1938 in direct contradiction to Sir Horace Wilson's earlier orthodoxy, 'was the introduction into the Areas of new industries.' The 'all important side of the commission's work', which the Ministry wished to protect with permanent legislation, was, therefore, the provision of inducements especially through private site companies and trading estates. On the grounds that new industries needed 'not so much bribes but facilities', the estates indeed became the symbol of the Ministry's new commitment to diversify the structure of industry in the special areas. They were vigorously defended from attack by the Treasury (which disliked certain financial irregularities), the Board of Trade's industrial advisers (who disliked the concentration of new industries on one site), and the FBI (which resented positive discrimination in favour of the depressed areas). Ernest Brown was also constantly at pains to stress their essential economic purpose. 'The main purpose of the estate', he knowledgeably informed the Cabinet in 1938, for example, 'is to attract new industries and the main attraction is not the sentimental desire to relieve unemployment but the business desire to make profits.'[85]

This transformation of the Ministry's policy was truly revolutionary. Amidst its initial negativism in 1934 there had, admittedly, been even more unorthodox views. An increase in unemployment benefit in place of the Government's proposed reduction of income tax had, for instance, been advocated on the grounds that:

not only would men's physical fitness and employability be improved but the increased spending power would give back a valuable stimulus to local trade and put many people back in employment ... There is a market

[84] For the Ministry's eventual positivism, see Lab 23/180 and Wolfe's evidence to the Royal Commission on the Distribution of the Industrial Population, *Evidence*, 10th and 11th days. The Ministry's rejection of Rowntree is noted in M. E. Daly, 'Government policy and the depressed areas in the inter-war years' (unpublished D.Phil. thesis, Oxford University, 1979), p. 263.

[85] Cab 27/578/DA (34) 20. For the battle in which Portal's views were dismissed as 'very prejudiced', see Lab 23/180, T 161/992 and SRO, DD 10/176. See also Royal Commission on Industrial Population, *Evidence*, 10th and 11th days, q. 2684.

ready to hand if only people are given purchasing power to make their demands effective.[86]

The new departmental policy itself, however, did—in line with much 'middle opinion'—directly challenge orthodox faith in the rationality of market decisions. It questioned both the competence of businessmen (who neither enjoyed perfect knowledge nor acted for purely economic motives) and the automatic identification of private with the public interest. 'The economic interest of a given manufacturer', Wolfe asserted before the Barlow Commission, 'is not necessarily a national interest.' It also maintained that, by the provision of tariffs and above all social services, government had already in practice started to distort the market. 'The responsibility of the state has now gone so far in social legislation of all kinds', remarked another official, 'that it must claim the right to exercise some control over industrial development also.'[87] The corollary of such views was that, whereas other government departments (and especially the Treasury) regarded regional policy as a temporary expedient to bring conditions in the special areas up to the national average, the Ministry wished (as the Treasury had originally promised) to consolidate the successful innovations into more general legislation permanently to assist the depressed regions. 'I feel certain that some form of control and direction is bound to come', Brown argued again in 1938, 'and that "inaction" ... is no longer suited to modern conditions. In my opinion we must have in due course a policy of industrial planning.' Such a conclusion was of course anathema to representatives of orthodox economic policy, such as Chamberlain and the Chancellor of the Exchequer, who equated any modification of market forces with a descent into 'state socialism'.[88]

Special areas legislation, therefore, transformed the Ministry's economic thinking, but did it succeed in the rather more important task of bringing relief to the depressed regions? In retrospect the Ministry thought not, admitting in 1943 that legislation 'cannot be regarded as an adequate contribution to the problems of the special

[86] Lab 18/28. The author was S. L. Besso, a Sephardic jew whose unorthodox habits no doubt led to the discounting of his often incisive memoranda.

[87] Royal Commission on Industrial Population, *Evidence*, q. 2651; SRO, DD 10/174.

[88] Cab 27/578, memo. 30 and minute 15. Regional policy, like rationalization, could of course be projected as the salvation, not the supercession, of capitalism.

areas'; and certainly there is little evidence that direct government action significantly improved either the relative or the absolute level of unemployment in these areas.[89] Whereas, for example, in December 1934 the respective rates of insured unemployment in Great Britain, the Scottish and the three other special areas were 16.6, 29, and 35 per cent, in December 1938 they were still 13.6, 20, and 29 per cent; and, whereas there had been a halving of the absolute level of insured employment from 442,000 in November 1934 to 222,000 in August 1939, the number of jobs actually created by the Commissioners' expenditure of some £10m. has been estimated as follows:

	Scotland	England and Wales
Transference	4,353	45,225
New factory employment	6,137	21,101
Public works	13,726	54,460
TOTAL	24,216	120,786

Too pessimistic a conclusion, however, should not be drawn from these figures because it would be neither reasonable in practice nor legitimate in principle to have expected quick, easy results. In practice, effective legislation was only passed in 1937 and there was consequently little time for it to become fully operative before the war. It was also concentrated on the most 'derelict' areas and overshadowed by government rearmament contracts which the Ministry, with the full backing of the Treasury, sought to direct to the special areas.[90] In principle, moreover, the Ministry (as its evidence to the Barlow Commission made plain) was concerned not just with the short-term relief of unemployment but with the long-term diversification of the regions' industrial base, which sometimes militated against immediate results. It was committed to support, and not to supplant, local initiative.

It was, indeed, this latter consideration which most impeded the

[89] Cab 87/63/EC (43) 5. For the later assessments, see Lab 8/257 and D. E. Pitfield, 'Labour migration and the regional problem in Britain, 1920–39' (unpublished Ph.D. thesis, Stirling University, 1974), table 32 and 34 b. Pitfield's estimate of employment includes wastage (from transference) and the multiplier effects, whilst the financial estimates include expenditure only, not future commitments.

[90] See, for example, Cab 24/268/CP 62(37) and the Treasury view expressed in T 172/1827. The increasing effectiveness of the 1937 legislation is demonstrated by the fact that 17 per cent of new factories were located in special areas in 1938 whereas only 4.5 per cent had been in 1937; but, to avoid unfair competition, the areas still included only the most derelict localities and excluded any town that might reasonably have acted as a growth pole.

short-term effectiveness of policy. New experiments had constantly to be delayed for fear of discriminating against existing profitable industry; and aid, wherever possible, had to be channelled from and to private institutions—be it social assistance (via the National Council of Social Services), the provision of capital (from the Bank of England and the Nuffield Trust) or its expenditure (via privately owned site companies and trading estates). Policy was dependent for its success, therefore, on the initiative of others, and this was by no means always forthcoming. In Scotland during the early 1930s, for example, all state intervention was automatically spurned by the influential Sir James Lithgow, who remarked with characteristic vigour:

The trouble in all the Depressed Areas ... reminds me of the fabled city of Hamlin where the Mayor and corporation did nothing while the people girned at them. In the end the Pied Piper came along and rid them of their troubles, but at the same time he so misled their children by promises of a rosy future that they were also spirited away: surely a reminder that it is safer for people to do their own rat-catching without recourse to experts wearing shirts of various hues.[91]

After the sluggish response of Scottish industrialists to rearmament contracts, his views mellowed; but in England there was no such change of heart. There was a veritable stampede of bankers and industrialists from the depressed regions in the late 1930s. It was this failure of private enterprise which finally convinced the Ministry in its pragmatic way that, if each region were to have a balanced industrial structure, some measure of state control over the location of industry was inevitable.

Throughout the 1930s, therefore, the Ministry matured rapidly as an economic department. It was assisted, admittedly, by the development of new economic theories (well reflected in the work of the Economic Advisory Council) and was propelled into action by parliamentary pressure; but economic theory was little concerned with the micro-economic problems with which the Ministry was faced, and the continuing dominance (if perhaps not dogmatism) of the orthodox Treasury view made it difficult to translate

[91] Lithgow papers, 74. In England both the City and Lord Nuffield declined to renew their support once the resources of the Special Areas Reconstruction Association and the Nuffield Fund were exhausted, and Portal's role as the Board of Trade's industrial adviser was to resist as far as possible the implementation of policy. See, in particular, Lab 23/180.

parliamentary pressure into positive action. This, however, the Ministry achieved with the discrediting of the pre-Keynesian attack on unemployment insurance, the attainment of a counter-cyclical programme of public works, and the provision of financial assistance to profit-making industries in the depressed regions. The Ministry's success should not be exaggerated. Too often it mistakenly embraced individual policies as the single remedy for unemployment. In 1934, it was reluctant to experiment. A certain gulf also existed, as contemporary commentators such as S. R. Dennison noted, between its evolving ideas and its actual practices.[92] After 1934, however, it was at the forefront of pragmatic experiment. Long-discussed ideas were at last put into practice and, when they failed, more unorthodox policies had—by default—to be embraced.

The Ministry as an Economic Department

In contrast to its role as an industrial relations and social services department, the Ministry was ill-equipped both politically and administratively to be an 'employment department'. Given the prevailing assumption that government should not intervene directly in the economy, it was theoretically consistent that such a department should have few powers. Politically, however, it was highly embarrassing and the Ministry was consequently forced, despite its consistent denials of responsibility, to address the underlying economic causes of mass unemployment.[93] From Wilson's identification of structural unemployment and Eady's flirtation with Keynesianism (of which Steel-Maitland was the political beneficiary) to the imaginative unorthodoxy of Wolfe and the stolid pragmatism of Tribe (of which Ernest Brown was the beneficiary), it developed, with characteristic administrative enthusiasm, a

[92] S. R. Dennison, *The Location of Industry and the Depressed Areas* (1939), p. 199. Before the Barlow Commission, the Ministry argued that, if properly co-ordinated, the policy of transferring the unemployed from and inducing industry into the special areas need not be incompatible. Dennison replied: 'the whole difficulty has been, of course, that the policies have not been "properly conducted", and thus they have been, and continue to be, incompatible.' As a wartime civil servant, however, Dennison fared no better: his sole remedy for regional imbalance was transference.

[93] See Prem 1/365 for the Ministry's rearguard action against Chamberlain's assertion in the House of Commons on 19 July 1939 that 'questions relating to employment should ordinarily be addressed to my right honourable friend the Minister of Labour'.

distinctive departmental view which was impressed with increasing authority upon Whitehall.

Did, however, the very existence of a separate Ministry of Labour, symbolizing the demise of the pre-war Board of Trade as a comprehensive 'ministry of labour and industry', weaken the administrative response of government to mass unemployment? Undoubtedly it did. Unemployment on the scale of the early 1920s was by no means inevitable. There were adequate statistics from which its nature and causes might have been analysed. The germs of new economic ideas existed, as was demonstrated by the early use of such terms as 'effective demand' and 'natural aggregate demand'. In Keynes, inter-war governments also had at their potential service one of the most practical and original economic thinkers, against whose ideas they could have reformulated and developed their own policies. Within Whitehall, however, statistics were never adequately analysed; new ideas were, in general, neither sought nor welcomed; and little effort was made to co-ordinate the various strands of policy—monetary, physical, trade, and relief—from which an effective 'employment' policy had to be fashioned. In December 1939, a senior Treasury official mused that his department had 'almost unconsciously assumed the role of a co-ordinating department in the economic as well as the purely financial sphere'.[94] Such a development should have been consciously seized many years before. What inter-war Whitehall desperately needed was a powerful 'employment' ministry to collate information and ideas; to challenge (far more substantially than had Steel-Maitland) Treasury assumptions; to provide constructive help for innovative politicians (such as Mosley); and to introduce economists (far more intimately than did the Economic Advisory Council) to the political and cultural constraints on policy. As was demonstrated by its uneasy relationship to the Board of Trade in the 1920s and its reluctance to trespass on the preserve of the Treasury in the 1930s, the Ministry was clearly unable to fulfil such a role.

Administrative reform could not alone, of course, have produced an effective employment policy. Such an achievement was dependent also on the leadership of politicians, the responsiveness of industry, the expertise of economists, the acceptance of the public

---

[94] T 175/117 (part 1). Critics of the Ministry might equally note that, as its establishment and confidence increased in the 1930s, it did not immediately seek to expand—as had the pre-war Board of Trade—its statistical expertise.

and, above all perhaps, the amenability of the international economy. Inter-war Whitehall might at least, however, have addressed itself more systematically to the right questions. 'The most remarkable feature of government economic activity between the wars', as A. J. Youngson has noted, may well have been 'the rate of its extension'; but the vast majority of initiatives (such as protection and the managed exchange rate) were involuntary and defensive. There was no bold attempt by officials to make, in the words of another commentator, 'the extension of the franchise substantive in economic terms'.[95]

What was the appropriate cure for mass unemployment and how closely did the Ministry's own policy equate with it? Undoubtedly the Ministry was correct in the late 1920s and early 1930s to reject both the Keynesian proposals for public works and pre-Keynesian strictures on unemployment insurance and industrial conciliation. Keynesian public works proposals in 1929 and again in 1935 were—as has been seen—theoretically unsound, administratively impractical, and culturally unacceptable. Keynes's characteristic concern was with the short and not the long term, but even in the short term—to the despair of practical administrators—he could be dangerously cavalier.[96] The pre-Keynesians, although they too addressed themselves to immediate problems, suffered from a different fault. To the equal despair of administrators, 'analysis took precedence over policy', with the result that, before the 1929-31 Macmillan Committee for example, Pigou was reduced to admitting that the measures he considered theoretically best for the country (such as employment subsidies and temporary inflation) were impractical because of the danger of political abuse.[97] The pre-Keynesians knew what they did not like: high unemployment insurance benefit, and industrial conciliation, which, in their opinion, created unemployment by inducing wage rigidity. The Ministry, however, was able to reject proposals for their reform as both impractical and irrelevant. The pre-Keynesians, it rightly divined, had identified a symptom and not the cause of Britain's *malaise*.

[95] A. J. Youngson, *Britain's Economic Growth* (1967), p. 265; W. H. Janeway, 'The economic policy of the second Labour Government, 1929-31' (unpublished Ph.D. thesis, Cambridge University, 1971), p. 297.

[96] See R. Middleton, 'The Treasury and public investment', *Public Administration*, 61 (1983), 368.

[97] Casson, *The Economics of Unemployment*, pp. 151-2.

Was the Ministry's *via media* between Keynesian and pre-Keynesian policies any more effective: a programme of counter-cyclical public works, industrial transference, and financial induce-ments to industry in the depressed areas, supplemented by unemployment insurance (to help maintain demand and the em-ployability of workers) and good industrial relations (which min-imized the threat of wage inflation which pre-Keynesians thought would accompany reflation)? Clearly so limited a policy was wholly inadequate to resolve the underlying causes of mass unemployment, which lay with the lack of co-operation in the world economy and the structural weakness of British industry. What was really re-quired was a restoration of international economic co-operation (which was achieved after the Second World War) and a concen-tration of investment in correctly identified areas of industrial growth (which questionably was not). Within its limited sphere of influence, however, the Ministry successfully identified the varied causes of unemployment, gave substance to expedients often thoughtlessly conceded by Cabinet, and championed pragmatic ex-periment. It both anticipated Keynes's temporary concern with re-gional unemployment and progressed beyond the pre-Keynesians' obsession with industrial transference.

The Ministry's achievement as an economic department was, therefore, relative rather than absolute. The ever-willingness of its officials to experiment gave them a growing and largely unrivalled experience which was well reflected by their monopoly over regional policy in the late 1930s. In the drafting of the 1944 *Employment Policy* white paper, it was also significant that three of the eight officials (Phillips, Barlow, and Eady) had served long apprenticeships within the Ministry. As their contribution to the white paper made plain, however, officials remained highly sceptical about academic economics. Eady likened the theoretical justification for demand management to 'a voyage in the stratosphere', and simultaneously Leggett, with characteristic bluntness, expressed his considered view of the utility of economists thus:

the arguments concerning wages which convince pure economists and fin-ancial experts make little appeal to workers, the great majority of whom are not receiving such high wages as those who receive so much promi-nence. Indeed, seeing that so many of those who advocate restrictions are much better off than themselves, they are less ready to consider their arguments.[98]

Such scepticism is perhaps understandable in the light of conflicting inter-war advice, but it did limit officials' perception and often prevented them from rising above a preoccupation with the immediate practicalities of policy. However, that they were the acknowledged experts in such practical problems, was testimony to the fact that in economic, as in social, policy the Ministry had acted as an irresistible magnet for new responsibilities, as the state, through an irresistible combination of democratic electoral pressure and mass unemployment, was obliged to intervéne more widely in the economy.

[98] *The Collected Writings of John Maynard Keynes*, vol. 27 (1981), p. 371; Lab 10/135. On the control of post-war inflation, the Ministry was noticeably more realistic than both economists and the Treasury, see R. Jones, 'The wages problem in employment policy, 1936–1948' (unpublished M.Sc. thesis, Bristol University, 1983).

CHAPTER 7

CONCLUSION

THIS study of the inter-war Ministry of Labour has had two principal objectives. The first has been to reassess the role of the Ministry and, in particular, to resolve the paradox of how so seemingly weak a department was able successfully to discharge such all-important responsibilities during the Second World War. The second, rather more ambitiously, has been to use the Ministry as a case-study of the response of government, both politically and administratively, to the effective advent of democracy in 1918. The realization of these objectives has raised methodological and ideological problems. Methodologically, how—from the records that survive—can the respective contribution to policy of politicians and officials be distinguished? Ideologically, on what assumptions should a study of the state and its bureaucracy be based?

In the conventional history of inter-war Britain, the Ministry (whenever its presence has been noticed) has been depicted as a drudge, as the mechanical provider of inadequate benefit for the unemployed and of inadequate statistics for the historian. Moreover, to those few historians who have had reason to assess its particular influence, it has also appeared (as to Bullock) as 'one of the least important home departments' and (as to V. L. Allen) as a 'second-rate Ministry ... occupied by a stodgy, uninspiring people'.[1] Such descriptions, however, are inadequate, having been unduly influenced either by such highly publicized events as the retrenchment of the early 1920s or, as in the latter case, by inappropriate comparisons with the 'exceptional qualities' of the pre-war Board of Trade. Significantly, Allen never asked why the Board's labour policies were publicly rejected in 1916 or why its 'enthusiastic' pre-war presidents—Lloyd George and Churchill—were peculiarly reluctant, when in office in the inter-war years, to extend their earlier experiments. The Ministry, it is true, never enjoyed the established status, or ministerial salary, of the historic

[1] Bullock, *Ernest Bevin*, vol. 2, p. 119; Allen, *Trade Unions and the Government*, p. 63.

secretaryships of state. Nor did it ever enjoy exceptional political leadership as did other newly-established departments, such as the Ministry of Health under Neville Chamberlain. By the late 1930s, however, its weight in Cabinet was considerable as both the foremost social services department and a distinctive influence on economic policy. It had become, on Neville Chamberlain's authority, a key to an understanding of the 'home front' and was starting to be recognized for what it was to become in the 1950s and 1960s, an essential training ground for ambitious young politicians.[2] In Whitehall, its authority was also considerable, as was reflected by the rise through its ranks of the second head of the civil service, Sir Horace Wilson. By the mid-1930s, its officials had established a virtual monopoly over such important initiatives in domestic policy as unemployment assistance and regional policy—a monopoly which later assured them an influential (if somewhat conservative) role in the implementation of the two main pillars of the welfare state, the Beveridge Report and the *Employment Policy* white paper. There is, therefore, little mystery as to how, especially under Bevin's exceptional leadership, the Ministry was able to rise to the challenge of the Second World War.

The key to the Ministry's burgeoning strength was its close identification with the government's response to the advent of democracy. After 1918, British politics became unquestionably more pluralistic. It was also dominated by the problem of mass unemployment. As the department responsible for industrial relations, the Ministry quickly became the acknowledged authority on the opinions of industry and, in particular, of organized Labour, of which government previously had had little knowledge. As a social services department, it became expert in the reconciliation of executive efficiency with democratic accountability, through the payment of unemployment relief. As an informal 'employment' department, it also slowly developed an understanding of not just the social consequences but also the economic causes of unemployment. The Ministry discharged its extremely varied responsibilities with apparent efficiency. Industrial unrest decreased. 'Economic security' was provided for the vast majority of the unemployed

---

[2] Butler, *Art of the Possible*, p. 61; A. Eden, *Full Circle* (1960), p. 318. Through its post-war portals, for example, have trooped the young and not-so-young hopefuls Butler, Bevan, Robens, Macleod, Heath, Castle, Shirley Williams, Whitelaw, Foot, Prior, and Tebbit.

and, by the late 1930s, an efficient, flexible system of relief had been devised (in the shape of the UISC and UAB) which was to survive long after the inter-war period. The limitations of orthodox economics were also recognized and, in an attempt to alleviate structural unemployment, a wider range of regional policies adopted than was to become available again before the 1960s.[3] Just as pre-1914 Board of Trade officials had visited Germany to study social experiments there, so, in the wake of the New Deal, American social scientists came to Britain to study how government in general, and the Ministry in particular, were responding to the social and economic dislocation of the 1930s.

The Ministry's achievement, and the 'silent revolution' in economic and social policy which it symbolized, can be exaggerated. In industrial relations, attitudes on the shop-floor were never significantly affected by the Ministry's conciliators and the positive ideal of 'ordered freedom', which the Ministry had initially sought, was gradually abandoned. In social policy, although there was (in contrast to Edwardian England) some modest redistribution of income, there were still major imperfections as the Beveridge Report demonstrated: above all, the stigma of the household means test discouraged many from claiming their legal rights. In economic policy, despite significant increases in public investment and economic management to compensate for the imperfections of the market, there also remained—as the 1944 *Employment Policy* white paper demonstrated—the need for a new macro-economic strategy.[4] In each area of policy, government as a whole continued to cling to certain fundamental, traditional beliefs. In industrial relations, it declined to act as a model employer to secure minimum standards. In social policy, it refused openly to abandon the principle of less eligibility. In economic policy, the annual budget was never deliberately unbalanced. Only the shock of war was to make more acceptable the full logic of the pragmatic changes which had evolved in the inter-war years.

The extent to which the Ministry was responsible for the relative successes and failures of inter-war policy depends necessarily on the fine judgement of what one ministry and, in particular, on what officials within that ministry could have achieved. Politically, the

---

[3] McCrone, *Regional Policy*, p. 99.

[4] For a summary of the evidence, see D. H. Aldcroft, *The Inter-War Economy* (1970), pp. 369–74; Middleton, 'The Treasury and public investment', 352–5.

Ministry symbolized the unheroic response of government to the advent of democracy. Ministers never sought, as syndicalists had feared, to regiment Labour, but equally they never had the weight to persuade their Cabinet colleagues to lead the newly-enfranchised electorate by example and thereby prove beyond doubt the efficacy of parliamentary democracy. Consequently, they failed to seize the opportunity to achieve the democratic ideal either of correlating 'economic facts with social aspirations' (as defined by Conservative planners in the 1920s), or of raising the whole standard of working life by the establishment of a 'code of conduct, inspection, enforcement and welfare' (as defined by Harold Butler and later Bevin).[5] Rather, as in the collation of the 1929 *Memoranda on Certain Proposals Relating to Unemployment*, they were obliged by the convention of collective responsibility to support policies with which they did not wholly agree and thereby lay themselves open to ill-judged ridicule. Ministers could, of course, protest that they were bound by powerful cultural constraints. Lack of industrial consensus, for example, prevented any major institutional advances in the conduct of industrial relations (as the emasculation of the 1919 Industrial Courts Bill demonstrated). Suspicion of central government and the growth of bureaucracy also compromised many social and economic reforms such as trade boards and the public works programmes of Lloyd George and Mosley. Vested interests and the electorate alike were seemingly unwilling to accept that, were the new ideals of greater economic efficiency and social justice to be achieved, some of their traditional freedoms—of necessity—had to be restricted. Ministers failed to make the need for such a choice explicit.

Contemporary cultural values, and the convention of ministerial responsibility, equally constrained the civil service. With what success, however, did Ministry officials discharge their constitutional role, which may be taken to be (in the formulation of policy) the gathering of information, consultation with relevant interests, the marshalling of arguments, and the presentation to ministers of a full range of policy-options and (in the implementation of policy) the execution of parliament's general wishes in the most equitable and cost-effective way? In the preparation and presentation of policy advice, they unquestionably lacked the wide-ranging expertise and the intellectual grasp of their predecessors at the Board of

[5] See above, pp. 30, 78–9.

Trade when, before 1914, it had effectively been a 'ministry of labour and industry'. Faced with the need to develop long-term interventionist policies, under alternating governments of different political philosophies, they also developed in all three areas of their responsibility a strong departmental view which restricted the options presented to ministers. Only the strongest ministers (amongst whom, most surprisingly, was Betterton in 1934) were able to reopen questions which officials had closed. However, Ministry officials did enjoy three collective virtues. First, owing to the Ministry's extensive regional organization and outside contacts, they developed—as far as their limited resources would allow—a keen awareness of economic and social problems and displayed considerable open-mindedness in seeking their resolution. Secondly, in the implementation of policy, a high standard of humane efficiency was attained, despite the inevitable instances and rumours of maladministration. Informed commentators all agreed that the executive achievement of unemployment relief was one of the major accomplishments of inter-war government. Finally, officials displayed a ready responsiveness to public opinion, a quality which had not been amongst the most prominent characteristics of the paternalistic Board of Trade. Herein, however, lay a major source of danger for the Ministry. Constrained by political vacillation and public conservatism, officials were tempted to retreat into a 'stoical realism' in which long-term objectives became lost beneath lowered horizons. Outside expert advice came to be increasingly resisted, be it from lay advisers (such as Violet Markham on the UAB) or from academics (such as, after 1933, Keynes). 'Criticism is received with impatience and swept aside as amateur opinion,' complained Markham, 'argument does not take place between equals.'[6] There was the danger, therefore, as Bagehot had foreseen for all bureaucracies, that the Ministry might be spoilt by its own initial success. 'Marvelling at its own merits', was it about to confuse routine for results and consequently provide the 'most unimproving and shallow of governments'?[7]

Before 1939, this danger was largely averted and—as was demonstrated by their increasing authority in Whitehall—Ministry officials responded well to the challenge of democracy; but did their increasing authority mean that they were exceptional? Is it legiti-

[6] Markham papers, VM 13/4.
[7] W. Bagehot, *The English Constitution* (1878 ed.), pp. 193-4.

mate to generalize about the inter-war civil service as a whole from the particular example of the Ministry? Coincidentally with the extension of the franchise, the civil service had been reformed under the direction of the Treasury and the administrative machine made ready for any new task that might be placed upon it. Wartime extravagance was duly checked, potential corruption forestalled, and a common purpose of public service instilled. The inherent weakness of any hierarchical structure, however, is that it becomes increasingly dependent for its success on the quality of leadership; and the inter-war civil service undoubtedly lacked the requisite quality of leadership from both successive Cabinets and Treasury officials, who (as members of a finance department) were prepared to act with speed and a disregard for formal rules only when reductions in public expenditure and state responsibilities were called for. One of the first victims of this limited vision was the Ministry's Statistics Department, on which the Ministry's successful emulation of the intellectual achievements of the Board of Trade crucially depended. Despite its extension, however, Treasury control in the inter-war years was never complete.[8] Senior officials had been appointed long before the greater standardization of recruitment in 1919; the installation of the specialist Phillips and the outspoken Wolfe as the Ministry's permanent and deputy secretaries demonstrated that the Treasury's administrative wishes could be defied; and the Ministry's victories over the constitution of the UAB, the extension of special areas legislation, and the planning of public capital expenditure equally demonstrated that the Treasury could be politically frustrated. Any final assessment of its typicality must await further case-studies, but the Ministry would seem to be but one example of the essential heterogeneity of the inter-war civil service.

The more general theories of the state and bureaucracy would both ignore this heterogeneity and dispute many of the assumptions on which the preceding conclusions have been based. Despite the richness of the archives and the wealth of relevant theories, there has in fact been little sustained, mutually informed work by historians and theorists on the nature of government during this period. Historians have been discouraged by, amongst other things,

---

[8] See H. Heclo and A. Wildavsky, *The Private Government of Public Money* (1974), p. 345: 'After fifty years of hard-fought, though publicly inaudible battles, the Treasury in the 1970s can be said to have gained the high ground.'

the tautological nature of much theory and the seemingly inherent inability of any general theory to allow for the particular nature of a particular state at a specific historical time. As an old truth has been recently restated, there are 'intrinsic limits' to all theories of the state since all governments are 'autonomous entities with their own interests and historically specific capacities for action'.[9] (Perhaps historians—especially British historians—have also been discouraged by the language requirements.) Many theorists and, in particular, functionalists—be they of a liberal, corporatist, or Marxist complexion—have also seen little value in the detailed study of administrative and political history. Given that a state exists to serve some particular function, whether it be to preserve social order and facilitate capital accumulation or to rationalize the complexities and compensate for the 'diswelfares' of advanced industrial society, its actions and their consequences (whatever the local colour) are necessarily predetermined.

However, just as any theory which can never be related to a concrete historical situation is of little intrinsic value, so no history can be a-theoretical. Some assumptions, explicit or implicit, must determine the criteria by which evidence is selected and the argument structured. The basic assumptions underlying this study have been what is termed 'incrementalism' and pluralism—although many insights have been provided by other theories and much evidence has been found which would (superficially at least) support these rival theories. Policy has been seen to be typically determined, not by some far-seeing, rational blueprint, but by small adjustments, often governed by expediency and limited objectives, which frequently have unforeseen consequences. Hence the importance of the variety of opinions expressed by ministers and civil servants, both within and without the Ministry, and—in contrast

[9] S. Tolliday and J. Zeitlin (eds.), *Shop Floor Bargaining and the State* (Cambridge, 1985), p. 25. The succeeding paragraphs are largely based on the summaries provided in chapter 1 of this book, in chapter 2 of Higgins, *The Poverty Business*, and the references cited therein, especially the work of T. Skocpol and F. Block on the New Deal in the USA. Functionalism 'normally represents little more than unsubstantiated claims that the systematic needs of capitalism generate the means of their own satisfaction or tautological claims that *any* development which retrospectively appears to be advantageous for or even compatible with the survival of capitalism can be explained by reference to the latter's functional requirements'. Analysis based on the 'relative autonomy of the state' would appear to be equally in danger of tautology. Either the state is autonomous or it is not. See Tolliday and Zeitlin, *Shop Floor Bargaining*, pp. 22, 25.

perhaps to the pre-war Board of Trade—the essentially pragmatic way in which the Ministry responded to the immense political and administrative challenge of democracy. Society has also been seen as typically stable, with the essential role of the state being to mediate between competing interest groups—although (despite the assumptions of some pluralists) effective power is not equally distributed between these groups and the state is never wholly disinterested. Hence the Ministry was not just a passive agency, through which government was informed of and adjusted to the needs of the newly enfranchised and, in particular, organized Labour; it was also (as illustrated by its championing of 'responsible' trade-unionism and 'controlled' localism and discretion) an active, and interested, influence on the nature of the ultimate adjustment.

Some theorists of bureaucracy, most notably the 'public choice' school, would argue that the principal determinant of government growth at this time was not the need of government to adjust to outside change but the self-interest of officials.[10] As earlier chapters have deliberately demonstrated, there is indeed much circumstantial evidence to support this assertion, from the Ministry's sudden embrace of Whitleyism in 1917 (when its own future was threatened) to officials' final acceptance of the UISC and UAB (which so enhanced their career prospects). In every area of policy, the importance of personal and departmental interest should never be underestimated. Neither should it be exaggerated. In the formulation of policy, the foremost objective of Ministry officials in championing, for example, 'home rule for industry', contributory unemployment insurance, and the market economy was to maximize the freedom of individual and thereby minimize state intervention. By so acting, they were working directly against their own career interests. In the implementation of policy, the verdict of those who actually studied bureaucracy at work in the inter-war years was equally decisive. 'Officials', concluded Burns, 'have in the main subordinated mechanical administrative convenience to considerations affecting the welfare of the unemployed.'[11] Vested interest was neither the sole, nor even the main, motivation of Ministry officials.

The concept of corporatism provides an alternative interpreta-

---

[10] For a brief summary, see W. A. Niskanen, *Bureaucracy: Servant or Master?* (1973).

[11] Burns, *British Unemployment Programs*, p. 324.

tion of the Ministry's history and, in particular, the variant of 'corporate bias' which Keith Middlemas has developed specifically to explain the relative political stability of inter-war Britain. Following the crisis of the First World War, Middlemas has argued, governments fostered national organizations of employers and Labour and, by sharing with them real power and authority, transformed them from ordinary pressure groups into 'governing institutions'. In return, these organizations agreed to control their own members and thereby marginalize dissent. Under this secret compact, the authority of parliament was eroded; each party became so constrained that 'crisis avoidance' became the only political option; and, most importantly for this study, the power of the civil service increased because, in the ensuing political stalemate, officials became the final arbiter of the 'national interest' and the repository of 'accumulated knowledge, expertise and hence residual power'.[12] Since the Ministry was at the heart of industrial politics, its history not surprisingly provides much evidence that could be taken to support this view. Leading officials, during the First World War, were undoubtedly interested in corporatism and both the NIC and ILO were, in part, a consequence of this interest. Legislation, such as the 1919 Industrial Courts Act, was discussed with the TUC and NCEO, and significantly amended, before submission to parliament. Leading members of the TUC and NCEO were invited to sit on government bodies (such as the UISC and the Amulree Committee) and, in the absence of industrial consensus, several important policy decisions (such as the amendment of the Fair Wages Resolution) were either evaded or postponed.

Corporate bias, however, is a thesis that cannot be sustained on either general or particular grounds. On the one hand, the assumption that political stability was the achievement of high politics (rather than the consequence of more fundamental forces, such as rising living standards) is extremely questionable. On the other, the history of the Ministry can neither sustain nor be explained by it. Between the wars, the TUC and NCEO were never more than ordinary pressure groups. Employers and trade-unionists may have

---

[12] Middlemas, *Politics in Industrial Society*, pp. 23, 327; and see above, p. 124. For a fuller examination of Middlemas's treatment of the Ministry, and a summary of the factual inaccuracies which make his book so unreliable a quarry of information for other historians, see R. Lowe, 'The Ministry of Labour: fact and fiction', *Bulletin of the Society for the Study of Labour History*, 41 (1980), 23.

been consulted by government more regularly than in the past, but this was largely because government was entering new areas of policy where the specialist knowledge and active goodwill of both sides of industry were valuable. Their views may also have influenced the detail of legislation but, despite the propaganda of the TUC and NCEO (which, in order to attract new members, naturally exaggerated their influence with government), they rarely affected its underlying principles (as the history of unemployment insurance illustrates). After 1919, detailed legislation was purposely not submitted to the TUC and NCEO before parliament. Members of both organizations were invited to sit on government bodies not as representatives, let alone delegates, but as individuals—just as were members of other 'interest groups' such as women and Scots (hence the appointment of Violet Markham and Reynard to the UAB). Moreover, as was demonstrated by the UAB standstill and the extension of special areas legislation in 1937 (which was bitterly opposed by the NCEO), back-bench parliamentary opinion was still a potent influence on legislation. Rather than there being 'triangular harmony', there was in fact a distinct triangular disharmony as the NCEO pilloried Baldwin in the 1920s, the TUC helped to bring down the Labour Government in 1931, and the Mond–Turner talks ground to a halt; and the most significant fact about corporatist experiments, such as the NIC, is not that they occurred, but that they failed. Significantly, it was the Ministry's policy after 1920 that they should fail. Leggett, in particular, zealously opposed the revival of the NIC, and the policy of 'home rule for industry' was designed to favour individual trade unions and employers' associations rather than the TUC and NCEO. It was thus the exact antithesis of corporate bias. Its purpose was not to transform national organizations into 'governing bodies' but individual industries into self-governing entities, over which government could judiciously watch in order to safeguard 'the public interest'.

Marxist analysis offers a far more substantial alternative interpretation, both in its 'instrumentalist' guise (as applied to inter-war Britain by Ralph Miliband) and in its neo-Marxist form (whereby the state is deemed to be 'relatively autonomous' from the dominant class, or the dominant fraction of that class, but structurally constrained to act in capital's long-term interest). Again, preceding chapters have deliberately provided much evidence which superficially supports these views. Personal and cultural links grew ever more strong between employers and civil servants, who implicitly accepted the inevitability and legitimacy of capitalism. In industrial relations, the abandonment of reform in 1922 and the calculated support of moderate trade unions apparently confirm Marxist assumptions about the 'neutrality of the state'. The provision of social services, subject always to the principle of less eligibility, may be seen as a palliative to help divide the working class and thereby maintain social peace. Similarly, the encouragement of industrial rationalization and regional planning may be interpreted as an attempt to facilitate capital accumulation.

When applied to concrete historical situations, however, each variant of Marxism appears inadequate. The constant lack of a coherent, class-conscious capitalist élite effectively in control of the state machine has encouraged neo-Marxists theoretically to discredit instrumentalists. Equally, serious doubts have been raised about neo-Marxist theory itself by the constant evidence of capitalists' resistance to reform (such as the opposition of both industrialists and financiers to uncovenanted benefit in the 1920s and the extension of special areas legislation in the 1930s). Neo-Marxists have had increasingly to resort to tautological functionalism and a highly selected use of evidence in their search for

structural mechanisms which [can] explain how a state which is independent of direct capitalist control [can] both be able to implement reforms essential for the long-term stability of capitalism even in the face of determined resistance from capitalists themselves, and yet be constrained to act in the general interests of the capitalist class.[13]

Given that capitalism has survived, every action of the state is too easily assumed to have furthered its interests. Moreover, evidence (such as that provided by the history of unemployment relief) is ignored which suggests that the constraints under which ministers and officials worked were not solely 'the needs of capitalism' but electoral and, in particular, the search for 'democratic legitimacy'. Marxist theory would seem to be too heavily influenced by how its own proponents would wish to use state-power to achieve an alternative hegemony, rather than by the given actions of particular

---

[13] Tolliday and Zeitlin, *Shop Floor Bargaining*, p. 22. Miliband's most recent historical critique is *Capitalist Democracy in Britain* (Oxford, 1982).

governments at specific historical times. It provides a powerful antidote to traditional liberal faith in the political neutrality and powerlessness of the state and its bureaucracy, but, as a comprehensive form of historical explanation, it is itself equally simplistic and naïve.

Finally, what lessons—if any—does the history of the inter-war Ministry have for the present-day civil service and in particular for its beleaguered successor, the Department of Employment? Deprived of responsibility for regional policy and social security at the peak of its power in the 1940s, the Ministry was briefly translated into the Department of Employment and Productivity between 1967 and 1970, only to be quickly deprived of responsibility for productivity (as in 1920) and finally of its vital contacts with the public (through the hiving-off in the 1970s of the Advisory, Conciliation and Arbitration Service and the Manpower Services Commission). The most obvious lesson is that smooth, civilized order—which is, ironically, one of the principal goals of bureaucracy—should be avoided at all costs. Order breeds complacency, whilst tension provides for dynamism. Creative tension can be provided in three ways. Ideally it can be provided, as desired by Bagehot and achieved in the Ministry under Bevin, by the constructive partnership of administrative expertise and political leadership: 'a due mixture of special and nonspecial minds—of minds which attend to the means, and of minds which attend to the end.'[14] In the inter-war period it was the latter not the former that was seriously lacking. Secondly, it can be provided within a ministry by the collegiate pooling of generalist and specialist advice, preferably from relatively young officials who have ready access to policymaking and are not hopelessly bound by precedent. Roche and Sachs have emphasized this point in their own distinctive way: 'Both the bureaucrat and the enthusiast supply ... vital components. Each by himself works badly; left alone the bureaucrat simply goes in concentric circles while the enthusiast rushes unsheathed from one ideological orgasm to another.'[15] Thirdly, given the inherent vulnerability of research departments within the civil service (as demonstrated by the inter-war Ministry), there is the need to maintain vital two-way contact between civil servants and

---

[14] Bagehot, *English Constitution*, p. 197.
[15] J. P. Roche and S. Sachs, 'The bureaucrat and the enthusiast', *Western Political Quarterly*, 8 (1955), 261.

outside research institutions, be they attached to political parties, vested interests, or academic institutions: the 'animation' of the official can thereby be achieved simultaneously with the education of the 'expert'. As was well illustrated by the failures of inter-war economic policy, democratic government needs to benefit from, and under the cover of secrecy should not be embarrassed by, a plurality of ideas.

Such suggestions, however, are largely commonplace. They have been the standard recommendations of individuals from Bagehot to Crossman and of official inquiries from the 1918 Haldane Committee to the 1968 Fulton Report. The really distinctive lesson driven home by the history of the under-financed, underestimated and consequently under-researched inter-war Ministry of Labour is that, in the achievement of administrative success, it is not any formal system but the quality of individual officials that matters.

ADMINISTRATION

A PERSONNEL

Ministers

	Minister	Parliamentary secretary
1916 (Dec.)	J. Hodge	W. C. Bridgeman
1917 (Aug.)	G. H. Roberts	
1919 (Jan.)	Sir R. Horne	G. J. Wardle
1920 (Mar.)	T. J. Macnamara	Sir C. A. M. Barlow
1922 (Oct.)	Sir C. A. M. Barlow	A. Boyd-Carpenter
1923 (Mar.)		H. B. Betterton
1924 (Jan.)	T. Shaw	Margaret Bondfield
(Nov.)	Sir A. Steel-Maitland	H. B. Betterton
1929 (June)	Margaret Bondfield	J. Lawson
1931 (Aug.)	Sir H. B. Betterton	M. Gray
(Nov.)		R. Hudson
1934 (June)	O. Stanley	
1935 (June)	E. Brown	A. Muirhead
1937 (May)		R. A. Butler
1938 (Feb.)		A. Lennox-Boyd

Officials

	Permanent secretary	Second/Deputy secretary	Principal assistant secretary*
1916	Sir D. J. Shackleton		
1917			H. B. Butler (HQ)
1919		E. C. Cunningham	F. G. Bowers (F)
			T. W. Phillips (UI)
			A. W. Watson (Estab.)
			H. J. Wilson (IR)
1920	Sir J. Masterton-Smith		H. Wolfe (Gen.)
1921	Sir H. J. Wilson		
1924		T. W. Phillips	J. A. N. Barlow (IR)
1929			J. F. G. Price (UI)
			C. W. G. Eady (E&T)
			F. W. Leggett (IR)
1930	Sir F. Floud		
1933			J. A. Dale (Estab.)
1935	Sir T. W. Phillips	Sir J. F. G. Price	J. S. Nicholson (UI)
1938		H. Wolfe	J. M. Glen (E&T)
			C. B. Hawkins (Gen.)
			G. H. Ince (Gen.)
1939		F. W. Leggett	

*Departments given in the final column are the ones to which principal assistant secretaries were initially appointed. For the earlier years, when there was incessant change, departmental names have been standardized.

B ORGANIZATION CHARTS

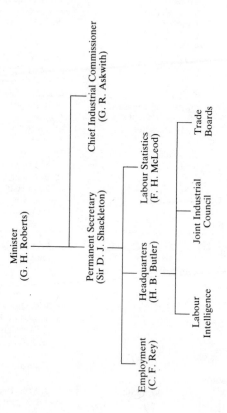

Minister
(G. H. Roberts)

Chief Industrial Commissioner
(G. R. Askwith)

Permanent Secretary
(Sir D. J. Shackleton)

Employment
(C. F. Rey)

Headquarters
(H. B. Butler)

Labour Statistics
(F. H. McLeod)

Labour
Intelligence

Joint Industrial
Council

Trade
Boards

December 1917

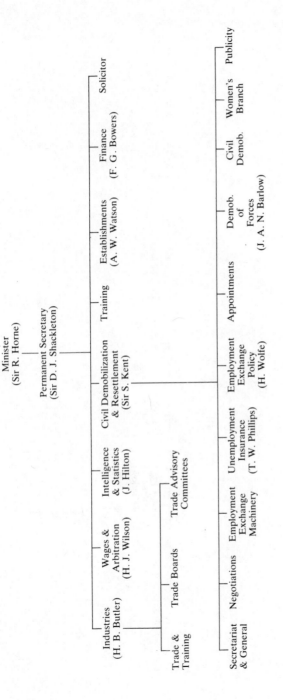

Minister
(Sir R. Horne)

Permanent Secretary
(Sir D. J. Shackleton)

Industries
(H. B. Butler)

Wages & Arbitration
(H. J. Wilson)

Intelligence & Statistics
(J. Hilton)

Civil Demobilization & Resettlement
(Sir S. Kent)

Training

Establishments
(A. W. Watson)

Finance
(F. G. Bowers)

Solicitor

Trade & Training

Trade Boards

Trade Advisory Committees

Secretariat & General

Negotiations

Employment Exchange Machinery

Unemployment Insurance
(T. W. Phillips)

Employment Exchange Policy
(H. Wolfe)

Appointments

Demob. of Forces
(J. A. N. Barlow)

Civil Demob.

Women's Branch

Publicity

April 1919

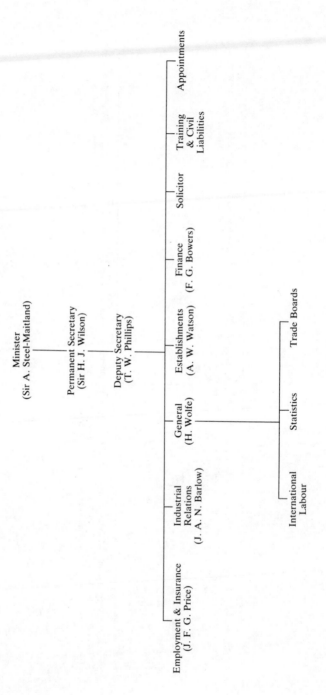

Minister
(Sir A. Steel-Maitland)

Permanent Secretary
(Sir H. J. Wilson)

Deputy Secretary
(T. W. Phillips)

Employment & Insurance
(J. F. G. Price)

Industrial Relations
(J. A. N. Barlow)

General
(H. Wolfe)

Establishments
(A. W. Watson)

Finance
(F. G. Bowers)

Solicitor

Training & Civil Liabilities

Appointments

International Labour

Statistics

Trade Boards

December 1924

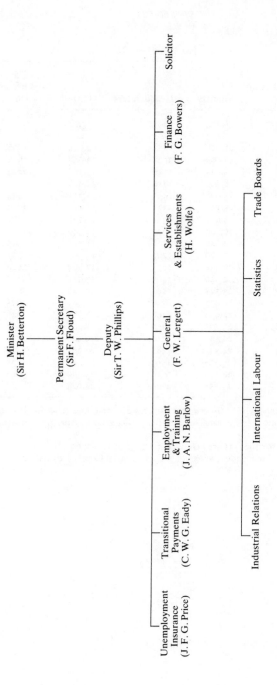

Minister
(Sir H. Betterton)

Permanent Secretary
(Sir F. Floud)

Deputy
(Sir T. W. Phillips)

Unemployment Insurance
(J. F. G. Price)

Transitional Payments
(C. W. G. Eady)

Employment & Training
(J. A. N. Barlow)

General
(F. W. Lergett)

Services & Establishments
(H. Wolfe)

Finance
(F. G. Bowers)

Solicitor

Industrial Relations

International Labour

Statistics

Trade Boards

January 1933

C ESTABLISHMENT

	Non-industrial civil service	Ministry	Headquarters	Outstations	Claims & Record Office
1914	282,420	5,824	495	5,320	–
1918	420,510	7,113	1206	5,907	–
1919	397,825	26,318	3587	21,025	1696
1920	380,963	18,904	3208	13,988	1673
1921	366,894	25,525	2450	19,388	3670
1922	317,721	18,400	1818	12,906	3663
1923	304,998	15,678	1453	11,311	2893
1924	296,621	15,548	1332	11,123	3070
1925	298,960	16,041	1341	11,706	2971
1926	296,258	16,709	1323	12,549	3813
1927	296,887	14,946	1288	11,001	2635
1928	297,140	17,320	1263	13,366	2665
1929	302,140	17,354	1413	13,264	2644
1930	306,154	22,540	1465	17,921	3113
1931	315,139	25,521	1442	20,940	3094
1932	316,229	24,632	1330	20,283	2975
1933	312,897	22,953	1298	18,775	2846
1934	311,874	23,502	1358	19,449	2662
1935	327,417	23,532	1416	19,348	2737
1936	338,604	24,541	1484	20,241	2816
1937	356,339	25,874	1559	21,448	2837
1938	376,491	28,175	1629	23,449	3063
1939	374,301	29,754	4726	25,028	–

Sources: *Staff Employed in Government Departments* and *Report of the Ministry of Labour* for various years. Figures for the civil service refer to April, for the Ministry to December.

Ministry figures for 1921–31 are taken from T 165/52, 54, 57, 60.

Figures for small independent offices (e.g. the Industrial Court) are omitted.

D EXPENDITURE (EM)

	Net Expenditure				Gross Expenditure		
	Civil service (Civil & Revenue Depts.)	Ministry of Labour	UAB (& Unemployment Assistance Allowance)	Special Areas (& Finance Assistance)	Admin.	UI (& Transitional Employment payment)	& Training
1917	112.8	1.7			–	–	–
1918	130.7	2.7			–	–	–
1919	616.0	49.5			4.4	0.9	–
1920	523.3	28.6			5.1	2.3	–
1921	517.9	21.2			6.7	8.7	7.6
1922	351.9	17.1			4.2	12.2	4.4
1923	306.2	16.0			3.6	12.9	2.8
1924	290.1	15.1			3.7	13.3	2.0
1925	310.3	14.6			3.9	13.7	1.2
1926	304.7	11.5			4.0	11.0	0.5
1927	299.4	12.2			3.8	12.1	0.3
1928	292.6	12.9			4.2	11.9	0.8
1929	317.5	20.4			4.3	19.6	0.9
1930	376.1	36.3			5.1	35.4	0.9
1931	391.4	50.3			5.3	50.0	0.8
1932	414.5	78.6			5.5	80.3	0.7
1933	409.9	71.3			5.4	72.9	0.7
1934	419.9	66.0			5.4	67.6	0.8
1935	441.0	23.6	46.7		5.5	22.4	1.4
1936	453.1	23.6	41.9	3	5.7	21.8	2.0
1937	481.4	23.8	41.4	3.6	6.0	22.0	1.9
1938	521.0	24.4	39.6	7.9	6.7	22.5	1.9
1939	535.5	25.2	32.2	0.6	7.0	22.6	1.6

Sources: *Civil Appropriation Accounts* for relevant years. Ministry figures for 1921–31 are based on a more detailed breakdown of the cost of services rendered to the Ministry by other departments (T 165/54, T 165/60). Expenditure on small services (e.g. the ILO) are omitted from the breakdown of gross cost.

APPENDIX 2

INDUSTRIAL RELATIONS

A   INDUSTRIAL UNREST AND TRADE UNION ORGANIZATION

	a	b	c	d	e	f
		No. of workers involved direct & indirect (000)		Working days lost excluding coal (000)	TU membership (m.)	% of total workforce
	No. of stoppages		Working days lost (000)			
1916	532	276	2,446	2,135	4.6	25.6
1917	730	872	5,647	4,476	5.5	30.2
1918	1,165	1,116	5,875	4,710	6.5	35.7
1919	1,352	2,591	34,969	27,528	7.9	43.1
1920	1,607	1,932	26,568	9,144	8.3	45.2
1921	763	1,801	85,872	13,179	6.6	35.8
1922	576	552	19,850	18,604	5.6	31.6
1923	628	405	10,672	9,489	5.4	30.2
1924	710	613	8,474	6,911	5.5	30.6
1925	603	441	7,952	4,499	5.5	30.1
1926	323	2,734	162,233	15,799	5.2	28.3
1927	308	108	1,174	486	4.9	26.4
1928	302	124	1,388	936	4.8	25.6
1929	431	533	8,287	7,711	4.9	25.7
1930	422	307	4,399	3,736	4.8	25.4
1931	420	490	6,983	4,135	4.6	24.0
1932	389	379	6,488	6,201	4.4	23.0
1933	357	136	1,072	626	4.4	22.6
1934	471	134	959	594	4.6	23.5
1935	553	271	1,955	587	4.9	24.9
1936	818	316	1,829	977	5.3	26.9
1937	1,129	597	3,413	1,917	5.8	29.6
1938	875	274	1,334	637	6.1	30.5
1939	940	337	1,356	791	6.3	31.6

Sources: a–d, Department of Employment, *British Labour Statistics*, T 197
e–f, A. H. Halsey, *Trends in British Society*, table 4.12.

B   CONCILIATION AND ARBITRATION

	Arbitration settlements			Conciliation settlements	Court of Inquiry
	Industrial Court	Single arb.	*Ad hoc* Board		
1920	540	73	15	286	3
1921	122	19	7	123	1
1922	37	9	8	48	1
1923	113	14	6	33	1
1924	143	7	12	83	7
1925	165	8	8	73	3
1926	104	5	4	24	–
1927	82	6	1	14	–
1928	52	10	5	42	–
1929	39	14	3	38	–
1930	43	6	3	31	1
1931	35	7	6	48	–
1932	28	3	1	45	–
1933	26	3	1	22	–
1934	30	6	4	29	–
1935	29	10	–	41	1
1936	35	9	1	45	–
1937	20	6	2	66	2
1938	26	6	2	83	–

Figures refer only to agreements where Ministry of Labour arranged final meeting.
Sources: R. V. Vernon and N. Mansergh (eds.), *Advisory Bodies* (1940), p. 305, supplemented by *Annual Reports* of the Ministry of Labour.

UNEMPLOYMENT

A NUMBER OF PERSONS UNEMPLOYED AND ON UNEMPLOYMENT RELIEF IN GREAT BRITAIN

	a Unemployment	b Insured unemployment	c Unemployment insurance	d Supplementary national systems	e Total national relief	f Poor Law
	(million)			(thousands)		
1916						
1917	0.1					
1918	0.1					
1919	0.7					
1920	0.4					
1921	2.2					
1922	1.9		954	153	1,107	239
1923	1.6	1.3	800	261	1,061	174
1924	1.4	1.1	544	491	1,035	113
1925	1.6	1.4	–	–	971	162
1926	1.8	1.8	–	–	1,141	264
1927	1.4	1.0	–	–	943	154
1928	1.5	1.3	973	119	1,092	112
1929	1.5	1.2	–	–	1,126	94
1930	2.4	1.9	1,973	383	2,356	59
1931	3.3	2.7	1,345	762	2,107	101
1932	3.4	2.8	1,200	1,039	2,239	168
1933	3.1	2.5	854	936	1,790	192
1934	2.6	2.1	952	728	1,680	222
1935	2.4	2.0	822	688	1,510	173
1936	2.1	1.7	744	579	1,323	144
1937	1.8	1.4	896	556	1,452	30
1938	2.2	1.9	1,076	554	1,630	28
1939	1.3	1.4	–	–	–	–

Sources: a. C. H. Feinstein, *Statistical Tables of National Income, Expenditure and Output of the U.K. 1855-1965*, T 126.

b. Department of Employment, *British Labour Statistics*, T 163.

c–f. E. M. Burns, *British Unemployment Programs, 1920-1938*, pp. 347, 360. Figures refer to December of each year except cols. c–e for 1922 and 1923 which refer to November and April respectively. Col. f refers to the number of persons (excluding dependants) receiving relief on account of unemployment only.

B EXPENDITURE ON UNEMPLOYMENT RELIEF

	a	b	c	d	e	f	g
	Insurance system			Supplementary system			Poor relief on the unemployed
	Benefits	Admin.	Total	Payments	Admin.	Total	Total
		£m.			£m.		£m.
1921	34.1	1.1	35.4				–
1922	53.0	4.8	59.8				–
1923	41.9	4.5	51.6				12.1
1924	36.0	4.1	50.4				8.4
1925	44.6	4.6	54.4				5.4
1926	43.7	4.9	51.4				7.0
1927	38.7	3.5	42.9*				13.7
1928	36.4	4.9	46.6				8.1
1929	46.7	5.1	54.4				5.9
1930	42.3	5.7	54.2	3.7	0.3	4.0	4.8
1931	73.0	5.3	81.0	19.2	1.0	20.3	2.6
1932	80.2	5.4	90.5	30.7	1.6	32.4	4.0
1933	54.2	4.2	64.0	50.4	3.4	53.8	6.5
1934	40.2	3.8	57.8	48.4	3.7	52.1	8.1
1935	43.8	4.1	54.1	42.2	4.0	46.2	9.7
1936	42.7	4.6	52.7	42.4	4.3	46.7	9.6
1937	35.3	4.9	45.8	37.4	4.4	41.8	7.8
1938	36.7	5.1	67.3	36.7	4.7	41.4	2.5
1939	55.1	6.3	68.9	35.3	4.3	39.6	–

Source: E. M. Burns, *British Unemployment Programs, 1920–1938*, pp. 361, 367.
Col. c includes expenditure on travelling expenses, approved courses instruction, and repayment of Treasury advances and interest (especially heavy in 1924, 1934, and 1938).

* 9-month period only.

C GOVERNMENT TRAINING PROGRAMMES, 1929–1938

	1929	1930	1931	1932	1933	1934	1935	1936	1937	1938
Government training centres										
number	11	10	9	9	8	9	9	11	14	16
persons completing course	4,768	6,204	7,170	4,843	4,432	5,087	7,205	10,693	10,761	9,175
persons placed in employment	4,429	5,160	5,290	3,440	3,728	4,819	7,059	10,398	10,424	8,315
premature terminations	792	1,611	1,709	1,047	844	1,134	1,663	3,083	3,939	3,550
Training courses for women										
number	39	38	37	33	32	32	37	39	37	38
persons completing course	3,800	3,906	5,640	5,133	4,682	4,078	4,050	3,286	3,407	3,775
persons placed in employment	3,435	3,463	4,437	4,178	3,940	3,403	3,313	3,275	2,789	1,926
premature terminations	489	480	564	653	566	498	523	517	454	540
Instructional centres										
number	5	10	6	11	12	15	17	15	24	25
persons admitted	3,518	9,886	7,652	6,654	10,545	16,248	18,077	20,872	20,588	23,772
persons placed in employment/ transferred to other programmes	1,725	6,718	5,734	2,865	1,571	2,602	3,119	4,312	3,474	3,037
premature terminations	1,029	2,487	1,724	736	855	1,280	2,609	3,959	5,285	7,571
Juvenile instruction centres										
number of centres and classes	87	114	163	170	138	124	205	209	187	194
persons attending during year	60,750	88,300	143,900	136,700	101,600	113,500	169,000	191,000	20,013	23,732

Source: E. M. Burns, *British Unemployment Programs, 1920–1938*, p. 373.

SELECT BIBLIOGRAPHY

A UNPUBLISHED SOURCES

1 Public Records (at the Public Record Office (PRO), London)

1.1 Ministry of Labour

The only certain thing about the records of the inter-war Ministry of Labour is that it is impossible to be certain as to the class, if any, in which a file on a particular topic can be located. The following comments are no substitute for the relevant guides and handbooks at the PRO and in particular for B. Swann and M. Turnbull (eds.), *Records of Interest to Social Scientists, 1919–39* (3 vols., 1971–8).

The most important class is Lab 2, to which access is easiest—all terms being relative—through the original docket-books preserved in Lab 7. Its 2,191 boxes contain most of the important *policy* files for the period 1916–33, although it also includes the labour records of the pre-war Board of Trade and—inevitably—some files for the period after 1933. Many files, opened before 1933, have also been extracted and placed in other classes, the most important being Lab 8 and 10 and, outside the Ministry, Pin 3, 6 and 7 of the Ministry of Pensions and National Insurance's records. The bulk of the records after 1933 have been preserved in classes organized by subject, as listed below. Files originating in the Ministry can also be found in the records of other ministries, in particular those of the Ministry of Health (MH 61) and of the Assistance Board (Ast 7).

The main classes of Ministry records used in this study were, with approximate dates:

Lab 2   General Correspondence, 1897–1933
Lab 3   Industrial Court, 1919–56
Lab 4   Unemployment Grants Committee, 1920–51
Lab 7   Docket-books to Lab 2
Lab 8   Employment, 1909–62
Lab 9   Finance, 1912–64
Lab 10 Industrial Relations, 1917–59
Lab 12 Establishments, 1915–61
Lab 16 Solicitor's Department, 1928–60
Lab 17 Statistics, 1918–65
Lab 18 Training, 1922–62
Lab 23 Special Areas, 1934–46
Lab 27 Coal Mining Industry Dispute and 1926 General Strike, 1918–29
Lab 31 Holidays with Pay, 1938

Files in Lab 2 are classified according to the department in which they originated (details of which are on pp. 54–5 and Appendix 1, B). The main sequences used with their approximate dates were:

HQ (Headquarters), MH (Montagu House), ML (Ministry of Labour), CS (Council Secretariat): major policy, 1916–21
WA (Wages and Arbitration), IR (Industrial Relations): industrial relations, 1918–33
L (Labour), LE (Labour Exchanges): Board of Trade records, pre-1917
ED ((Employment Department), ET (Employment and Training): 1916–33
EI (Establishments), CEB (Central Establishments Branch), S and E (Services and Establishments), OP (Premises): 1918–1933
F (Finance): 1919–33
DR (Demobilization and Resettlement): 1918–19
I and S (Intelligence and Statistics), Stats (Statistics): 1917–33
TB (Trade Boards): 1917–33
IL (International Labour): 1921–33

To assist the PRO's computer, and typesetters, Lab 2 records are being recatalogued. The changes, at the time of publication, affect the first six file sequences listed above and consist of substituting a single number (based on the file's position in its box) for the original file reference. Hence file ML 12475/2/1919 in box 254 of the class Lab 2, which was previously catalogued as Lab 2/254/ML 12475/2/1919 is now Lab 2/254/12. It is no longer possible, therefore, immediately to identify from which department and at what date a file originated; but despite this, and the consummate skill with which the PRO timed its announcement to coincide with the completion of the book's final draft, the changes have been incorporated. Guides exist at the PRO to permit reconversion.

For the wary, selections from the records of the Ministry (principally Lab 2, 10) and the Assistance Board (Ast 12) are available on microfilm from the Harvester Press: *Conflict and Consensus in British Industrial Relations, 1916–48* (1985) and *The Origins of the Welfare State in Britain, 1934–48* (1985).

1.2 *Other Government Records*

Cabinet (Cab 23, 24, 26, 27, 33, 37, 42, 87)
Prime Minister's Office (Prem 1, 4)
Treasury (TI, 126, 161, 162, 163, 172, 175)
Assistance Board (Ast 7, 9, 12)
Board of Trade (BT 13, 56)
Home Office (HO 45)
Ministry of Health (MH 61)
Ministry of Munitions (Mun 5)

Ministry of Pensions and National Insurance (Pin 1, 6, 7)
Scottish Office (DD 10, at the Scottish Record Office, Edinburgh)

2 Private Papers

Asquith	(Bodleian Library, Oxford)
Baldwin	(Cambridge University Library)
Beveridge	(British Library of Political & Economic Science)
Bevin	(Churchill College, Cambridge)
Bonar Law	(House of Lords Record Office)
Bridgeman	(Viscount Bridgeman)
Austen Chamberlain	(Birmingham University Library)
Neville Chamberlain	(Birmingham University Library)
Floud	(Birkbeck College, London)
Grigg	(Churchill College, Cambridge)
Haldane	(National Library of Scotland)
Henderson	(Labour Party Library)
Tom Jones	(National Library of Wales)
Lithgow	(Glasgow University)
Lloyd George	(House of Lords Record Office)
MacDonald	(Public Record Office)
Markham	(British Library of Political & Economic Science)
Milner	(Bodleian Library, Oxford)
Passfield	(British Library of Political & Economic Science)
Rey	(Bodleian Library, Oxford)
Samuel	(House of Lords Record Office)
Steel-Maitland	(Scottish Record Office)
Tribe	(Dr C. R. Tribe, Bristol)
Weir	(Churchill College, Cambridge)

Dock, Wharves, Riverside and General Workers' Union (Modern Records Centre, Warwick University)
Labour Party
Labour Party Executive Committee (British Library of Political and Economic Science)
Mass Observation (Sussex University)
National Confederation of Employers' Organisations (Modern Records Centre, Warwick University)
Trades Union Congress (Congress House, London)

3 Interviews and Correspondence

Viscount Bridgeman	(private sec., Parliamentary Secretary, 1917–18)
Lord Butler	(Parliamentary Secretary, 1937–8)
C. J. Dennys	(Assistant Secretary; principal private sec., Minister, 1938)

Sir James Dunnett	
*Sir Harold Emmerson	(Assistant Secretary; Secretary, English Special Areas Commission, 1938–9)
Sir Alan Hitchman	(principal private sec., Minister, 1939)
Sir Frederick Leggett	(Deputy Secretary, 1939)
C. J. Maston	(assistant private sec., Minister, 1937–9)
F. Pickford	(Assistant Principal)
H. Rossetti	(Principal; principal private sec., Minister, 1937)
N. Singleton	(private sec., Permanent Secretary, 1938–9)
*C. H. Sisson	(Assistant Principal)
Sir John Walley	(Principal)
P. H. St. John Wilson	(Principal; private sec. to Minister and Parliamentary Secretary, 1934–6)

*denotes interview. Positions given are the most important held in, or before, 1939.

4 Theses

Booth, A. E., 'The timing and content of government policies to assist the depressed areas, 1920–39' (Ph.D., University of Kent, 1975).

Caldwell, J. A. M., 'Social policy and public administration' (Ph.D., Nottingham University, 1956).

Daly, M. E., 'Government policy and the depressed areas in the inter-war years' (D.Phil., Oxford University, 1979).

Davidson, R., 'Sir Hubert Llewellyn Smith and labour policy' (Ph.D., Cambridge University, 1971).

Jacques, M., 'The emergence of "responsible" trade unionism: a study of the "new direction" in TUC policy, 1926–1935' (Ph.D., Cambridge University, 1976).

Janeway, W. H., 'The economic policy of the second Labour Government, 1929–31' (Ph.D., Cambridge University, 1971).

Jones, H., 'The Home Office and working conditions, 1914–40' (Ph.D., London University, 1983).

Jones, R., 'The wages problem in employment policy, 1936–1948' (M.Sc., Bristol University, 1983).

Lowe, R., 'The demand for a Ministry of Labour, its establishment and initial role, 1916–24' (Ph.D., London University, 1975).

O'Halpin, E., 'Sir Warren Fisher, head of the civil service, 1919–39' (Ph.D., Cambridge University, 1982).

Pitfield, D. E., 'Labour migration and the regional problem in Britain, 1920–39' (Ph.D., Stirling University, 1974).

Roberts, R., 'The Board of Trade, 1925-39' (D.Phil., Oxford University, 1985).

Rodgers, T., 'Work and welfare: the National Confederation of Employers' Organisations and the unemployment problem, 1917-36' (Ph.D., Edinburgh University, 1982).

Scheps, A., 'Trade unions and Governments, 1925-7' (D.Phil., Oxford University, 1972).

Shaw, S., 'The attitude of the TUC towards unemployment in the inter-war period' (Ph.D., University of Kent, 1979).

Sims, D.J., 'Juvenile unemployment programmes in England, 1909-1979' (M.Phil., Southampton University, 1982).

Stacey, S.R., 'The Ministry of Health, 1919-29: ideas and practice in a government department' (D.Phil., Oxford University, 1984).

Wrigley, C.J., 'Lloyd George and the Labour movement' (Ph.D., London University, 1973).

B PUBLISHED SOURCES

The place of publication is London unless otherwise stated.

1 Official Publications

1.1 Annual Reports of the Ministry of Labour

1923-4	(Cmd. 2481), PP (1924-5), xiv.
1925	(Cmd. 2736), PP (1926), xiii.
1926	(Cmd. 2856), PP (1927), x.
1927	(Cmd. 3090), PP (1928), xi.
1928	(Cmd. 3333), PP (1928-9), vii.
1929	(Cmd. 3579), PP (1929-30), xv.
1930	(Cmd. 3859), PP (1930-31), xv.
1931	(Cmd. 4044), PP (1931-2), xi.
1932	(Cmd. 4281), PP (1932-3), xiii.
1933	(Cmd. 4543), PP (1933-4), xiii.
1934	(Cmd. 4861), PP (1934-5), x.
1935	(Cmd. 5145), PP (1935-6), xiii.
1936	(Cmd. 5431), PP (1936-7), xii.
1937	(Cmd. 5717), PP (1937-8), xii.
1938	(Cmd. 6016), PP (1938-9), xii.
1939-46	(Cmd. 7225), PP (1946-7), xii.

1.2 Other Publications Cited (in chronological order)

Report of the Royal Commission on Labour (C. 7421), PP (1894), xxxv.

Report of the Royal Commission on the Poor Laws (Cd. 4499), PP (1909), xxxvii.

*Final Report on the (Whitley) Committee on Relations between Employers
and Employed* (Cd. 9153), PP (1918), viii.
Report of the (Haldane) Machinery of Government Committee (Cd. 9230),
PP (1918), xii.
*Final Report of the (Aberconway) Committee of Inquiry into the Scheme of
Out-of-Work Donation* (Cmd. 305), PP (1919), xxx.
Evidence to the (Aberconway) Committee ... (Cmd. 407), PP (1919), xxx.
*Report of the Provisional Joint Committee presented to the Meeting of the
Industrial Conference* (Cmd. 501), PP (1919), xxiv.
*Report of the (Peel) Committee on the Staffing and Methods of Work of the
Ministry of Labour* (Cmd. 1069), PP (1920), xxv.
Reports of the (Geddes) Committee on National Expenditure (Cmd. 1581,
1582, 1589), PP (1922), ix.
*Report of the (Cave) Committee appointed to enquire into the Working and
Effects of the Trade Boards Act* (Cmd. 1645), PP (1922), x.
Memoranda on Certain Proposals Relating to Unemployment (Cmd. 3331),
PP (1928-9), xvi.
Report of the (Tomlin) Royal Commission on the Civil Service (Cmd. 3909),
PP (1930-1), x.
*First Report of the (Gregory) Royal Commission on Unemployment Insur-
ance* (Cmd. 3872), PP (1930-1), xvii.
Report of the (May) Committee on National Expenditure (Cmd. 3920), PP
(1930-1), xvi.
Final Report of the Royal Commission on Unemployment Insurance (Cmd.
4185), PP (1931-2), xiii.
Minutes of Evidence to the Royal Commission on Unemployment Insurance
(1932).
Final Report of the Unemployment Grants Committee (Cmd. 4354), PP
(1932-3), xv.
*Report of the (Barlow) Royal Commission on the Distribution of the Indus-
trial Population* (Cmd. 6153), PP (1939-40), iv.
Minutes of Evidence to the (Barlow) Royal Commission (1938).
Social Insurance and Allied Services (the Beveridge Report, Cmd. 6404),
PP (1942-3), vi.
Employment Policy (Cmd. 6527), PP (1943-4), viii.
*Report of the (Donovan) Royal Commission on Trade Unions and Employers'
Associations* (Cmnd. 3623), PP (1967-8), xxxii.
Report of the (Fulton) Committee on the Civil Service (Cmnd. 3638), PP
(1967-8), xviii.

2 Memoirs and Biographies

2.1 Ministry of Labour Personnel

Askwith, Lord, *Industrial Problems and Disputes* (1920).

Bondfield, M., *A Life's Work* (1948).
Bullock, A., *The Life and Times of Ernest Bevin*, (vols. 1-2, 1960-7).
Butler, H. B., *The Confident Morning* (1950).
Butler, R. A., *The Art of the Possible* (1971).
Church, R., *The Golden Sovereign* (1957).
—— *The Voyage Home* (1964).
Harris, J., *William Beveridge* (Oxford, 1977).
Hilton, J., *Rich Man, Poor Man* (1944).
Hodge, J., *Workman's Cottage to Windsor Castle* (1931).
Joad, C. E. M., *The Book of Joad* (1935).
Morris, Sir H., *Back View* (1960).
Munro, C. K., *The Fountains in Trafalgar Square* (1952).
Nixon, E., *John Hilton* (1946).
Norman, F. A., *Whitehall to West Indies* (1952).
Scott, Sir H., *Your Obedient Servant* (1959).
Tallents, S. G., *Man and Boy* (1930).

2.2 Other Memoirs and Biographies

Addison, C., *Politics from Within* (2 vols., 1924).
——*Four and a Half Years* (2 vols., 1934).
Barnes, G. N., *From Workshop to War Cabinet* (1923).
Bevan, A., *In Place of Fear* (1961).
Blaxland, G., *J. H. Thomas: A Life for Unity* (1964).
Brown, W. J., *So Far* (1943).
Citrine, Lord, *Men and Work* (1964).
Crisp, Q., *The Naked Civil Servant* (1977).
Crossman, R., *Palestine Mission* (1946).
—— *The Diaries of a Cabinet Minister* (3 vols., 1975-7).
Dilks, D., *Neville Chamberlain* (vol. 1, Cambridge, 1984).
Eden, A., *Full Circle* (1960).
Feiling, K., *The Life of Neville Chamberlain* (1946).
Fisher, N., *Iain Macleod* (1973).
Fitzroy, A., *Memories* (2 vols., 1925).
Gilbert, M., *Winston S. Churchill* (vols. 3-5, 1971-6).
Griffith-Boscawen, A., *Memories* (1925).
Grigg, P. J., *Prejudice and Judgement* (1948).
Hamilton, M. A., *Arthur Henderson* (1938).
James, R. R., *Memoirs of a Conservative* (1969).
Jones, T. J., *A Diary with Letters* (1954).
—— *Whitehall Diary* (vols. 1-2, 1969).
Keynes, J. M., *The Collected Writings of John Maynard Keynes* (29 vols., 1971-83).
Markham, V. R., *Return Passage* (1956).

Marquand, D., *Ramsay MacDonald* (1977).
Marsh, E. H., *A Number of People* (1936).
Meynell, F., *My Lives* (1971).
Middlemas, K. and Barnes, J., *Baldwin* (1969).
Mosley, O., *My Life* (1968).
Percy, E., *Some Memories* (1958).
Riddell, Lord, *Lord Riddell's War Diary* (1933).
Roberts, R., *The Classic Slum* (Harmondsworth, 1973).
Stocks, M., *My Common-Place Book* (1970).
Taylor, A. J. P. (ed.), *Lloyd George: A Diary by Frances Stevenson* (1971).
Thomas, J. H., *My Story* (1937).
West, Maj.-Gen. Sir F., *Haldane* (2 vols., 1937).
Williams, F., *A Pattern of Rulers* (1965).
Wilson, Sir A., *Walks and Talks* (1934).

3 Contemporary Writings

3.1 Works on the Ministry or by Ministry Officials

Amulree, Lord, *Industrial Arbitration in Great Britain* (1930).
Beveridge, W. H., *The Public Service in War and Peace* (1920).
—— *Insurance for All and Everything* (1924).
—— *War and Insurance* (1927).
—— *Power and Influence* (1953).
Chegwidden, T. S., and Mynddin-Evans, G., *The Employment Exchange Service of Great Britain* (1934).
Clay, H., *The Problem of Industrial Relations* (1929).
Davison, R. C., *The Unemployed* (1930).
—— *What's Wrong with Unemployment Insurance* (1930).
—— *British Unemployment Policy: The Modern Phase since 1930* (1938).
Hilton, J., 'The public services in relation to the problem of unemployment', *Public Administration*, 15 (1937), 3.
HMSO, *Industrial Relations Handbook* (1944).
Ince, G. H., *The Ministry of Labour and National Service* (1960).
Leggett, F. W., 'The settlement of labour disputes in Great Britain', in E. Jackson (ed.), *Meeting of Minds* (New York, 1952).
Lockhead, A. V. S., 'The use of advisory bodies by the Industrial Relations Department of the Ministry of Labour', in R. V. Vernon and N. Mansergh (eds.), *Advisory Bodies* (1940).
Phelan, E. J., 'The peace conference: British preparations', in J. T. Shotwell (ed.), *The Origins of the International Labour Organisation* (vol. 1, New York, 1934).
—— *Yes and Albert Thomas* (1949).
Seymour, J. B., *The British Employment Exchange* (1928).
Wolfe, H., *Labour Regulation and Supply* (1923).

3.2 Other Works

Astor, J. J., *Unemployment Insurance in Great Britain* (1925).
Bakke, E. W., *The Unemployed Man* (1933).
—— *Insurance or Dole?* (Yale, 1935).
Boothby, R., Macmillan, H., Loder, J. de V. and Stanley, O., *Industry and State—a Conservative View* (1927).
Burns, E. M., *British Unemployment Programs, 1920–1938* (Washington, 1941).
Cato, *Guilty Men* (1940).
Cole, G. D. H. and Postgate, R., *The Common People* (1938).
Conservative Party, *A Great Social Reform* (1934).
Dale, H. E., *The Higher Civil Service in Great Britain* (1941).
—— *The Personnel and Problems of the Higher Civil Service* (1943).
Dennison, S. R., *The Location of Industry and the Depressed Areas* (1939).
EEF, *Unemployment—its Realities and Problems* (1933).
FBI, *Report of the Committee on the Organization of Industry* (1935).
Gannett, F. L. and Catherwood, B. F. (eds.), *Industrial and Labour Relations in Great Britain* (New York, 1939).
Gleason, A., *What the Workers Want* (1920).
Fabian Society, *The Reform of the Higher Civil Service* (1947).
Hewart, Lord, *The New Despotism* (1929).
Macassey, L., *Labour Policy—False and True* (1922).
Millett, J. D., *The Unemployment Assistance Board* (New York, 1940).
NCEO, *Report on Unemployment Insurance* (1924).
—— *The Industrial Situation* (1931).
Owen, A. D. K., 'The social consequences of industrial transference', *Sociological Review*, 29 (1937), 331.
PEP, *Report on the British Social Services* (1937).
Rankin, M. T., *Arbitration Principles and the Industrial Court: An Analysis of Decisions, 1919–29* (1931).
Richardson, J. H., *Industrial Relations in Great Britain* (Geneva, 1938).
Robson, W. A. (ed.), *The British Civil Servant* (1937).
Sells, D., *British Wages Boards* (Washington, 1939).
Tillyard, Sir F., *Unemployment Insurance in Great Britain, 1911–48* (Leigh-on-Sea, 1949).
Vernon, R. V. and Mansergh, N. (eds.), *Advisory Bodies* (1940).
Webb, S. and B., *A Constitution for the Socialist Commonwealth of Great Britain* (1920).

4 Historical Studies

4.1 Reference

Department of Employment and Productivity, *British Labour Statistics* (1971).

Feinstein, C. H., *Statistical Tables of National Income, Expenditure and Output of the U.K., 1855-1965* (1976).

Halsey, A. H., *Trends in British Society* (1972).

Swann, B. and Turnbull, M., *Records of Interest to Social Scientists* (PRO Handbooks 14, 16, 18) 3 vols. (1971-8).

4.2 Conceptual

Albrow, M., *Bureaucracy* (1970).

Bagehot, W., *The English Constitution* (1878 edn.).

Block, F., 'Beyond relative autonomy: state managers as historical subjects', *Socialist Register* (1980), 227.

Carpenter, L. P., 'Corporatism in Britain, 1930-45', *Journal of Contemporary History*, 11 (1976), 3.

Crouch, C., *Class Conflict and the Industrial Relations Crisis* (1977).

Hall, P., Land, H., Parker, R. and Webb, A., *Change, Choice and Conflict in Social Policy* (1975).

Higgins, J., *The Poverty Business* (Oxford, 1978).

Hill, M., *The Sociology of Public Administration* (1972).

Jessop, B., *The Capitalist State* (Oxford, 1982).

Middlemas, K., *Politics in Industrial Society* (1979).

Miliband, R., *The State in Capitalist Society* (1973).

—— *Capitalist Democracy in Britain* (Oxford, 1982).

Niskanen, W. A., *Bureaucracy: Servant or Master?* (1973).

Roche, J. P. and Sachs, S., 'The bureaucrat and the enthusiast', *Western Political Quarterly*, 8 (1955).

Roth, G. and Willich, C., *Max Weber: Economy and Society* (3 vols., New York, 1968).

Skocpol. T., 'Political response to capitalist crisis: neo-Marxist theories of the state and the case of the New Deal', *Politics and Society*, 10 (1980-1), 155.

4.3 British Politics

Adams, W. S., 'Lloyd George and the Labour movement', *Past and Present*, 3 (1953), 55.

Armitage, S., *The Politics of Decontrol of Industry* (1969).

Blake, R., *The Conservative Party from Peel to Churchill* (1968).

Checkland, S. G., *British Public Policy, 1776-1939* (Cambridge, 1983).

Cowling, M., *The Impact of Labour, 1920-4* (1971).

Cronin, J. and Schneer, J. (eds.), *Social Conflict and the Political Order in Modern Britain* (1982).

Halévy, E., *The Rule of Democracy* (*History of the English People in the Nineteenth Century*, vol. 6) (1961 edn.).

—— *The Era of Tyrannies* (1967).

Johnson, P. B., *Land Fit for Heroes* (Chicago, 1968).

Marwick, A., *The Deluge* (1965).

Matthew, H. G. C., McKibbin, R. I. and Kay, J. A., 'The franchise factor in the rise of the Labour Party', *English Historical Review*, 91 (1976), 723.

Morgan, K. O., *Consensus and Disunity* (Oxford, 1979).

Mowat, C. L., *Britain Between the Wars* (1955 edn.).

Pugh, M., *The Making of Modern British Politics* (1982).

Ramsden, J., *The Age of Balfour and Baldwin* (1979).

Read, D., *England 1868–1914* (1979).

Skidelsky, R., *Politicians and the Slump* (Harmondsworth, 1970 edn.).

4.4 Public Administration

Beloff, M., 'The Whitehall factor: the role of the higher civil service', in G. Peele and C. Cook (eds.), *The Politics of Reappraisal* (1975).

Booth, A., 'An administrative experiment in unemployment policy in the 1930s', *Public Administration*, 56 (1978), 139.

Chapman, R. A. and Greenaway, J. R., *The Dynamics of Administrative Reform* (1980).

Chester, D. N. (ed.), *Lessons of the War Economy* (Cambridge, 1951).

Davidson, R., 'Llewellyn Smith, the Labour Department and government growth, 1886–1909', in G. Sutherland (ed.), *Studies in the Growth of Nineteenth-Century Government* (1972).

—— 'Social conflict and social administration', in T. C. Smout (ed.), *The Search for Stability and Wealth* (1979).

—— *Whitehall and the Labour Problem in Late-Victorian and Edwardian Britain* (1985).

—— and Lowe, R., 'Bureaucracy and innovation in British welfare policy, 1870–1945', in W. J. Mommsen (ed.), *The Emergence of the Welfare State in Britain and Germany* (1981).

Fry, G. K., *Statesmen in Disguise* (1969).

—— *The Growth of Government* (1979).

Greenaway, J. R., 'Warren Fisher and the transformation of the British Treasury, 1919–39' *Journal of British Studies*, 23 (1985), 125.

Harrison, E. M., 'Local Advisory Committees', *Public Administration*, 31 (1953), 65.

Heclo, H. and Wildavsky, A., *The Private Government of Public Money* (1974).

Howson, S. and Winch, D., *The Economic Advisory Council, 1930–1939* (Cambridge, 1977).

Kelsall, R. K., *Higher Civil Servants in Britain* (1955).

Lowe, R., 'The Ministry of Labour, 1916–1924: a graveyard of social reform?', *Public Administration*, 52 (1974), 415.

—— 'The erosion of state intervention in Britain, 1917–1924', *Economic History Review*, 2nd ser., xxxi (1978), 270.

—— 'The Ministry of Labour: fact and fiction', *Bulletin of the Society for the Study of Labour History*, 41 (1980), 23.

—— 'The Ministry of Labour, 1916–1919: a still, small voice?', in K. Burk (ed.), *War and the State* (1982).

—— 'Bureaucracy triumphant or denied? The expansion of the British civil service, 1919–1939', *Public Administration*, 62 (1984), 291.

Peden, G. C., 'The Treasury as the central department of government, 1919–39', *Public Administration*, 61 (1983), 371.

Showler, B., *The Public Employment Service* (1976).

Thomas, R., *The British Philosophy of Administration* (1978).

Williams, D. G. T., 'The Donoughmore Report in retrospect', *Public Administration*, 60 (1982), 273.

Williams, F. M. G., *The Organization of British Central Government*, (1968 edn.).

4.5 Industrial Relations

Allen, V. L., *Trade Unions and the Government* (1960).

—— *The Sociology of Industrial Relations* (1971).

Anderson, A., 'Political symbolism of the labour laws', *Bulletin of the Society for the Study of Labour History*, 23 (1971), 14.

—— 'The labour laws and the Cabinet Legislative Committee of 1926–7', *Bulletin of the Society for the Study of Labour History*, 23 (1971), 39.

Bercusson, B., *Fair Wages Resolutions* (1978).

Blank, S., *Government and Industry in Britain* (Farnborough, 1973).

Burgess, K., *The Challenge of Labour* (1980).

Charles, R., *The Development of Industrial Relations in Britain, 1911–1939* (1973).

Clegg, H. A., *The History of British Trade Unions since 1899* (vol. 2, Oxford, 1985).

Davidson, R., 'The Board of Trade and industrial relations, 1896–1914', *Historical Journal*, 21 (1978), 571.

Fox, A., *History and Heritage* (1985).

Gospel, H. F., 'Employers' labour policy: a study of the Mond–Turner talks, 1927–33', *Business History*, 21 (1979), 180.

Hinton, J., *The First Shop Stewards' Movement* (1973).

Jeffrey, K. and Hennessy, P., *States of Emergency* (1983).

Jenkins, P., *The Battle of Downing Street* (1970).

Knowles, K. G. J. C., *Strikes—A Study of Industrial Conflict* (Oxford, 1954).

Lowe, R., 'Review article', *British Journal of Industrial Relations*, 13 (1975), 115.

—— 'The failure of consensus in Britain: the National Industrial Conference, 1919-21', *Historical Journal*, 21 (1978), 649.

—— 'Hours of labour: negotiating industrial legislation in Britain, 1919–39', *Economic History Review*, 2nd ser., xxxv (1982), 254.

McDonald, G. W. amd Gospel, H. F., 'The Mond-Turner talks, 1927-33: a study in industrial co-operation', *Historical Journal*, 16 (1973), 807.

Martin, R. M., *TUC: The Growth of a Pressure Group* (Oxford, 1980).

Mason, A., 'The Government and the General Strike, 1926', *International Review of Social History*, 14 (1969), 1.

Parker, R. A. C., 'British rearmament, 1936-9: Treasury, trade unions and skilled labour', *English Historical Review*, 96 (1981), 306.

PEP, *British Trade Unionism* (1948).

Phillips, G. A., *The General Strike* (1976).

Reader, W. J., *Imperial Chemical Industries* (vol. 2, 1975).

Sharp, I. G., *Industrial Conciliation and Arbitration in Great Britain* (1950).

Tolliday, S. and Zeitlin, J. (eds.), *Shop Floor Bargaining and the State* (Cambridge, 1985).

Turner, J. (ed.), *Businessmen and Politics* (1984).

Wigham, E., *The Right to Manage. The History of the Engineering Employers' Federation* (1973).

—— *Strikes and the Government, 1893-1974* (1976).

4.6 Social Policy

Abrams, P., 'The failure of social reform', *Past and Present*, 24 (1963), 43.

Benjamin, D. K. and Kochin, L. A., 'Searching for an explanation of unemployment', *Journal of Political Economy*, 87 (1979), 441 and multiple replies in 90 (1982).

Briggs, A., 'The welfare state in historical perspective', *European Journal of Sociology*, 2 (1961), 221.

Briggs, E. and Deacon, A., 'The creation of the Unemployment Assistance Board', *Policy and Politics*, 2 (1973), 43.

Crowther, M. A., 'Family responsibility and state responsibility in Britain before the welfare state', *Historical Journal*, 25 (1982), 133.

Deacon, A., *In Search of the Scrounger* (1976).

—— 'Concession and coercion: the politics of unemployment insurance in the twenties', in A. Briggs and J. Saville (eds.), *Essays in Labour History* (vol. 3, 1977).

Fulbrook, J., *Administrative Justice and the Unemployed* (1978).

Gilbert, B. B., *British Social Policy, 1914-1939* (1970).

Harris, J., 'Did British workers want the welfare state? G. D. H. Cole's survey of 1942', in J. Winter (ed.), *The Working Class in Modern British History* (Cambridge, 1983).

Lynes, T., 'Unemployed Assistance Tribunals', in M. Adler and A. Bradley (eds.), *Justice, Discretion and Poverty* (1976).

—— 'The making of the unemployment assistance scales', in *Low Incomes* (Supplementary Benefits Administration Papers, 6, 1977).

Macnicol, J. S., *The Movement for Family Allowances, 1918-45* (1980).

Miller, F. M., 'National assistance or unemployment assistance?', *Journal of Contemporary History*, 9 (1974), 163.

—— 'The British unemployment assistance crisis of 1935', *Journal of Contemporary History*, 14 (1979), 329.

Prosser, T., 'The politics of discretion', in M. Adler and S. Asquith (eds.), *Discretion and Welfare*, (1981).

Walley, Sir J., *Social Security: Another British Failure?* (1972).

Whiteside, N., 'Welfare legislation and the unions during the First World War', *Historical Journal*, 23 (1980), 857 and debate in 25 (1982), 437.

4.7 Economic Policy

Aldcroft, D. H., *The Inter-War Economy* (1970).

Booth, A., 'The "Keynesian Revolution" in economic policy-making', *Economic History Review*, 2nd ser., xxxvi (1983), 103.

—— and Glynn, S., 'Unemployment in the interwar period: a multiple problem', *Journal of Contemporary History*, 13 (1978), 65.

Campbell, R. H., 'The Scottish Office and the special areas in the 1930s', *Historical Journal*, 22 (1979), 167.

Casson, M., *The Economics of Unemployment* (Oxford, 1983).

Floud, R. and McCloskey, D. (eds.), *The Economic History of Britain since 1700* (vol. 2., Cambridge, 1981).

Glynn, S. and Howells, P. G. A., 'Unemployment in the 1930s: the "Keynesian solution" reconsidered', *Australian Economic History Review*, xx (1980), 28.

Hancock, K. J., 'Unemployment and the economists in the 1920s' *Economica*, 27 (1960), 305.

—— 'The reduction of unemployment as a problem of public policy, 1920–29', *Economic History Review*, 2nd ser., xv (1962), 328.

Hannah, L., *The Rise of the Corporate Economy* (1976).

Kahn, Lord, 'Unemployment as seen by the Keynesians', in G. D. N. Worswick (ed.), *The Concept and Measurement of Involuntary Unemployment* (1976).

McCrone, G., *Regional Policy in Britain* (1969).

Mackay, D. I., Forsyth, D. J. C. and Kelly, D. M., 'The discussion of public works programmes', *International Review of Social History*, 11 (1966), pt. 1, 8.

Middleton, R., 'The Treasury in the 1930s: political and administrative constraints to acceptance of the "new economics', *Oxford Economic Papers*, new ser., 34 (1982), 48.

—— 'The Treasury and public investment', *Public Administration*, 61 (1983), 351.

Miller, F. M., 'The unemployment policy of the National Government, 1931-36', *Historical Journal*, 19 (1976), 453.

Moggridge, D. E., *Return to Gold* (Cambridge, 1969).

Parker, H. M. D., *Manpower* (1957).

Peden, G. C., 'Keynes, the Treasury and unemployment in the later nineteenth-thirties', *Oxford Economic Papers*, new ser., 32 (1980), 1.

—— 'Sir Richard Hopkins and the "Keynesian Revolution" in employment policy', *Economic History Review*, 2nd ser., xxxvi (1983), 281.

—— '"The Treasury View" on public works and employment in the inter-war period', *Economic History Review*, 2nd ser., xxxvii (1984), 167.

Pigou, A. C., *Aspects of British Economic History, 1918-45* (1947).

Tawney, R. H., 'The abolition of economic controls', *Economic History Review*, 2nd ser., xiii (1943), 1.

Youngson, A. J., *Britain's Economic Growth* (1967).

INDEX